GREAT PREACHING ON
REVIVAL

GREAT PREACHING ON
REVIVAL

COMPILED BY
SHELTON L. SMITH

SWORD of the LORD PUBLISHERS

P. O. Box 1099 • Murfreesboro, TN 37133
(800) 247-9673 (615) 893-6700
FAX (615) 848-6943 • E-mail: 102657.3622@compuserve.com
1997

ISBN 0-87398-340-8

Printed and Bound in the United States of America

Dedication
to
Dr. Curtis W. Hutson
1934 - 1995

Dr. Hutson served as president and editor of the SWORD OF THE LORD for over fourteen years. As a pastor and as an evangelist he preached the themes of revival and soul winning often and with great conviction. During his lifetime he led thousands of people to Christ and sparked a fire in the hearts of Christian workers the world over to do the same.

When this "Great Preaching" series was begun in 1984, it was Dr. Hutson's vision to have a twenty-volume set of the greatest sermons available in print on certain vital subjects. He saw sixteen of those volumes completed, and the seventeenth was published shortly after his death. With God's help the Sword of the Lord Publishers will complete the twenty-volume series just as Dr. Hutson intended.

Because this current volume, *Great Preaching on Revival,* so epitomizes the life and ministry of this great preacher, we are pleased to dedicate it to his memory and with a prayer that it will stir the hearts of preachers and Christian workers everywhere for genuine, Heaven-sent revival.

Table of Contents

Preface

When the people of God lose their zeal, grow cold, and start cavorting with worldlings, there is a need for revival.

When the work of God wanes, crowds diminish, pulpits are dry, very few souls are being converted, and the baptistry is a haven of cobwebs, there is a need for revival.

When the men of God (the preachers) are weary of forbearing, listless in preaching, faithless in their devotions, fruitless in their work, and more concerned over their salary than they are soul winning, there is a need for revival.

When the church of God is consumed over buildings and budgets, occupied in committee, yawning through every service, and hardly open on Sunday night and Wednesday night, there is a need for revival.

When the Word of God is not given the highest priority, there is a need for revival.

When the will of God is not the center focus of a Christian's life, there is a need for revival.

When the way of God is shelved and replaced with other pursuits and interests, there is a need for revival.

It is the need for the United States, for Canada, for Mexico and the world.

It is the need of preachers and laymen alike.

It is the burden of our time.

Dr. Curtis Hutson, pastor, evangelist, preacher and editor of the SWORD OF THE LORD (1980-1995), said:

> There is nothing better than old-fashioned revivals where half-asleep Christians wake up; where those who have lost their burden for souls get it back; where those who have quit tithing start again; where those who fail to attend church on Sunday night become faithful.

While the defeated religionists whimper like crybabies that it can't be done, the stalwart soldiers in the Lord's army, the genuine servants of Christ, live by faith, breathe in hope and press for revival. They "cry aloud" and "spare not" in making their case. It doesn't take many—only a few. Is there not a cause? Our nation and our families are precious to us. Can we not be motivated by the Saviour to do for Him what will give life to the dying and rescue the perishing?

Dr. John R. Rice, the beloved founder of the Sword of the Lord Publishers, a great preacher and evangelist, said:

> I say that we can have great revivals now, as great revivals as the world ever saw. I mean we can have mass evangelism shaking whole cities, with thousands saved in a single campaign. I say that the Gospel can again grip whole communities, whole areas, and affect the moral standards, the philosophy of life of the general public. I say that as a result of such mass revivals, we may have a new and mighty missionary impetus that will win millions of souls around the world, that will build and support great Christian institutions like those that came with the ministry of great evangelists of the past—I mean an evangelism led by men called of God as evangelists, anointed with power from Heaven; men with the gifts needed for mighty mass movements, backed by Bible-believing pastors and people.

Revival should be our prayer, our passion and our priority. It should be the normal state of things in every church. What should be, could be and will be—when we believe God as we should and give ourselves devotedly to His cause.

In this volume, *Great Preaching on Revival*, we have included great sermons on revival and great sermons from men who experienced great revivals.

As you read these sermons, do so with a prayer in your heart for God to ignite the fires of revival in your own soul. May the stirring of the fires begin even now.

The Sword of the Lord Publishers

WILLIAM ASHLEY SUNDAY
1862-1935

ABOUT THE MAN:

William Ashley (Billy) Sunday was converted from pro baseball to Christ at twenty-three but carried his athletic ability into the pulpit.

Born in Ames, Iowa, he lost his father in the Civil War and lived with his grandparents until age nine when he was taken to live in an orphanage. A life of hard work paid off in athletic prowess that brought him a contract with the Chicago White Stockings in 1883. His early success in baseball was diluted by strong drink; however, in 1886 he was converted at the Pacific Garden Mission in Chicago and became actively involved in Christian work.

Sunday held some three hundred crusades in thirty-nine years. It is estimated that a hundred million heard him speak in great tabernacles, and more than a quarter million people made professions of faith in Christ as Saviour under his preaching. His longtime associate, Dr. Homer Rodeheaver, called him "the greatest gospel preacher since the Apostle Paul."

Billy Sunday was one of the most unusual evangelists of his day. He walked, ran or jumped across the platform as he preached, sometimes breaking chairs. His controversial style brought criticism but won the admiration of millions. He attacked public evils, particularly the liquor industry, and was considered the most influential person in bringing about the prohibition legislation after World War I.

Many long remembered his famous quote: "I'm against sin. I'll kick it as long as I've got a foot, and I'll fight it as long as I've got a fist. I'll butt it as long as I've got a head. I'll bite it as long as I've got a tooth. And when I'm old and fistless and footless and toothless, I'll gum it till I go home to Glory and it goes home to perdition!"

Those who heard him never forgot him or his blazing, barehanded evangelism.

The evangelist died November 6, 1935, at age 72. His funeral was held in Moody Church, Chicago; the sermon was preached by H. A. Ironside.

I.

Making the Case for Revival

BILLY SUNDAY

(Preached in Richmond, Indiana, 1922)

"O Lord, revive thy work in the midst of the years. . . in wrath remember mercy."—Hab. 3:2.

It is a good thing to take an occasional retrospective view, then an introspective view, then a prospective view, and try to discover by the introspective what caused you to do the things that make you hang your head in shame, the things that loom up out of the midst of the past, like the periscope of a submarine.

A good many things remind us that the sands of the hourglass of time are fast shifting for all of us. It will not be long until the undertaker will pump us full of embalming fluid and a quartet will sing,

Lead, kindly Light,
Amid th' encircling gloom,
Lead Thou me on!

The Prophet Habakkuk was a contemporary with Jeremiah, and his prophecy was uttered in anticipation of the Jewish captivity, which was the result of the people of God mingling, mixing and amalgamating with those whom God told them to pass up, like a bum would a pay car or a hobo a woodpile. But they wouldn't listen to God. They thought they could give the Lord cards and spades, that He was a little too old fogyish. They imagined His religion was a little out of date.

So the prophet looked down and saw, by the laws and conditions that were then operative, that there was but one inevitable outcome from all that conglomerate mixture and amalgamation—the Babylonian captivity and the baring of their backs to the blows of their taskmasters. So he prayed, "O Lord, revive thy work." The only way to keep that crowd safe is to revive them.

Is what the world needs today more money? Oh, no! It isn't conservation of natural resources, irrigation projects, free silver, or the gold standard that the old world needs; it is a baptism of the old-time religion that has warmed the world's cold heart for over two thousand years.

There are people who suppose—I suppose they always will suppose—that the only way to promote religion is to move along uniformly in the same old rut.

There are two crowds in every church—the ruts and the anti-ruts. So long as they will deliver the goods, I don't care how old the methods nor if they are moss-covered. But if they don't deliver the goods, there is but one place for them—the scrap pile.

Some people are scared to death that somebody may do something out of the ordinary that will keep a sinner out of Hell. Some of you would rather see a person go to Hell than for things to be done differently.

Now what is the nature of a revival? An increase in religious things. We are facing the growing dominance of the material over the spiritual. You can take a basket of money on your arm, walk down the average street, scatter it, and lead the bunch who follow so close to Hell that they can smell the sulphur fumes vomiting from the inferno below.

This is a busy age in which we live. Man hardly has time to stop and comb his hair or get shaved.

This is a day of *isms*, schisms and *ologies*. There never was a time when there were more *isms* wriggling their carcasses out of the pit of Hell to lead people off on a tangent from the true God than in our day. The Devil has transformed himself into an angel of light. A few years ago he was assaulting the church through infidelity, led by the archangel of infidelity, Bob Ingersoll. But today the church is being assaulted by *isms* and schisms. There isn't religion enough in them to float their dirty fallacies!

The Devil is a smart guy; he's been preying on this old world for six thousand years. He never gets appendicitis or peritonitis or cancer; he's always Johnny-on-the-spot.

It's an axiom in regard to all enterprises that the measure of one's preparedness will, in a degree, determine the measure of his success. Just in proportion as you are prepared to have the Spirit of God move upon your heart and through your heart into the community, in that proportion will the Spirit of God move to bring this city to its knees in repentance.

Years ago when Moody was in New York, some of the preachers were knocking him, saying he was crude and a jabberer. His eccentricities and idiocyncrasies greatly astonished and alarmed them.

That reminds me of a lady who came to my tabernacle. When she was asked, "What do you think of Mr. Sunday?" she drew in her diaphragm and replied:

> Well, he seems to be desperately in earnest. He is a man of contrast. He is January and he is June. He is Mount Vesuvius in a hemorrhage of lava; now he's raining daffodils. Now he's refined and as chaste as a lamb; now he's as slangy as a hobo in a beer joint asking for a handout.

I try to be all things to all people that I might win some to God! (If I don't stick to my text, I still try to stick to my crowd!)

Dr. Booth got up before the Ministerial Association of New York and said of Moody:

> Here's a man who has done for weeks what all the Methodist preachers combined could not do. He has arrested, gripped and held the attention of this pleasure-mad community. Instead of growling and grumbling, I think it's up to us to pray.

Dr. Booth said:

> I went home with that conviction and prepared a sermon on the text, "Come; for all things are now ready." I had two heads—**Come** and **Come Now.** I preached and gave the invitation. Three young men went into an afternoon meeting weeping their way from sin to salvation.

That was three more than they had had for years in that great religious refrigerator.

The man who magnifies the Word of God and the blood of Jesus Christ in his preaching is one whom God will hurl like a thunderbolt against the forces of error!

Why is it that the names of Wesley, Whitefield, Jonathan Edwards, Finney, Moody and multitudes of others stand out as clean-cut as a cameo upon the pages of history? I will tell you! They were conspicuous because of their fearlessness in their assaults upon every form of evil and evildoers—rich, poor, black, white, native-born or foreign-born. They hurled the anathemas of God into the ranks of sin, irrespective of who might sit and listen. That kind of man God will honor, no matter who he be.

I want to say to this city right at the kickoff that I believe the Bible is the Word of God from cover to cover. I believe it, not because I can harmonize it with the philosophies of men, but because the mouth of the Lord hath spoken it, and it has delivered the goods for all these centuries.

When some bigwig who has dreamed his theories over the beer mugs, tobacco smoke and the battle fumes of Heidelburg and Leipzig butts into me and says, "Mr. Sunday, the consensus of the latest scholarship has decreed thus and so regarding the divine origin of the Scriptures," I say, "When the consensus of the latest scholarship says one thing and the Word of God another, the latest scholarship can go plumb to Hell for all I care."

We may determine tonight whether we will have a spiritual awakening and put the Devil in the hospital before the Fourth of July. The responsibility has never been with God—never! And it never will be!

I used to say, "I can see a revival cloud the size of a man's hand." I used to say, "There is a coming revival," but, bless God, I have learned that the promises of God are in the present tense. We can have it now if we will do what God tells us.

If your city sags morally; if men are staggering, reeling, vomiting, spewing down the street; if girls are selling their womanhood; if they hang around your bars, hotels and restaurants overperfumed, overjeweled, overfed and underdressed, it is your fault. A man couldn't look at one of them very long with prayer-meeting thoughts, and don't you forget it! I wonder today that as many fellows keep their decency and morals as do, with what is flaunted in their faces.

If the city sags morally, the trouble is not with God but with its citizenship. It's up to you.

If the church is losing her power, degenerating into a third-rate amusement bureau, and reducing religion to form and ceremony, ritual and an ethical code, the trouble is not with God. If the preachers preach to wood and varnish instead of folks, the trouble isn't with God. If the Devil can scare up more church members at a leg show than come to prayer meeting, the trouble isn't with God. It is with the members of these churches. You can't blame the Lord for these things.

I plead not for a modern revival. I don't know anything about your modern stuff. Mine is as old as the cross of Jesus, as old as the nails that were driven through His hands. I plead for an old pentecostal revival that will make drunkards sober; that will cause thieves to steal no more; that will make blasphemers pray; that will make men who are keeping someone on the side and disgracing their wives and children, go home and be decent; that will make deadbeats pay their debts; that will transform this old God-forsaken, whiskey-soaked, Christ-hating, Lord-damning, harlot-ridden world into a paradise of peace, benediction and blessing.

Some people say, "A revival is an abnormal condition." Not so! A revival is a normal condition. This low, dead, lifeless condition is abnormal.

Do you mean to insult God by saying that anything that makes a man pray, kiss his wife instead of beating her, and pay his debts instead of being a deadbeat is an abnormal condition? Do you mean to say that it is normal when a man goes home drunk? Or that it is abnormal when he is sober and decent?

You say, "It is followed by reaction." I say again, "That's a lie!"

Even if it were true, it is worth all the money spent, all the energy put forth, all the sleepless nights, and all the meals you neglect; for by and through a revival, the hearts and minds of a community will be gripped and turned toward God, and the tide will be turned from the whiskey joints toward the church, toward Sunday school, toward decency, sobriety and virtue.

When your child is ill, you summon a physician. He diagnoses the difficulty, then prescribes something for the malady. The medicine binds up the disintegrating tissue, puts the bloom of health on the cheek of your little one so that he may stay in your arms longer than if the doctor had not come. It is worth every dollar that you paid the doctor for the happiness and joy you have experienced in kissing your baby twelve months longer than if the doctor had not come.

If some man will stagger down that aisle, give me his hand, walk home sober for a year, give his wife his pay, let his children climb on his knees and run their hands through his hair—if at the end of a year he again staggers home drunk, it was worth every dollar spent to let that wife sleep for twelve months.

I. IS THERE A CASE TO BE MADE FOR REVIVAL?

"O Lord, revive thy work"! The history of the church is a history of revival. How can any minister have the audacity to insult God by lifting himself against revivals and still claim to be a preacher? In my opinion he is a disgrace to the church, whether he buttons his collar in front or behind.

Ask the man or woman who sits by your side, "When did you turn to Jesus Christ?" You will be dumbfounded to discover that about seven out of every ten will say, "At a time of special awakening." So I take issue with you right there.

The economy of nature provides for the occasional copious downpour of rain, but you would be a fool to grumble because it didn't rain all the time.

It is never unwise to have revivals in business—not at all! I have never heard of a community or a commercial club saying they were doing too much business.

It isn't unwise to have a revival in politics—not at all! The government spends billions of dollars on educational buildings, books and teachers. Once every four years we hire halls, newspapers, editors, magazines and orators; this republic becomes a university in which to train voters.

A number of them have backslidden; therefore, some Democrats are going to vote the Republican ticket, and some Republicans are going to vote the Democratic ticket, while some are utterly indifferent. So we have a political revival and political evangelists chasing up and down the country spouting their doctrines from the rear end of a train. It is nothing but a great political revival or awakening—that's all! So on it goes, no matter what it may be.

In the business world you have to make a market for the goods as well as to make the goods. A man may be an automaton and make the goods, but it takes a higher grade of intelligence to make a market for the goods than to make the goods. The highest grade of intelligence you can find in any one class must be the traveling salesman, for he has to have a good head on him to sell the goods.

Every community has a Chamber of Commerce to create a business revival.

We have an auto show—which is nothing more than an auto revival—to show us the new designs.

We have a horse show—which is nothing but a horse revival—to show how magnificently we are developing horse flesh to a standard of perfection.

Colleges observe commencements—that keeps up the spirit of loyalty.

What commencement is to colleges, revival is to religion. What health is to an individual, revival is to religion. What education is to culture, a revival is to religion.

The mission of the church is to create a spirit of unrest in the hearts of the people and so disgust them with sin that they will forsake their iniquities.

Cut the day of Pentecost out of civilization; cut Peter and Paul out of civilization—what you have left wouldn't do to make a rummage sale.

If a man opens his soul toward business, he becomes a businessman; toward politics, a politician; toward dishonesty, a thief; toward the saloon, a booze hoister; toward Jesus Christ, a Christian.

My challenge to you, Sir, is this: show me your faith by your works.

A boy can pick up a stone and break the cathedral window, but it takes an artist to build it.

A fool can light a match and burn down a structure, but it takes a skilled contractor and architect to erect it.

Anybody can yank the leaves from a rose, but it takes God to make it and kiss it with the sunlight.

A mob spat in the face of Jesus Christ and nailed Him to the cross; but God wakened Him, and He rose from the dead.

Let those who sneer at revivals find something that has produced a blessing and benefit equal to that of a revival of religion before they open their big mouths.

When the preaching is faithful, the prayers earnest, the lives pure, a revival will follow as naturally as the sun will shine.

Somebody says, "A revival causes disrespect or brings disrespect to the cause of Christ." It does not! Because by and through the revival we confess that we have declined spiritually and need something to arouse us. You don't put the community in possession of some information they haven't already on tap—not at all! Honest confession is good for the soul!

You say, "A revival is temporary." So is a rain shower. So was Pentecost. So was the Reformation under Martin Luther, but the world feels the benefit of its blessings today.

A revival temporary? So is a bath! Take one; it will do you good!

You say, "It exalts the evangelist." It does nothing of the kind! The evangelist has his place in the divine economy as much as the pastor.

I am sick and disgusted with a lot of fellows knocking somebody who doesn't do the same thing just the way he would. I've got my place in God's divine economy just as much as January and February and October and November have in the calendar in the swinging of the sun. Where the word *pastor* is mentioned once in the Bible, *evangelist* is mentioned twice.

Now hold on a minute! I've got a great admiration for a man who can serve the church year in and year out and build his people up in their faith. God bless him! He has my prayers. But God hasn't called me to do it. Many a man whom God honors and blesses as pastor of a church would fizzle as an evangelist.

A revival is a conviction of sin in the church. Backsliders are aroused, sinners are brought to Christ, and one's faith is strengthened. The average man or woman today is blind to these conditions. If you will get your own heart and life right, then you will long to see that others are right toward Jesus Christ and His truth.

The truths of the Bible are a dream, a mirage to a great many people. They never become a reality to them because they are in such a backslidden state and condition themselves.

I was in a town in Iowa preaching in a tent. An old farmer, a rich old fellow, asked me to go out to his house for dinner. I went one time.

As we sat in the parlor, he was pulling his bird-tail whiskers and trying to hit the spittoon thirty feet away! Pretty soon he got up, walked across to the wall, took down a copy of *Jayne's Almanac,* and began to turn the leaves. "I am looking to see when the moon changes."

I said, "What for?"

"I want to mark my calves. I cut the slits out of the ears of some of them, and they bled to death. I was told if I marked them at a certain time of the moon, they would be all right."

"Do you believe that?" I asked.

"Yes. I've had one of these almanacs in the house for twenty years."

I said, "That's strange that you will believe that. Let's see. You have two kids. If you were to put them on the market tomorrow, they wouldn't bring as much as one of those black-polled steers you have out in the field."

The trouble with people is, they spend too much time getting their hogs and cattle ready for market and too little time getting boys and girls ready for Heaven.

Revival? Get right yourself! You begin to realize that without Jesus

Christ you are lost and drifting away from Christ and His truth!

"O Lord, revive thy work in the midst of the years. . . in wrath remember mercy."

II. WHEN IS REVIVAL NEEDED?

A. When Religion Is Not Ideal

When is a revival needed? When religion is not ideal. Christianity does not consist of certificates of church membership. Christianity does not consist of trotting out to church Sunday morning, keeping a little spot seventeen inches square warm for a half hour, listening to a sermonette, putting a few coins into the collection plate, then singing, "When the Roll Is Called Up Yonder."

A preacher came to me out in Iowa and said, "Bill, I thought I had done my duty when I held up the bleeding form of Jesus Christ and dilated upon His precepts. I find now that I've got a right to preach against sin."

I owe more to Dr. J. Wilbur Chapman that I became a preacher, than to any other man. I traveled with him as an assistant for two years. He picked me out of the corn rows of Illinois.

One time we went to a town in Kansas to conduct a series of meetings. We were accustomed to having union meetings; but when we arrived on the scene in this town, we found they could have had a union meeting had it not been for a quarrel with the Presbyterian church. They had had a fuss.

A few alive and awake, up-to-date people said they would withdraw. They went down to the bank of the river, built a church, got a good live-wire preacher there who was going at a good gait all the time in high gear, while the other fellow had the brakes set.

We were being entertained in the home of this preacher in whose church we were holding the meeting. These two preachers lived side by side on the bank of the river. They had a board fence right on the line, nine feet high, so the kids and wives couldn't scrap back and forth.

I said to Doc one day, "I'd like to meet the pastor of the other church, the Presbyterian church."

He said, "Well, perhaps."

We were strolling down the street one day. His white necktie was flapping back and forth. He was wearing a silk hat and twirling a cane.

"Yonder comes the pastor of the other church," he said.

"I'd like to meet him."

When we got in close quarters, the two turned, looked in the opposite direction, as though the world or one another smelled bad.

"It's evident that you two fellows don't speak as you pass," I commented.

"No, sir! I haven't spoken to him for eight years."

"Have you been preaching in the interim?"

"Yes, sir."

"Have you been administering the ordinances of communion and of baptism?"

"Yes, sir."

"What sort of a Bible have you? My Bible says, 'If you forgive not men their trespasses, neither will your Father forgive your trespasses.' I would like to see the theological gymnastics that you display to sidestep that."

We stayed there a week, and nobody got converted. We packed our trunks and left since the Spirit of God had fled from that scene of strife and discord.

You might as well expect a mummy to speak and bear children, as to expect people to be converted in a cold world of fault-finding, growling preachers.

A friend of mine was preaching in a town in Iowa when he had to go to the hospital for an operation. The ministerial association asked me to come and take the meeting in his absence.

I was scheduled to begin another meeting in another town on the Lord's day, but I said, "If you can fix it up with the preachers in that other town, I'll be glad to do it." They did, and wired me.

They sent a man up there to preach in the interim, and he preached a week; then I went up and preached a week. But there wasn't a man, woman or child converted—not a one!

When I preached, they seemed to sit spellbound.

While I was there, a minister came to see me, looking sad. "Bill, one of my leading members, Doc Stewart, asked for a letter of dismissal."

"I wouldn't give it to him," I replied.

"Well, we've done everything we can, but we can't convince that bullheaded Scotchman that he is wrong. You can't move him."

"What's the trouble?" I asked.

"Doc Stewart was a steward of our church. The mayor of the town was also a steward in the church. The school board was looking around for a site upon which to erect a new school building, and Doc Stewart had a site to sell. A man who owed the mayor $400 had a site to sell. The school board voted to buy the site from this man who owed the mayor. Doc charged the mayor with pulling strings so he could get his money.

"You couldn't convince him that he was wrong. You couldn't turn Doc. When they met on the street, they put up their dukes and went at it. The mayor gave an upper cut that sent Doc to the mat. He painted his eye."

One night I turned to the preacher and asked, "Whom will I ask to pray?"

"Ask Doc Stewart to pray."

I asked Doc Stewart to pray, and he was game. He got up, cleared his throat and went at it.

Did you ever hear a threshing machine start up in the fall after it had stood out all winter and all summer without any grease? Well, you could know that Doc was going some when he sweated out a celluloid collar.

He staggered through. I said to the preacher, "Now get those fellows together and see if you can't fix it up."

He got them and a number of the leading men together. Finally these two shook hands and buried the hatchet.

Everybody in town knew about their squabble.

The courthouse was in the middle of the town, and the town was built around it. I said, "Lock arms, walk around town, around the courthouse square, and let everybody know you've made up."

They locked arms, walked around the courthouse square, then catercornered through it. Everybody in town stretched their necks to see what was happening.

That night you couldn't get within a hundred feet of the building. I preached, but nobody was converted. People sat crying. I saw a woman get up and start down the aisle—a big woman who had to move in sections—she went through a cross aisle, stopped by another woman, threw her arms around her and let out a yell like a Comanche Indian. She threw her arms up in the air like a Dutch windmill.

I asked, "What's the matter?"

(Two society women had been scrapping for three or four years to see who would be recognized as society leader.)

A pastor said, "They are about to settle the scrap."

I announced the next day would be a day of fasting and prayer. That afternoon two other women who hadn't spoken to one another for years got into the same home to pray. They spoke to everybody there and were cordial to everyone *except each other*. I heard about it and mentioned the fact. "It's a disgrace; I'm ashamed to hear it," I said.

One woman sitting in the back near a post got up and said, "Brother Sunday, I feel horribly chagrined. I'm one of the two to whom you refer. I have made up my mind that I am going to get right tomorrow."

I said, "Sis, you had better do it now. You might die before tomorrow."

She got up and beat it.

That night when I gave the invitation, fifty-seven men and women came weeping down the aisle. When the revival ended, hundreds had been swept into the kingdom of God.

Out of that crowd they built a church that cost hundreds of thousands of dollars. The church community was stirred.

Oh, the Spirit of God flees from strife and discord.

B. When There Is a Worldly Spirit

It isn't necessary to do something grossly inconsistent with the standards of morality and decency. No!

A ship will ride the waves until the water gets into her; she was made to ride the water and not for the water to be in her. The church is all right as long as she is in the world; she is all wrong when the world is in her.

One of the troubles of the church today is that she has joined the world, and that is just the reason why the world won't join the church. This has lowered the standard of the church in the universe. Oh, the world is lousy with humbugs today. The churches are full of sour-faced religious crabapples who are trying to hand God a lemon.

Whoever works for the Devil will get his pay from the Devil. He will give you hell here and Hell when you are through; and you play both ends against the middle! What a big fool you are to follow the Devil! I tell you, religion has done too much good for this old world for any buckeyester and sawdust-filled fellow to knock. Don't forget that! Some men in some churches are bigger rogues than some of the convicts in Sing Sing.

Live the way you ought to for God. Hell is seldom preached nowadays, and that may be one reason we have so much hell here on earth. If you don't want to hear about Hell, don't come around here. I don't preach Gehenna or Hades; I believe in plain, old-fashioned *H-e-l-l*—Hell.

It is no argument against religion that there are black sheep in the flock. Please remember that the Devil at one time lived in Heaven. He had a chance, but he passed it up. So if you mind your own faults, you will have less time to find fault with others. It will keep you busy looking out for yourself!

"O Lord, revive thy work."

C. When There Is Spiritual Desolation Among the Multitude

You will find them in every denomination—the Presbyterian, the Episcopal, the Methodist, the Baptist, the Lutheran, the Reformed and all!

Oh, we need a panic in religion! The world doesn't need reformation; it needs transforming by the blood of Jesus Christ! Mighty few people are being saved.

Every church has its constituency. Some men go to church—you, a Methodist; you, a Reformed; you, a Lutheran; you, an Episcopalian; you, a Presbyterian—why? Oh, your wife goes there, your mother was a member there, your children go to that Sunday school; so you have your property and your religion in your wife's name!

Every church has its constituency; whenever you go, you go there. If you feel at home under these circumstances, all right.

Take the Sunday school. How few of the Sunday school scholars are being saved and brought into the church! How few people are being saved! Most men are touched by church influence sometime, but they are allowed to drift away—no family altars in their homes!

Oh, we are letting our children grow up like wild asses' colts today. With no family altar no wonder they are going to the Devil. No wonder that, with the dew of youth on their brows, your girls feed the red light districts! No wonder the age of the prostitute in the last few years in this country has fallen lower and lower. Most of our criminals are young men under eighteen.

"O Lord, revive thy work."

May God yield the success that attends the preaching of the Word. If the preacher stands up to speak the truth, some God-forsaken old mountebank will object. Take it from me, Bud; you have no more business running the church because you have money than that fellow who sits there who hasn't a dime. You can dictate to some preachers because you've got a little money, but you have put your eyeball on one whom you can't tell how to preach. I know I am preaching for God, and preaching what He wants me to preach to the people. There is a big difference between preaching for God and preaching to God.

"O Lord, revive thy work."

D. When Sinners Are Careless, Licentious, Grafting

My friends, without a general religious awakening in this country, it means the dissolution of the home, the church, the state. I am no pessimist about that, either. You have to judge by past history, and America is up against it good and strong.

I don't know why it should be. I don't know why people are sick. I don't know why God wants us to plant seed in March or April. I don't know why God had to have a blood sacrifice to save the world. The history of the world reveals that you can find the lowest state of morals in individuals and communities and nations at the greatest height of prosperity. The highest standard of morals has walked hand-in-hand with periods of great affliction or of war or of something that has chastised the nation.

God Almighty will start the suffering. You can't work a shell game on God all your life! You can't hand Him the hot end of the poker all your days!

"O Lord, revive thy work."

Against this revival here, you will find every black-legged gambler, every brewer of the state, every madame of the red light; you will find every gunman, good-for-nothing, God-forsaken hobo, riffraff, plug-ugly rag-tag and bobtail of society who feeds and fattens and gormandizes upon the virtues, the manhood, the womanhood of others. They will lift themselves against this revival. Think twice if you want to line up with a dirty bunch like that.

III. WHY IS REVIVAL DELAYED?

Now, why haven't we had a revival? Listen!

A. Because You Have No Faith in Them

You thought you could get along without God's way of doing things.

Oh, but wait a minute! God won't allow the church nor the preachers nor the community to lose faith in this form of service.

Some fellows with their mutton-chop whiskers, their white neckties and their bell-bottomed trousers have said the days of revivals are over. Oh, bless them!

One day God stopped making worlds, fell down, leaned over the battlements of Glory, called down into the coal mine and said: "O-h-h, Roberts, come here."

That Welsh coal miner, with his cap on, with face grimed with coal and burnt powder, with his lamp burning, crawled up out of the bowels of the earth and said, "Who called me? What do You want, Lord?"

"I haven't got a preacher or a college professor in all Wales whom I can trust with the job, so I want you to start a religious awakening."

God, through that crude, illiterate coal miner, started one of the greatest religious awakenings that has been recorded in the history of the world since Peter preached at Pentecost.

God grabbed up the Welsh revival, hurled it into the faces of the critics and said, "Take that, you scoffer!"

That was when they were saying the days of revivals were over.

God poked His head in the door of a university and called for that infidel, agnostic professor, R. A. Torrey, and sent him out. I would rather sit at the feet of R. A. Torrey and hear him expound the Scriptures than any man I know of in America. God sent him preaching around the world. God picked up the Torrey-Alexander revival, hurled it into the faces of the critics and said, "Take that, you scoffer!"

That was when they were saying the days of revival were over.

God called to my friend, Dr. J. Wilbur Chapman, and sent him preaching up and down the land, across the seas and to the antipodes: China, Japan, the Malay peninsula. He held up the bleeding form of Jesus Christ until thousands came weeping into the kingdom of God. God said, "Oh, take that, you scoffer!"

"The days of revivals are over," so you say. When you come to the place that you believe in revivals, then you can have them.

B. Because the Preacher Has Lost His Concern

Nobody ever heard me say an unkind word against the ministerial institution, and they never will. All I preach against is the fellow who doesn't preach the truth. I preach the truth with all the vim I've got.

Nobody has ever heard me ridicule a minister. Nobody has ever heard me argue with any man who differs from me religiously or any other way. I haven't any time to stop to argue with every little yellow dog that barks along the highway.

Yet the responsibility for no revival has got to be thrown at the door of the preachers of the country. If you will stop fighting theological sham battles and go to preaching God's truth, you will see the greatest religious awakening the world has ever looked at.

If people have lost their spirit of concern, it's because you preachers have lost yours. That's sure!

I will allow no man on earth to go beyond me in paying tribute to culture, intellectual greatness and social distinction; but the man who stands in the pulpit must have the mind and Spirit of God and of Christ. He has to speak with a passion for souls.

I love the church with every drop of blood, every corpuscle, every cell, every molecule, vein, artery, hair and cuticle in and on my body. She's the best institution on the top of God's dirt, but I know her weakness.

What kind of man would you consider me if I would accept the invitation of the ministers of the churches, then stand up and knock the church of God Almighty and the ministry as an institution? Not I! Not with all the strength that God gives me! Never! The church is a blessing.

But I'll tell you this: You have had no revivals because the church of God has been indifferent to them. You have had no revival because the church has been cold and formal. You can't scald a hog in ice water.

You pastors have had no revival because you have been as dignified, stiff, staid, cold as tombstones. You have had no revival because you have been worldly.

Spurgeon once preached a sermon, "How Saints May Help the Devil." One way is to discourage the efforts that are being put forth to beat the Devil.

The Devil hates a revival, but he is dead stuck on the attitude that some preachers and church members take toward it: to try to weaken the hands of those who are trying to make headway against the Devil; to dampen the ardor of those who are against the Devil; to discourage others from uniting their efforts and influence.

If I knew all the devils on earth were here and sitting in the seats to leer at me with their hot, wilting, burning breaths, led by the cohorts of Hell, I would keep shooting away God's truth into their ranks with all the power I possess.

I repeat: the most effective means, in my opinion, that you can employ to publicly demonstrate your insensibility as a citizen and your absolute indifference to decency is to oppose a great work and a great campaign like this that has for its only purpose the making of men and women as God Almighty wants men and women to be.

If it were not for that purpose, you couldn't get me to come. You haven't got money enough in your bank vaults or in the government treasury to hire me to come and work on that basis, if I didn't believe people were lost and on the road to Hell.

"O Lord, revive thy work."

C. Because Christians Care for Other Things More Than Revival

One reason it is so difficult to have the work of God advanced is that there are so many people in the church who care more about other things than about a revival—more about politics, more about business, more about society.

Some of you women break your fool necks to keep your name on the calling list of some society woman to get the opportunity to stick your feet under her mahogany and drink her booze and champagne, then stagger home drunk. You work more at that than to please Jesus Christ. That's your ideal of life and the way to live in the world.

I tell you, there is hardly a city on earth that doesn't need to be taken down to God's bathhouse and have the hose turned on it for righteousness and truth in the name of the Lord.

One preacher came to me out in Iowa and said, "Mr. Sunday, what we need is an ethical revival."

I said, "Forget it! You can starve to death on this ethical stuff. What we need is a revival that will give us better homes."

Oh, there is a great tendency today to break down the family altar. Father forgets that he is the priest. Mother forgets that she represents the church. They turn their kids over to some governess or nurse or babysitter who is only interested in sitting with their children because it means so many dollars.

This revival is one tide from an old sea that has swept the world since Pentecost.

"O Lord, revive thy work."

We need a revival that will give us more men for the ministry. We are facing a crisis in the ministry today. More are leaving the ministry than ever before. I have been trying to preach in my crude, illiterate, jabbering jargon for twenty years up and down the land, ever since I put off the spikes as a professional baseball player for the Chicago White Stockings. For twenty years I have been going up and down the land, holding up the bleeding form of Jesus Christ as God's atonement for sin, and doing my best to help people to Jesus.

"O Lord, revive thy work in the midst of the years. . . in wrath remember mercy."—Hab. 3:2.

RAYMOND W. BARBER
1932-

ABOUT THE MAN:

Dr. Raymond Barber was the pastor of Worth Baptist Church, Fort Worth, Texas, for thirty-five years. Under his leadership the Sunday school averaged over 800, and the church saw many converts and decisions for service. Dr. Barber retired as pastor in 1997, entering the field of evangelism and working on publishing more of his writings.

He is president of Independent Baptist Fellowship International and an outstanding preacher of the Gospel. His message long remains in the minds and hearts of all those who hear him in conferences and special meetings.

Dr. Barber is a member of the Board of Directors of the Sword of the Lord Foundation, and he is a greatly respected man of God.

Dr. Barber has printed many fine books, including *What the Bible Teaches, A Dozen Diamonds From Daniel, Family Portraits* and *Ten Commandments for Teenagers.*

II.

Our Greatest Need Is Revival

What, Why, and When

RAYMOND BARBER

(Preached at the National Sword of the Lord Conference on Revival and Soul Winning, Highland Park Baptist Church, Chattanooga, Tennessee, July 23, 1986)

"Thou, O Lord, remainest for ever; thy throne from generation to generation. Wherefore dost thou forget us for ever, and forsake us so long time? Turn thou us unto thee, O Lord, and we shall be turned; renew our days as of old."—Lam. 5:19-21.

You have heard man after man refer to the days of yesteryear, the ministries of great men like Dr. John Rice, Dr. Bob Jones, Sr., Dr. B. R. Lakin, Dr. J. Frank Norris.

I heard these men talk about the years and what has happened. Oh, we must make it our prayer that God will bring us some of the revival that they had in yesteryear. The great need of this hour is revival.

Surely you are familiar with the background of the book of Lamentations, but let me bring you up to date. Lamentations has several poetic names. It is called "a poem of pity," "a symphony of sadness," "a song of sorrow," "a funeral dirge." It is also referred to as "the wailing wall of the Bible."

Written by Jeremiah in the year 586 B.C., the prophet portrays his reaction to the fall of Jerusalem and the end of the Judean monarchy. For 18 months—from December in 588 B.C. until July in 586 B.C.—the armies of Babylon under Nebuchadnezzar surrounded and besieged the city of Jerusalem. The water and food supply was cut off. The famine was so intense that the people resorted to cannibalism. Mothers actually boiled their babies and ate them.

But far greater than the physical famine was the spiritual famine that plagued the Holy City. Scarcely could a righteous man be found within her walls.

Our Jerusalem is also besieged by the enemy. We are in a state of spiritual apathy. We are suffering from a severe case of spiritual malnutrition. We are in a spiritual stupor. We are sinking into a coma of depression, despondency and despair.

A dark cloud of judgment looms over the horizon for America. Lethargy, laziness and lukewarmness have taken their toll. Needless to say, we have had many remedies offered us for our dilemma and our disease—bigger budgets, more powerful programs, positive promotions, gimmicks, gadgets, giveaways—you will undoubtedly agree that these have not worked. Yet we go on searching with the same lameness, tameness and sameness for the answers to our dilemma.

We have heard from the psychologists. (Do you know the difference between a psychotic, a neurotic and a psychiatrist? The neurotic builds the castles in the air; the psychotic lives in them; the psychiatrist collects the rent!)

The psychologist and the psychiatrist tell us if we will just psyche ourselves up into believing that we are good, we will be good. But the Bible tells us,

"There is none righteous, no, not one: There is none that understandeth, there is none that seeketh after God. . . there is none that doeth good, no, not one."—Rom. 3:10-12.

"All our righteousnesses are as filthy rags" in His sight.

The economists have told us to balance the budget and to spend our way out of the dilemma. But the Bible says:

". . . ye were not redeemed with corruptible things, as silver and gold, from your vain conversation received by tradition from your fathers; But with the precious blood of Christ, as of a lamb without blemish and without spot."—I Pet. 1:18, 19.

The politicians have also spoken. They have said to us in essence, "Vote for us, put us in office, and we'll put you in the driver's seat." But the Bible says:

"Promotion cometh neither from the east, nor from the west, nor from the south. But God is the judge: he putteth down one, and setteth up another."—Ps. 75:6, 7.

The educators have told us they can educate us to God. But the Bible says, "The wayfaring men, though fools, shall not err therein" (Isa. 35:8).

The philosophers tell us to follow the teachings of the great minds of yesteryear. But the Bible tells us,

"Let this mind be in you, which was also in Christ Jesus: Who, being in the form of God, thought it not robbery to be equal with God: But made himself of no reputation, and took upon him the form of a servant, and was made in the likeness of men: And being found in fashion as a man, he humbled himself, and became obedient unto death, even the death of the cross. Wherefore God also hath highly exalted him, and given him a name which is above every name: That at the name of Jesus every knee should bow, of things in heaven, and things in earth, and things under the earth; And that every tongue should confess that Jesus Christ is Lord, to the glory of God the Father."—Phil. 2:5-11.

The environmentalists have spoken to us and said, "If we could just create the proper environment, we could establish a Utopia on earth." Well, Adam and Eve blew that argument out the window 6,000 years ago!

The religionists tell us to do good and we will be in good standing with God. But the Bible tells us, "Not by works of righteousness which we have done, but according to his mercy he saved us" (Titus 3:5).

When are we going to learn that the teachings of God supersede the traditions of men? We have tried all of these panaceas for our illness, yet we are sicker than we have ever been.

We don't need to hear from the psychiatrists or the economists or the politicians or the educators or the philosophers or the environmentalists or the religionists. We need to hear from God! We need to go beyond the veil. We need to take hold of the horns of the altar. We need to bow down before the awesome splendor of the Shekinah glory until the beauty of Jesus is seen in us.

We have been to the courthouse, to the state house, to the White House; but we need to go to the powerhouse. There is no power shortage in Heaven, no energy crisis up there.

I read in Isaiah 59:1, 2:

"Behold, the Lord's hand is not shortened, that it cannot save; neither his ear heavy, that it cannot hear: But your iniquities have separated between you and your God, and your sins have hid his face from you, that he will not hear."

The powerhouse is always there, so push the button labeled "prayer."

The winepresses of Heaven are full and running over. The cruse is full of oil, and the barrel is full of meal.

I. WHAT IS REVIVAL?

There are many diversified opinions about revival. My text says, "Turn thou us unto thee." "Revive us again." "Renew our days." Webster says to *revive* means "to restore consciousness of life."

The most abnormal monstrosity in all the world is a cold, decaying, disintegrating, dying church. The church was meant to be a living, vibrant, militant body of believers, not an invisible, inanimate, indefinable mass of exoplasm. It is a local coming together of a body of baptized believers in Christ.

The church of Jesus Christ is on the march. So many churches have icicles hanging from the ceiling because they have a polar bear in the pulpit. Not many people are attracted to a church as cold as ice with a preacher as dry as dust.

Let me say this as I pass along. Jesus said, "Upon this rock I will build my church." He did not say, "You'll build your church." He said, "I will build my church." Preachers, when are we going to stop using people to build a church and start using the church to build people?

Revival is a rebirth. Revival is a reawakening. Revival is a renewal. Revival is a resuscitation. Revival is a renaissance.

The Devil has vaccinated many Christians with a needle of apathy. We could not care less if men go to Hell. While we sleep, the world rushes headlong into eternity. While we live in comfort, men die in consternation. While we walk in pleasure, men agonize in pain.

We sing:

> **Revive us again; fill each heart with Thy love;**
> **May each soul be rekindled with fire from above.**

The revival we need in this hour comes from God. So what is revival? It is a renewal, a rebirth, a renaissance.

II. WHY DO WE NEED REVIVAL?

Fourteen teenagers will commit suicide in America today—and Friday and Saturday and Sunday and every day of the week the year 'round.

In America, 100,000 children ages 10 and 11 get drunk every week. We need revival when we are so indifferent and apathetic and when we fail to realize what is happening in our world.

America is at the crossroads. We are bankrupt religiously, educationally, socially, morally, spiritually. We are about to have a national nervous breakdown. We would be hard put to find the moral pulse of the spiritual heartbeat of our so-called "nation under God." We are weak and growing weaker. I am persuaded that nothing short of an old-fashioned, God-honoring, Christ-exalting, Devil-killing, sin-skinning, soul-winning, Bible-preaching revival will save America.

Let me emphasize that preaching for a moment. Paul said:

"For the preaching of the cross is to them that perish foolishness; but unto us which are saved it is the power of God. For it is written, I will destroy the wisdom of the wise, and will bring to nothing the understanding of the prudent. Where is the wise? where is the scribe? where is the disputer of this world? hath not God made foolish the wisdom of this world? For after that in the wisdom of God the world by wisdom knew not God, it pleased God by the foolishness of preaching to save them that believe. For the Jews require a sign, and the Greeks seek after wisdom: But we preach Christ crucified, unto the Jews a stumblingblock, and unto the Greeks foolishness; But unto them which are called, both Jews and Greeks, Christ the power of God, and the wisdom of God."—I Cor. 1:18-24.

We must no longer play down, put down or water down preaching. Preaching has been so de-emphasized in the average pulpit that you could cut it out altogether and nobody would miss it. And there are a lot of sorry, shallow substitutes for preaching.

I have come to tell you, you can substitute for the preacher, but you cannot substitute for preaching.

Paul said to young Timothy, "Preach the word." Somebody said it well a long time ago, "We have had so many 'sermonettes' in so many 'churchettes' by so many 'preacherettes' that we have developed a generation of 'Christianettes,' and we are all about to be 'et up' by the Devil."

Where is the backbone? Paul said:

"Preach the word; be instant in season, out of season; reprove, rebuke, exhort with all longsuffering and doctrine. For the time will come when they will not endure sound doctrine; but after their own lusts shall they heap to themselves teachers, having itching ears; And they shall turn away their ears from the truth, and shall be turned unto fables."—II Tim. 4:2-4.

Paul said, "Preach the word." To preach the Word is to preach Christ.

"In the beginning was the Word, and the Word was with God, and the Word was God.

"The same was in the beginning with God. . . .

"And the Word was made flesh, and dwelt among us, (and we beheld his glory, the glory as of the only begotten of the Father,) full of grace and truth."—John 1:1, 2, 14.

When we preach Christ, we preach the Word. When we preach the Word, we preach Christ. "They that were scattered abroad went every where preaching the word" (Acts 8:4).

By the way, the Bible does not say, "Preach about Christ." The liberals do that. You can preach about Socrates, about Aristotle, about Plato, but you cannot know them. But you can and you must preach Christ and His blood.

What can wash away my sin?
Nothing but the blood of Jesus.

There is pow'r, pow'r,
Wonder-working pow'r
In the blood of the Lamb.

The only thing that stirs up the Devil, the only thing that gets the Devil's attention, is the blood of Jesus Christ. Do not in any way de-emphasize the blood. Preach Christ. Preach Him as a Babe in yonder manger, but do not stop there. Preach Him as a Boy in the Temple, but do not stop there. Preach Him as the blessed Sacrifice upon a cross, bearing our sins in His own body on the tree, but do not stop there. Preach Him as a Body in the tomb, but do not stop there. Preach Him as a Priest at the right hand of God, making intercession for us, but do not stop there. Preach Him until you hear the trumpet sound and see the Son of God coming with great clouds of glory to establish His kingdom upon the earth. Preach Him in season and out of season.

Your pulpit is not a throne from which you rule with an iron fist. Preachers are not to tell people where to get off; they are to tell people where to get on.

Your pulpit, pastor, is not a stage from which you act or enact a theatrical drama. Your pulpit is not a bargain counter where you merchandise the wares of the world. Your pulpit is not a laboratory where you experiment with the latest scientific findings. Your pulpit is not a university chair where you expound the latest philosophical pronouncements. Your pulpit is not a bookstand where you review the latest books from off the press. **Your pulpit is a table from which you feed the flock of God.**

Pastor, do not forget that your calling is not to entertain the goats but to feed the sheep.

Everybody is made in the image and likeness of God. God help us! We have tried to westernize God, Americanize God, provincialize God, tribalize God. But He is the God of the whole world. When God loved, He loved the world. When He sent His Son, He sent Him to the world. When He gave us the Great Commission, it was to evangelize the world.

Ninety-eight percent of the world's population remains unevangelized. We need revival. The Gospel of Jesus Christ is the greatest story ever told, yet many Christians never tell it.

By the way, when is the last time you told it?

> **Tell it again! Tell it again!**
> **Salvation's story repeat o'er and o'er,**
> **Till none can say of the children of men,**
> **"Nobody ever has told me before."**

We need revival because every time you breathe, four souls go into eternity who have never heard the name of Christ. We need revival because, in our modern world of global communication and worldwide travel, there are 2,500 languages and dialects in which not one single word of this Book has ever been translated.

We need revival in America! While preachers plan bigger budgets, nurse old wounds and watch soap operas, myriads of souls are dying and going to Hell.

Wake up, preacher! Time is running out. Wake up, preacher! Eternity is drawing nigh. Wake up, preacher! God is ringing your number. Please do not send back a busy signal.

The greatest need in America is a revival among preachers. Moral purity! Our preachers are moral wimps when we ought to be moral giants. God help us to know why we need revival in America today!

III. WHEN WILL REVIVAL COME?

Let me submit to you first—revival will not come through the testimony of a converted athlete with bulging muscles and big-time contracts. I certainly do not have anything against bulging muscles, and

I know little about big-time contracts; but we have to come to the place where we realize that bringing in the stars of Hollywood and television and all the rest is not going to convert this world. God said, "Preach the word."

Revival will not come through the appeal of a beauty queen with tear-filled eyes and a sexy smile. Revival will not come through professional singers singing contemporary gospel songs in Hollywood style or to a Nashville beat.

Our churches are so full of this gospel rock. We have desecrated music. God give us some music men who know what music really is.

I was lifted to the ninth heaven awhile ago when the dear lady sang about the Potter and when Curt Davis played, "What a Friend we have in Jesus! / All our sins and griefs to bear." That music has a message, that music exalts, that music does something to the heart and not just to the flesh.

Revival will not come through eloquent sermons from the lips of university-trained orators. Revival will not come through lifestyle evangelism. We must get back to the basics in America. We must get back to confrontational evangelism.

Jesus confronted Nicodemus, did He not? Paul confronted the Philippian jailer, did he not? Philip confronted the Ethiopian eunuch, did he not? John the Baptist confronted Herod Antipas and lost his head. Confrontation is telling men why they are sinners and how they can be saved.

Revival will come when Christians have such a burning zeal to know God that the fires of revival reach out in the pulpit and in the pew all over America.

Unless there is within us a power from above, we will succumb to everything around us; and our foundation will crumble beneath us.

I am in my thirty-fifth year in the ministry. I have been pastoring the same church for twenty-five years, and it is too late for me to try to start making an impression. It is too late for me to become a professional. It is too late for me to seek acceptance by the National Council or the World Council, or the Ministerial Council, or the Security Council, or any other council. I am determined, more than I have ever been, to cry aloud and spare not. I am determined to tell it like it is to people like they are.

I have a new zeal, a new dedication, a new commitment. I will unequivocably, unhesitatingly, unapologetically, unreservedly, uncompromisingly tell the world there is only one way to God, and that is through Jesus who said, "I am the way, the truth, and the life."

I will tell them there is only one way to be saved, and it is written in Acts 4:12: "Neither is there salvation in any other: for there is none other name under heaven given among men, whereby we must be saved."

I will tell them there is only one way to find rest for their weary souls—accepting the invitation of Jesus who said, "Come unto me, all ye that labour and are heavy laden, and I will give you rest. Take my yoke upon you, and learn of me; for I am meek and lowly in heart: and ye shall find rest unto your souls" (Matt. 11:28, 29).

I will tell them there is only one way to have revival, and that is to incorporate the formula of God into our program. It is written: "Pride goeth before destruction, and an haughty spirit before a fall" (Prov. 16:18). "God resisteth the proud, but giveth grace unto the humble" (Jas. 4:6).

Let us come down off our pedestals of pride. Let us be willing to come down on our faces before God and humble ourselves and pray.

Prayer makes the darkest cloud withdraw;
Prayer climbs the ladder Jacob saw,
Gives exercise to faith and love,
Brings every blessing from above.

Restricting prayer, we cease to fight.
Prayer makes the Christian's armor bright;
And Satan trembles when he sees
The weakest saint upon his knees.

If there is to be power in the pulpit, there must be praying in the pews; for powerful pulpits and praying pews make perfect partners. "If my people, which are called by my name, shall humble themselves, and pray, and seek my face, and turn from their wicked ways; then" (*then*, THEN!) "will I hear from heaven, and will forgive their sin, and will heal their land." We must go God's way!

Away with eloquence! Away with showmanship! Away with entertaining sermons! We do not need sermons that will cause us to stand up and applaud. We need sermons that will cause us to kneel down and weep.

"Knee"-ology will do a lot more for a sin-sick world than theology. The only theology that the thief on the cross had was a one-sentence prayer: "Remember me when thou comest into thy kingdom." Jesus answered, "To day shalt thou be with me in paradise." No intermediate stops, no purgatory, no "here" and "there" and "yon." This day! "To day shalt thou be with me in paradise."

"God is dead," the theologians say,
But I know He's not;
I talked with Him today.

"Dead, never to live again," they claim.
But alive to save
Through His Son's dear name.

"Alive, alive!" let it be said.
God will be living
When the theologians are dead.

I have a footnote, and I will be through: keep a sharp "Sword," brother!

And all the people said, "Amen."

CHARLES HADDON SPURGEON
1835-1892

ABOUT THE MAN:

Many times it has been said that this was the greatest preacher this side of the Apostle Paul. He began preaching at the age of 16. At 25 he built London's famous Metropolitan Tabernacle, seating around 5,000. It was never large enough. Even when traveling he preached to 10,000 eager listeners a week. Crowds thronged to hear him as they came to hear John the Baptist by the River Jordan. The fire of God was on him as on the Prophet Elijah facing assembled Israel at Mount Carmel.

Royalty sat in his Tabernacle, as did washerwomen. Mr. Gladstone had him to dinner; and cabbies refused his fare, considering it an honor to drive for this "Prince of Preachers." To a housewife kneading bread, he would say, "Have you ever tried the Bread of Life?" Many a carpenter was asked, "Have you ever tried to build a house on sand?"

He preached in all the principal cities of England, Scotland and Ireland. And although invited to the United States on several occasions, he was never able to visit this country.

HOW GREAT WAS HIS HEART: for preachers, so the Pastors' College was founded; for orphans, so the orphans' houses came to be; for people around the world, so his literature poured forth in an almost unmeasurable volume. He was a national voice; so every national issue affecting morals, religion or the poor had his interpretation, his counsel.

Oh, but his passion for souls! You can see it in every sermon.

Spurgeon published thousands of poems, tracts, sermons and songs.

HIS MESSAGE TO LOST SINNERS WILL LIVE AS LONG AS THE GOSPEL IS PREACHED.

III.

Spiritual Revival—
the Want of the Church

CHARLES HADDON SPURGEON

"O Lord, revive thy work."—Hab. 3:2.

If God should select out of His works that which He esteems most of all, He would select salvation. He regards the work of grace as being even more glorious than the works of nature. He is, therefore, especially careful that it always be known; and if any dare deny it, they do so in the teeth of repeated testimonies to the contrary, that God is, indeed, the author of salvation and that conversion is the effect of grace and the work of God.

I believe the Eternal might sooner forgive the sin of ascribing the creation of the heavens and of the earth to an idol than that of ascribing the works of grace to the efforts of the flesh or to anything else but God.

It is a sin of the greatest magnitude to suppose that there is aught in the heart which can be acceptable unto God save that which God Himself has first created there.

When I deny God's work in creating the sun, I deny one truth; but when I deny that He works grace in the heart, I deny a hundred truths in one; for in the denial of that one great truth—that God is the author of good in the souls of men—I have denied all the doctrines which make up the great articles of Faith and have run in the very teeth of the whole testimony of sacred Scripture.

Many of us have been taught that if there be anything in our souls which can carry us to Heaven, it is God's work; and if there is aught that is good and excellent found in His church, it is entirely God's work.

We firmly believe that it is God who quickens the soul which was dead, positively "dead in trespasses and sins," that it is God who maintains the life of that soul, that it is God who consummates and perfects that life in the Home of the blessed, in the land of the hereafter.

We ascribe nothing to man but all to God. The conversion of the soul is not effected either by its own effort or by the efforts of others. There are means and agencies employed, but the work is, both *alpha* and *omega*, wholly the Lord's. We think, therefore, that we are right in applying the text to the work of divine grace, both in the heart and in the church at large; and we think we can have no subject more appropriate for our consideration than the text, "O Lord, revive thy work."

First, trusting that the Spirit of God will help me, I shall endeavor *to apply the text to our own souls personally*, then *to the state of the church at large*, for it well needs that the Lord should revive His work in its midst.

I. TO OURSELVES

We should begin at home. We too often flog the church when the whip should be laid on our own shoulders. We drag the church like a colossal culprit to the altar; we bind her and try to execute her at once; we bind her hands fast and tear off handful after handful of her quivering flesh—finding fault with her where there is none and magnifying her little errors, while we too often forget ourselves. Let us, therefore, commence with ourselves, remembering that we are part of the church and that our own want of revival is in some measure the cause of that want in the church at large.

Now I directly charge the great majority of professing Christians—I take the charge to myself also—with a need of a revival of piety in these days. I lay the charge before you very peremptorily, because I have abundant grounds to prove it. The mass of Christians in this age need a revival, and my reasons are these:

First, look at *the conduct and conversation* of the many who profess to be children of God. It ill becomes any man who occupies the sacred place of a pulpit to flatter his hearers. The evil lies with too many of you who unite yourselves with Christian churches and in practicality protest against your profession.

It has become very common to join a church and go where you may find professing Christians who sit down at some Lord's table or another, but are there fewer cheats than there used to be? Are there fewer frauds committed? Do we find morality more extensive? Do we find vice entirely at an end?

No, we do not. The age is as immoral as any that preceded it. There is still as much sin, although it is more cloaked and hidden. The outside of the sepulcher may be whiter, but within the bones are just as rotten as before or more so. Society is not one whit improved.

Those men who, in our popular magazines, give us a true picture of the state of London life are to be believed and credited, for they do not stretch the truth—they have no motive for so doing. And the picture they give of the morality of this great city is certainly appalling. It is a huge criminal, full of sin. And if all the profession of those in London who call themselves Christians were true profession, it would not be nearly such a wicked place as it is.

My brethren, it is well known—and who dares deny it—that it is not a sufficient guarantee, even of a man's honesty, that he is a member of a church. It is a hard thing for Christian ministers to say, but we must say it. And if friends say it not, enemies will. Better the truth be spoken in our own midst, that men may see that we are ashamed of it, than that they should hear us impudently deny what we must confess to be true!

O sirs, the lives of too many members of Christian churches give us grave cause to suspect that there is none of the life of godliness in them at all! Why that reaching after money, why that covetousness, why that following of the crafts and devices of a wicked world, why that clutching here and clutching there, that grinding of the faces of the poor, that stamping down of the workman, if men are truly what they profess to be? God knows that what I speak is true. And too many here know it yourselves.

If they be Christians, at the least they need revival. If there be life in them, it is but a spark that is covered up with heaps of ashes and needs to be fanned and stirred, that some of the ashes may be removed and the spark have place to live. The church wants revival in the persons of its members. The members of Christian churches are not what once they were.

It is fashionable to be religious now. Persecution is taken away, and I almost said the gates of the church were taken away with it. The church has, with few exceptions, no gates now. People come in and go out just as they would march through St. Paul's Cathedral. They make it a very place of traffic instead of regarding it as a select and sacred spot.

If this be not true, you need not confess to sin you have not committed;

but if it be true in your case, humble yourselves under the mighty hand of God. Ask Him to search and try you that if you be not His child, you may be helped to renounce a false profession, lest it lead to Hell. If you be His, ask Him to give you grace to renounce these faults and follies and turn to Him with full purpose of heart.

Again, where the *conduct* of professing Christians is consistent, does not the *conversation* lead us either to doubt the truthfulness of their piety or else to pray that their piety may be revived?

Have you noticed the conversation of too many who think themselves Christians? You might live with them from the first of January to the end of December and never, from what you would hear of it, tire of their religion. They scarcely mention the name of Jesus Christ. On Sunday afternoon all the ministers are talked over, faults are found with this one and the other. All kinds of conversation take place under the name of religion, because it is concerning religious places. But do they ever talk of what Christ said and did and what He suffered for us?

Do you ever hear the salutation addressed to you by your brother Christian, "Friend, how doth thy soul prosper?" When we step into each other's house, is our talk concerning the cause and truth of God? Would God now stoop from Heaven to listen to our conversation, as once He did, when it was said, "The Lord hearkened, and heard it, and a book of remembrance was written before him for them that feared the Lord, and that thought upon his name"?

I solemnly declare, as the result of thorough and impartial observation, that the conversation of Christians, while it cannot be condemned on the score of morality, must invariably be condemned on the score of Christianity. We talk too little about our Lord and Master.

That word *sectarianism* has crept into our midst, and we must say nothing about Christ because we might be called sectarians. I am a sectarian and hope to be so until I die. Can a man be a Christian, thoroughly in earnest, without winning for himself that title?

We must not talk of this doctrine because perhaps such a one disbelieves it. We must not notice such and such a truth in Scripture because such and such a friend doubts or denies it. So we drop all the great and grand topics which used to be the staple commodities of godly talk and begin to speak of anything else, because we feel we can agree better on worldly things than we can on spiritual things.

Is it not a sad sin with some of us that we have need to pray, "O

Lord, revive Thy work in my soul, that my conversation may be more Christlike, seasoned with salt, and kept by the Holy Spirit"?

Yet a third remark here. There are some whose conduct is all that we could wish, whose conversation is for the most part unctuous with the Gospel and savory of truth. But even they will confess to a third charge, which I must now sorrowfully bring against them and against myself, namely, that there is *too little real communion with Jesus Christ*.

If we are able to keep our conduct tolerably consistent and our lives unblemished, still we must cry out against ourselves for lack of holy fellowship with Jesus, the high mark of the true child of God!

Brethren, how long is it since you have had a love-visit from Jesus Christ—how long since you could say, "My beloved is mine, and I am his: he feedeth among the lilies"? How long is it since 'He brought you into His banqueting house, and His banner over you was love'?

Perhaps some of you will be able to say, "It was but this morning that I saw Him. I beheld His face with joy and was ravished with His countenance." But I fear the greater part of you here will have to say, "Ah, sir, for months I have been without the shinings of His countenance."

What have you been doing? What has been your way of life? Have you been groaning every day? Have you been weeping every minute? "No!" Then you ought to have been. I cannot understand how your piety can be of any very brilliant order if you can live without the sunlight of Christ and still be happy.

Christians sometimes will lose the fellowship of Jesus; the connection between themselves and Christ will be at times severed, but they should always groan and cry when they lose the sense of Christ's presence.

What? Is Christ thy Brother, living in thine house, yet thou hast not spoken to Him for a month? Then I fear there is little love between thee and thy Brother. What? Is Christ the Husband of His church, yet has she had no fellowship with Him for all this time?

Brethren, let me not condemn you nor judge you, but let your conscience speak. Have you too much forgotten Christ? Have you lived too much without Him? Have you been contented with the world instead of desiring Christ? Have you been like that little ewe lamb that did drink out of the master's cup and feed from his table? Or have you been content to stray upon the mountains, feeding anywhere but at home?

I fear many of our troubles spring from want of communion with Jesus. We live too much without the light of His countenance and are too happy when He is gone from us. Let each of us, then, send up the prayer, "O Lord, revive thy work."

Ah! I hear one professor saying, "Sir, I need no revival in my heart; I am everything I wish to be." Down on your knees for him, my brethren! He is the one who most needs to be prayed for. He says that he needs no revival in his soul; but he needs a revival of his humility, at any rate. If he supposes that he is all that he ought to be, and if he knows that he is all he wishes to be, he has very mean notions of what a Christian is or of what a Christian should be, and very unjust ideas of himself.

Those are in the best condition who, while they know they want reviving, feel their condition and groan under it.

I think I have in some degree substantiated my charge. Now notice that the text has something in it which I trust that each of us has. Here is not only an evil implied in these words—"O Lord, revive thy work"—but there is an evil evidently felt. You see, Habakkuk knew how to groan about it: "O Lord, revive thy work."

Ah, many of us *want* revival, but few of us *feel* that we want it. It is a blessed sign of life when we know how to groan over our departures from the living God. It is easy to find hundreds of those who have departed, but you can count by ones those who know how to groan over their departure.

When the true believer discovers that he needs revival, he will not be happy; he will begin at once to cry and groan. This will prevail with God and bring down the blessing of revival. He will, days and nights, cry, "O Lord, revive thy work."

Let me mention some groaning times when a Christian needs revival. You will groan *when you look upon what the Lord did for you of old*. When you recollect the Mizars and the Hermons, those places where the Lord appeared of old to you, saying, "I have loved thee with an everlasting love," you will never look back to them without tears.

If you are what you should be as a Christian, or if you think you are not in a right condition, you will always weep when you remember God's lovingkindness of old.

Whenever the soul has lost fellowship with Jesus, it cannot bear to think of the "chariots of Amminadib"; it cannot endure to think of "the banqueting house," for he hath not been there so long; or when he does think of it, he says,

The peaceful hours I then enjoyed,
How sweet their memory still,
But they have left an aching void
The world can never fill.

When you hear a sermon which relates the glorious experience of the believer who is in a healthy state, you will put your hand upon your heart and say, "Ah, such was my experience once; but those happy days are gone! My sun is set; those stars which once lit up my darkness are all quenched. Oh, that I might again behold Him! Oh, that I might once more see His face! Oh, for those sweet visits from on high! Oh, for the grapes of Eshcol once more!" And by the rivers of Babylon you will sit down and weep. You will weep, when you remember your goings up to Zion—when the Lord was precious to you, when He laid bare His heart and was pleased also to fill your heart with the fullness of His love. Such times will be groaning times when you remember "the years of the right hand of the most High."

Again, to a Christian who wants revival, *ordinances* also will be groaning times. You will go up to the house of God; but you will say when you come away, "Ah, how changed! When I once went with the multitude that kept the holy day, every word was precious. When the song ascended, my soul had wings, and up it flew to its nest among the stars. When the prayer was offered, I could devoutly say, 'Amen!'

"Now the preacher preaches as he did before; my brethren are as profited as once they were, but the sermon to me is dry and dull. I find no fault with the preacher; I know the fault is in myself. The song is just the same—as sweet the melody, as pure the harmony; but my heart is heavy. My harp strings are broken, and I cannot sing."

The Christian will return from those blessed means of grace sighing and sobbing because he knows he wants revival.

More especially, at the Lord's Supper you will think, when you sit at the table, "Oh, what seasons I once had here! In breaking the bread and drinking the juice, my Master was present." You will recall how your soul was even carried to the seventh heaven and the house was made 'the very house of God and the gate of Heaven.'

"But now," you say, "it is bread, dry bread to me; it is juice, tasteless juice, with none of the sweetness of paradise in it. I drink, but all in vain. No thoughts of Christ. My heart will not rise; my soul cannot heave a thought halfway to Him!"

And then you will begin to groan again—"O Lord, revive thy work."

But I shall not detain you upon that subject. Those of you who know that you are in Christ but do not love Him enough and have not that faith in Him which you desire to have, I would just ask you this: Do you groan over it? Can you groan now? When you feel your heart is empty, is it "an aching void"? When you feel that your garments are stained, can you wash those garments with tears? When you think your Lord is gone, do you hang out the black flag of sorrow and cry, "O my Jesus! O my Jesus! art Thou gone?"

If you can, then I bid you do it. And may God be pleased to give you grace to continue to do it until a happier era dawns in the reviving of thy soul!

In the last place, when the soul is really brought to feel its own sad estate because of its declension and departure from God, *it is never content without turning its groaning into prayer* and without addressing the prayer to the right quarter: "O Lord, revive thy work."

Some of you, perhaps, will say, "Sir, I feel my need of revival. I intend to set to work this very afternoon to revive my soul."

Do not say it, and above all, do not try to do it, for you never can. Make no resolutions as to what you will do; your resolutions will as certainly be broken as they are made, and your broken resolutions will but increase the number of your sins. I exhort you, instead of trying to revive yourself, to offer prayers. Say not, "I will revive myself," but cry, "O Lord, revive *thy* work."

And let me solemnly tell you, you have not yet felt what it is to decline; you do not yet know how sad is your estate, otherwise you wouldn't talk of reviving yourself. If you did know your own position, you would as soon expect to see the wounded soldier on the battlefield heal himself without medicine or convey himself to the hospital when his limbs are shot away as you would expect to revive yourself without the help of God. I bid you not to do anything nor seek to do anything until first you have addressed Jehovah Himself by mighty prayer—until you have cried out, "O Lord, revive thy work."

Remember, He who first made you must keep you alive; and He who has kept you alive must restore more life to you. He who has preserved you from going down to the pit, when your feet have been sliding, can alone set you again upon a rock and establish your goings.

Begin, then, by humbling yourself—giving up all hope of reviving yourself as a Christian, but beginning at once with firm prayer and earnest supplication to God: "O Lord, what I cannot do, do Thou! O Lord, revive Thy work."

Christian brethren, I leave these matters with you. Give them the attention they deserve. If I have erred and in aught judged you too harshly, God forgive me, for I have meant it honestly. But if I have spoken truly, lay it to your heart and turn your houses into a "Bochim." Weep, weep, my brethren: "It is a sad thing to depart from the living God." Weep, and may He bring you back to Zion, that you may one day return like Israel, not with weeping but with songs of everlasting joy!

II. TO OUR CHURCHES

And now I come to the second part of the subject upon which I must be more brief. In the church itself, taken as a body, this prayer ought to be one incessant and solemn litany: "O Lord, revive thy work."

In the present era there is *a sad decline of the vitality of godliness*. This age has become too much the age of form instead of the age of life. I date the hour of life from this day one hundred years ago when the first stone of this building in which we now worship God was laid. Then was the day of life divine and of power sent down from on high.

God had clothed Whitefield with power. He was preaching with a majesty and a might of which one could scarcely think mortal could ever be capable, not because he was anything in himself but because his Master girded him with might.

After Whitefield there was a succession of great and holy men. But now we have fallen upon the dregs of time.

True men are the rarest thing in all this world. We have not many of them left now. We have hardly any men in government to conduct our politics and scarcely any men in religion. We have the men who perform their duties, as they are called; we have the good and, perhaps, the honest who in their regular routine go on like packhorses with their bells, forever in the old style; but men who dare to be singular, because to be singular is generally to be right in a wicked world—there are not very many in this age.

Compared with the puritanic times, where are our divines? Could we marshal together our Howes and our Charnocks? Could we gather together such names as I could mention about fifty at a time? I think not.

Nor could we bring together such a galaxy of brace and talent as that which immediately followed Whitefield. Think of Rowland Hill, Newton,

Toplady, Doddridge and numbers of others whom time would fail me to mention. They are gone. Their venerated dust sleeps in the earth.

And where are their successors? Ask where, and Echo shall reply, "Where?" There are none. Successors of them, where are they? God hath not yet raised them up, or if He has, we have not yet found out where they are.

There is preaching, and what is it? "O Lord, help Thy servant to preach, and teach him by Thy Spirit what to say." Then out comes the manuscript, and they read it—a pure insult to Almighty God! We have preaching of this order, but it is not preaching at all. It is speaking very beautifully and very finely, possibly eloquently, in some sense of the word; but where is the right down preaching such as Whitefield's?

Have you ever read one of his sermons? You will not think him eloquent. His expressions were rough, frequently very coarse and unconnected. There was very much declamation about him. It was a great part, indeed, of his speech. But where lay his eloquence? Not in the words you read but in the tone in which he delivered them, in the earnestness with which he felt them, in the tears which ran down his cheeks, and in the pouring out of his soul.

The reason why Whitefield was eloquent was just what the word means. He was eloquent because he spoke from his heart—from the innermost depths of the man. You knew when he spoke that he meant what he said. He did not speak as a trade or as a mere machine, but he preached what he felt to be the truth and what he could not help preaching. When you heard him preach, you could not help feeling that he was a man who would die if he could not preach. With all his might he called men to "Come! come! come to Jesus Christ and believe on Him!"

Now, that is just the lack of these times. Where is earnestness now? It is neither in pulpit nor in pew in such a measure as we desire it. And it is a sad, sad age when earnestness is scoffed at, when that very zeal which ought to be the prominent characteristic of the pulpit is regarded as enthusiasm and fanaticism.

May God make us such fanatics as most men laugh at—make us just such enthusiasts as many despise.

We reckon it the greatest fanaticism in the world to go to Hell, the greatest enthusiasm upon earth to love sin better than righteousness. And we think those neither fanatics nor enthusiasts who seek to obey

God rather than man and follow Christ in all His ways.

We repeat: one sad proof that the church needs revival is the absence of that deathlike, solemn earnestness which was once seen in Christian pulpits.

The absence of sound doctrine is another proof of our want of revival. The men who once were the orthodox are now the heretics. We can turn back to the records of our Puritan fathers, to the articles of the Church of England, to the preaching of Whitefield, and we can say of that preaching that it is the very thing we love; and the doctrines which were then uttered are—and we dare to say it everywhere—the very selfsame doctrines that he proclaimed. But because we choose to proclaim them, we are thought singular and strange; and the reason is that sound doctrine has to a great degree ceased.

We need a revival of sound doctrine once more in the midst of the land.

And the church at large, maybe, needs a *revival of downright earnestness in its members*.

Ye are not the men to fight the Lord's battles yet.Ye have not the earnestness, the zeal which once the children of God had. Your forefathers were oaken men; ye are willow men. Our people, what are they, many of them? Strong in doctrine when they are with strong-doctrine men but wavering when they get with others. They change doctrines as often as they change their company. They are sometimes one thing and sometimes another. They are not the men to go to the stake and die. They are not the men who know how to die daily and thereby are ready for death when it comes.

Look at our prayer meetings, with here and there a bright exception. Go in. There are about six women and a few men. Look at them. Prayer meetings they are called; *spare* meetings they ought to be called, for sparely enough they are attended. And very few go to our fellowship meetings or to any other meetings that we have to help one another. I would like to see a newspaper printed somewhere containing a list of all the persons who go to those meetings during the week in any of our chapels.

My friends, if they should comprise all the Christians in London, you might find that a chapel or two would hold them all. Few enough go.

We have not earnestness, we have not life as we once had. If we had, we would be called worse names than we are; we would have viler epithets thrown at us if we were more true to our Master. We would not have all things quite so comfortable if we served God better.

The church is getting to be an honorable institution of our land. And some think it a grand thing when the church becomes an honorable institution! I think it shows the church has swerved when she begins to be very honorable in the eyes of the world.

She must still be cast out, must still be called evil, must still be despised, until that day when her Lord shall honor her because she has honored Him—shall honor her, even in this world, in the day of His appearing.

Beloved, do you think it is true that the church wants reviving? Yes or no? "No," you say, "not to the extent that you suppose. *We* think the church is in a good condition. We are not among those who cry, 'The former days were better than these.'"

Perhaps you are not: you may be far wiser than we are, and therefore you are able to see those various signs of goodness which are to us so small that we are not able to discover them. You may suppose that the church is in a good condition; if so, of course you cannot sympathize with me in preaching from such a text and urging you to use such a prayer. But others of you are frequently prone to cry, "The church wants reviving." Let me bid you, instead of grumbling at your minister, instead of finding fault with the different parts of the church, cry, "O Lord, revive thy work."

"Oh," says one, "if we had another minister! Oh, if we had another kind of worship! Oh, if we had a different sort of preaching"—just as if that were all! But it should be our prayer, "O Lord, come into the hearts of the men we already have. O Lord, fill them with Thy power." We do not need fresh ways or fresh machinery; we need life in what we have.

There is an engine on a railway; a train has to be moved. "Bring another engine," says one, "and another, and another." The engines are brought, but the train does not move at all. To light the fire and get the steam up is what you want, not more or different engines.

To make the church better, we do not need fresh ministers or fresh plans or fresh ways, though many might be invented; we only need life in what we have.

Given, the very man who has emptied your chapel; given, the selfsame person who brought your prayer meeting low; God can make the chapel crowded to the doors yet and give thousands of souls to that very man.

It is not a new man that is wanted; it is the life of God in him. Do not be crying out for something new; it will no more succeed of itself than what you have. Cry, "O Lord, revive thy work."

I have noticed in different churches that the minister has thought first of this contrivance, then of that. He tried one plan and thought that would succeed; then he tried another; that was not it. Keep to the old plan but get life in it. We do not want anything new; "the old is better"—let us keep to it. But we want the life of the old.

"Oh," men cry, "we have nothing but the shell; they are going to give us a new shell." No, sirs, we will keep the old one, but we will have life in the shell, too. We will have the old thing, but we must have the life in the old. Oh, that God would give us life!

The church wants fresh revivals. Oh, for the days of Cambuslang again, when Whitefield preached with power. Oh, for the days when in this place hundreds were converted sometimes under Whitefield's sermons! It has been known that two thousand credible cases of conversion have happened under one solitary discourse. Oh, for the age when eyes would be strained and ears would be ready to receive the Word of God and when men would drink in the Word of Life—the very water of life which God gives to dying souls! Oh, for the age of deep feeling—the age of deep, thoroughgoing earnestness!

Let us ask God, plead with Him for it. Perhaps He has the man or the men somewhere who will shake the world yet. Perhaps even now He is about to pour forth a mighty influence upon men which shall make the church as wonderful in this age as it ever was in any age that has passed.

GEORGE WASHINGTON TRUETT
1867-1944

ABOUT THE MAN:

North Carolina was George Washington Truett's birthplace. By the time he was 18, he was educated well enough to begin teaching in a one-room public school on Crooked Creek in nearby Towns County, Georgia. It was during that two-year apprenticeship that George was converted. Then he established an academy at Hiawassee, Georgia, in 1887. The student body eventually numbered over 300.

When the Truett family moved to Texas in 1889, George went to college—Baylor University—though not as a student. He was offered the position of financial secretary and was instrumental in saving Baylor from bankruptcy. Afterward he became a student, graduated, and unbelievably was elected to become Baylor's president!

But the same year of his graduation he was called to the First Baptist Church of Dallas, remaining there for 47 years, or until his death in 1944. Under his leadership the church grew into the largest church in the world at that time, with 18,124 additions and 5,337 baptisms.

But Dr. Truett had many pulpits besides the pulpit at First Baptist Church. He instituted the Palace Theatre services, held each noon the week before Easter, with nearly 2,000 attending. He preached out in the country churches all across the South, and the common folk heard him gladly. He preached from the steps of our nation's Capitol, and in world centers in London, Stockholm, Paris, Berlin, Jerusalem, etc. Everywhere Truett's preaching produced souls for Christ.

In 1927 he was elected president of the Southern Baptist Convention, which office he served for three terms.

By any standard, he ranks as one of the most popular and influential preachers in America in the first half of the twentieth century. He was a world figure; was on close terms with presidents, senators and governors.

Dr. Truett was a great man, a great leader, and a great preacher of the Gospel. His biographers knew whereof they spoke when they explained the man and his ministry in two well-defined words: *"heart-power."*

IV.

A Prayer for Revival

GEORGE W. TRUETT

"Wilt thou not revive us again: that thy people may rejoice in thee?"— Ps. 85:6.

The text is a short prayer, but volumes of meaning are wrapped up in it.

David does not pray that conditions or circumstances may be changed, but he prays for people, God's people. "Wilt thou not revive us again: that thy people may rejoice in thee?" David had learned far back in that olden time that if there is to be any deep, great work of grace wrought for a lost world, then such work of grace must begin in the hearts of God's people. It is true—and does not need to be argued— that when God's people are right, things always go well with His work. When God's people are wrong, things always go badly with His work.

Prayer Always Essential to Revival

A lesson coming down to us through all the generations is that going before any great, deep work of grace, Christians have waited before God in confession of sin, in supplication for His grace, in the humbling of their hearts, in the submission of their wills to Him, that He might do for and with them according to His holy will.

That is surely the lesson that comes down to us, touching God's work and people all through the generations. There is no such thing as any great, deep, far-reaching work of grace anywhere, if God's people do not experientially know the mighty means of prayer touching such work of grace.

All history as it touches God's people and His work in the world is the confirmation of this statement.

It was when Israel down in Egypt prayed after the right fashion that deliverance came.

In the days of Nehemiah, when they prayed after the right fashion, the walls of God's house went up again.

It was so in the days of good King Josiah. The thing that preeminently characterized the revival for the glory of God in his time was the right waiting before God of His people.

And surely, from the human point of view, the one marvelous thing about the incomparable meeting on the day of Pentecost, the influence of which kept on in such wondrous fashion for a generation, was that for ten days God's people just prayed. For ten long days they tarried yonder in the quiet place, away from the crowd, waiting, with one accord, for power from on high.

When will we learn the lesson that it is time gained in all respects if we give ourselves very much to the blessed exercise of prayer in carrying on God's work in the world? For my part, I do not believe that in any of these "revivals" or "special meetings" we have that God is honored in them, or that people are really regenerated in them, if going through, and before, and after them there is not the moving of the hearts of Christians in prayer.

When will we rightly lay such great matter to heart? It is fundamental to the real success of all God-saving effort. And you yourselves are the witnesses that I speak the truth tonight. In your own Christian experiences, there come to you the memories of the occasions when you were specially blessed of God in the winning of souls. Those mighty spiritual blessings, those days of the right hand of God, those days when you heard His stately steppings, those days when you saw His mighty Spirit pierce the hearts of sinful men and bring them down—those were the times when your own hearts were empty of their self-sufficiency, and when, with a cry unto God from the deepest depths of the soul, you besought Him to arise and plead His own cause and save lost sinners.

You yourselves, I say, are witnesses to that same significant truth. When you have had special power with the unsaved to win them to God, it is always when you had power with God. Men do not have power with God—it is a thing unknown in His spiritual kingdom—if they be not men of prayer, men of real intercession, men who know the meaning of the secret place, where alone they look into the King's face until He speaks His message to them. There is no such thing as power to win the lost if God's people do not pray.

You yourselves, I say, are witnesses to that great fact. The times when you have had power with men so that they could not resist your appeals, so that you saw their faces humbled before you, and you saw the conquest of the soul go on before your very eyes—those were the times when you were in touch with the great King, when your soul had conscious fellowship with Him, when you took hold of Him and felt that you were one with Him. Those who come to realize that experience do so through the gracious medium of prayer.

A Burden for Souls Begets Powerful Prayer

"The burden of the Lord"—when that is upon us, then it is that we know the burden of prayer. O brethren, this light, easy, tearless, hop-skip-and-jump method in the matchless work of turning men to God is not the New Testament way. If the unsaved are turned to Almighty God in any blessed fashion, then the people of God know about it, and there is a cry unto Him; the deepest cry of their hearts is heard, that lost sinners may be saved. God's people always cry like that if any mighty movement of His Spirit and His saving grace is felt among the people.

When I was a little lad I recall how again and again I went to the old country church to their appointed "protracted meetings" every summer. Farmers would gather in at the morning meetings, then again at the evening meetings—two services a day—and they would thus daily gather together for several days. Great crowds came, but often nothing seemed to be done.

I have seen and heard those farmers as they would meet and chat under the great trees before the morning service. Often they would talk about this and that, then one would say to the other, "Neighbor, have you any burden for souls today?"

The answer would come back rather shrinkingly, "No, neighbor, I haven't any special burden yet for souls, I am sorry to say."

The next day that would be repeated. They would thus talk around on the edges of the meeting, maybe for days, then one would say, "Have you any burden about this meeting today? Have you a burden for souls today?"

The answer would be with trembling lip and with eyes suffused with tears, "I have, O neighbor, I have. God is my judge, how last night I felt to call upon Him through the long, long night. I saw my own boys lost, and I saw your boys lost, and I saw our neighborhood lost. Oh, I have a burden for souls I cannot describe."

I was at first too young to know what it all meant, but I can recall with what awe I would listen to it all, and even as a little child my soul was perfectly sure that God was somewhere near. And He was! And when we would go into the old country meeting house on such a day, and the meeting would begin, and trembling lips would lead the prayers, and the hymns would be sung, God would come down into that meeting, and men that day were brought down by the life-giving Spirit of God. Whereas for days before the meetings were perfunctory and stilted and cold, now they were kindled into a strange glow. Sobs were heard on every side, and lost men asked, "What must we do to be saved?"

What had happened, brethren? That "burden of souls" had come to God's people, without which soul-winning effort is largely in vain. Whenever they have that "burden of souls," things glorious always come to pass in the kingdom of God.

We had better wait; we had better betake ourselves to a quiet place; we had better search our hearts and beg Him to search them for us; we had better go alone, each one for himself or herself, and talk with God, each one pouring out his soul to this effect: "O God, give me to feel about Thy work like Thou wishest. Come down in Thine own way and open the gates to my soul, so that I shall feel about Thy work as Thou wishest."

You and I need to do that, brethren, and we need to do that tonight, with special reference to the work that is just now before us.

Prayer That Prevails With God

Some months ago a pastor was out in a vast country camp meeting. A large arbor was provided, and from night to night there gathered a mighty crowd, so that the pastor needed to put his voice out to the last limit to be heard. But for days, so far as could be judged, nothing much was done.

One night the preacher went to his room and was making ready to retire, when the gentleman with whom he was staying came in. The host had very little to say, and the preacher made ready for sleep, and now was in the bed, while the host sat on the cot on the other side of the room. (Both slept in the same room.) The good wife of the host had departed a few years before to be with the Lord. He had two grown daughters, popular and beautiful, but worldly—worldly, it seemed, after an unusual fashion.

He sat over there that night on his cot, and after awhile, just as the preacher was ready to sleep, a sob was heard. The preacher looked up and beheld his kindly friend with his face in his hands and his great body fairly quivering.

Said the preacher, "What is the trouble?" calling his host by name.

He answered, "You ought to know what the trouble is. You have been in my home for three or four days."

The preacher said, "Yes, I do; it is the girls."

The host replied, "It is even so. Their mother is gone, and the sense of responsibility for them comes over me tonight as I never felt it before." Then he added, "Oh, if Mary (the older one) would only come to Christ, the problem, I think, would be settled with Jennie. Jennie always does what Mary does."

The preacher said, "Well, we will pray for Mary tonight," and out of his bed he came. He knelt by his host. They talked to God about Mary, specifically, that the Almighty Saviour might Himself take hold of her heart and bring her to Himself. She was an amiable, beautiful girl, as has been said, but utterly indifferent about the claims of the Lord, so far as could be seen.

Then the preacher went back to his bed. After awhile the door stood ajar, and the anxious father was seen quietly going out into the moonlight, and then the door was closed. The preacher was soon asleep. In the early morning time the door was again quietly opened, and in came the host. A glance at his cot showed that he had been absent for the night.

The preacher asked, "Where have you been?"

And the answer was, "I will tell you about it, but you need not speak of it to the others. It is not a matter to be spoken of. I have been out there all night long talking to God about Mary. And that is not all. Mary will come to Christ today."

Said the preacher, "Do you look for that?"

He simply answered, "Yes, you will see that blessed result today."

And that day, when the preacher finished his sermon at the morning meeting and asked while they sang if anybody had found the Saviour to come and confess Him before all the people—before they could start the music, Mary came with smiling face and said, "I found Him while you preached."

Do you doubt that there was a vital connection between that man's prayer and that child's finding Christ? The very next day, before the preacher had preached ten minutes, the other daughter, Jennie, rose up in the midst of the great crowd and said, "Papa, I have found the Saviour, too."

I ask again, do you doubt that there was vital connection between that prayer and that child's finding Christ?

O God, burden us for souls! Paul had the "burden for souls." Hear him:

"I say the truth in Christ, I lie not, my conscience also bearing me witness in the Holy Ghost, that I have great heaviness and continual sorrow in my heart. For I could wish that myself were accursed from Christ for my brethren, my kinsmen according to the flesh."

The "burden for souls"—may God give it to us all! This is God's way—may His way be ours!

Why God Requires Burdened Prayer Before Soul-Winning Revival

Why is this God's way? The reasons for it could be multiplied. Here are some. This is God's plan. Because in His own infinite wisdom He chose that it should be His plan, that is enough for us. God has revealed all along that one of the mightiest instruments in His kingdom for the furtherance of His cause in this world, for the turning of men to Christ, is prayer.

See the injunctions to us to pray. We are to pray without ceasing. We are to pray for all men. We are not to so sin against the Lord, and so sin against men, as to cease praying for men. Behold, how the Scriptures magnify the place of prayer in the kingdom of God for the furtherance of His truth. It is God's plan, and we are to address ourselves to God's plan. Whenever we know God's mind about anything, then we have reached the end of the debate. We are to obey Him unreservedly.

Then we go further and see that as labor is good for us in the physical world, so is it in the spiritual world. Spiritual labor is an exercise of incalculable moment. In the physical world, physical labor is for our upbuilding. In the spiritual world, spiritual labor, the exercising of ourselves unto godliness, is the thing made very much of in the Scriptures.

Nor is that all. This kind of waiting upon God, this kind of confession of helplessness and of supplication for grace and power, fits us to take care of people when they are saved.

O brethren, how sad that our young Christians, so many times, get such a pitiful start in the Christian life! It is a great thing for a Christian to be well born. That is one reason why we need to guard the churches of Jesus Christ.

When Christ's church is spiritual and calls upon Him with all humility and with self-abnegation and He answers back and gives them a soul saved, then the church is ready to take care of that soul.

Why is it that in many of our churches vast numbers remain little spiritual babes all their lives? The answer is, their start was bad. Their surroundings were not of a gracious sort. They were not put on the right track and kept going in the right track. We are ready to take care of the young converts when they come to us in answer to the right sort of prayer.

What would become of that little newborn babe if he should be taken from his mother's arms and thrown into the snowbanks? And what will become of the little newborn child of God if he be ushered into a church where the atmosphere is lukewarm and worldly and indifferent to God's claims? There is likely to be one outcome only to that little religious life—the shipwreck of happiness and usefulness. Our God has ordained this great method of carrying on His work, so that when souls are given to us, we are able to take care of them after the right fashion.

Pray Because Salvation Is of the Lord

Not only that, but this is His plan, in order to teach us what we seem to forget most quickly of all—salvation is of the Lord. The truth that we seem to learn last of all, and the truth that we seem to forget most quickly of all is—salvation is of the Lord. Oh, we accept it theoretically. You ask if we believe it, and with great promptness we answer that we do, yet do we? How much do we believe it?

How soon we forget this vital truth: we can raise men from that cemetery yonder as easily as we can regenerate the most amiable child in your Sunday school to God; we can speak a world like this into life as easily as we can regenerate the most lovely soul in this city!

Salvation is a divine work. Regeneration is a divine work. Conviction for sin is a divine work. The turning of men to God is a divine work. The making of men ready for Heaven is a divine work.

We learn that when we are on our knees before God. When we are out talking and moving among men, we may go a great deal on the doctrine of salvation by works, but when we are on our faces before God, our helplessness is borne in upon us; then, with self-abnegation and a sense of our utter insufficiency, we humbly wait on God to do His work. Mark it: when our attitude is right before Him, He always uses us to do His work.

This is the crucial point I must ask you to face: Will we make this prayer of our text personal? "Wilt thou not revive us again, that thy people may rejoice in thee?" Do we wish for it to be personal? I ask you that direct question, and I ask you to answer it, beseech you to answer it in sincerity and truth. Is this our prayer tonight? Let us know full well that each one of us shall be a helper or a hindrance in this proposed work. All along we are one of these two things in Christ's work. I speak now to Christians, to those who have named Christ's name, who know and profess His cause to love. In Christ's work, we are either helpers or hinderers in giving salvation to the perishing around us.

How Christians Hinder Revival

Who hinders Christ's work? First, the idle Christian does. Christians are not made to be idle. They are not made to be mute. They are not made for their lips to be sealed so that they give forth no testimony to the dying around them. Christians are made to be busy. Christians are left in the world to be active for Jesus. The idle Christian, then, hinders the cause of God.

O Christian, if thou art idle, thou art hindering somewhere the advance of the great kingdom of God. The idleness of Christians surely hinders the march of the kingdom of God. Call to mind those solemn words of Jesus: "He that is not with me is against me; and he that gathered not with me scattereth abroad." What does your heart say to that?

Jesus cursed the fig tree because it was idle. It ought to have borne fruit, and it did not; therefore, He cursed it.

Meroz of old was cursed because Meroz was idle. She did not take up arms against the other tribes of Israel. She did not lift up the black flag and turn traitor to Israel. Meroz simply stayed home and left her brothers to go out and fight the battle. They went out, fought and won, but with their victorious refrain there was mingled the refrain of the curse of the angel of God: "Curse ye Meroz, . . . curse ye bitterly the inhabitants thereof; because they came not to the help of the Lord, to the help of the Lord against the mighty."

The idle Christian hinders God's work. Nor is that all. The Christian not right with God hinders His work. This is a matter of unspeakable gravity, if only we rightly knew it. If a saved person is not right in his outward conduct, we can see how that hinders God's work. But oh what wounds the Lord Jesus Christ receives in the house of His real friends, men who do love Him, men who, if they were crowded to the wall, would die for Him! What wounds He receives at the hands of such men, full many a time, by their inconsistent words and works!

We need not trouble so much about the attacks of some blatant infidel out yonder who rails against the Bible. He is not the supreme trouble at all. The trouble supreme to the advancement of our Lord's kingdom is with the people of His kingdom, with those who love it, who are of it, yet whose lives do not harmonize with it.

If we are saying wrong things or if we are doing wrong things; if in our lives inconsistencies may be seen; if there is marked worldliness; if we fall so far short of the characteristics of what a Christian ought to have so that those about us believe that our religion is just a theory and not the dominating passion of our lives, then are we hindering the cause of Christ to a very sad degree.

Nor is that all. We sadly hinder the cause of Christ, even though outwardly all may seem to be well with us, if inwardly it is not well with us. I do not know of any thought for the Christian more terribly serious than this: that the secret condition of his heart—which condition his wife does not, cannot know, nor his most intimate earthly companion know—which condition is known only to him and to God, is helping men in this city Heavenward or turning them Hellward. The secret condition of your heart, a condition where no other eye can look, save One, is now helping men up or dragging them down. If a man's heart is right with God, then one prayer prayed from such a heart will have more power with God and men than a thousand years of praying if the heart is all wrong with God.

No wonder David prayed, "Restore unto me the joy of thy salvation." Not salvation, mind you; he had that—but, 'Give me back again the *joy* of thy salvation, and then I will teach transgressors thy ways, and then sinners shall be converted unto God.'

When a man is right with God, there is power in his praying. When a man is right with God, he may lock the heavens, as did Elijah, or, like him, he may unlock them.

Mind you, it is the supplication of a "righteous" man that availeth much. So the secret condition of our hearts is helping or hindering now these appointed gospel meetings and will help or hinder them all along.

If there is one picture in the Bible more than another that is solemn in the extreme, it is the picture of Achan's secret sin and the doom that followed in Joshua's army in the olden time—a sin which was known only to Achan and to God until Achan was searched and exposed.

I had this night rather be nailed up in my coffin and buried alive than go through these gospel meetings with my heart all wrong and my soul out of harmony with God, for I will either help or I will hinder others. Death were preferable infinitely than that a man should go on as a Christian, himself hindering salvation, himself hindering the blessed current of life that comes from God to man.

Every Christian is one of these two things—a hinderer or a helper. He is a channel through which God is pleased to send His grace and blessings to lost men or a clog to stop up that channel.

Is this text our prayer tonight? "Revive us again"—do we pray it? Know this: God has a blessing for us here, if—if what? If only we wish it sufficiently.

There is a recipe for soul-winning effort given in chapter 7 of II Chronicles, the observance of which never fails: *"If my people, which are called by my name, shall humble themselves, and pray, and seek my face, and turn from their wicked ways; then will I hear from heaven, and will forgive their sin, and will heal their land."*

The observance of that recipe has never failed and never will. We shall have here a great blessing if we will faithfully live out the truth of this one verse.

The Sin of Not Caring for Souls

Are we going to be satisfied if Christ's people are not revived? Then they will not be. Are we going to be satisfied if men all about us are not convicted for sin and turned to Christ? Can we be satisfied if that result does not come? Then it will not come. Any preacher who can complacently preach month in and month out, year in and year out, without seeing men converted—who can preach on and eat heartily and sleep soundly—will not see many converts under his ministry.

I tell you, it is a life and death business in which we are engaged. Any church that can sit with folded hands and be satisfied if men are not turned to God, that can be at ease with such a condition, will not have men added unto her.

Do we wish to be revived? We shall have a great turning to God here if we wish it enough.

May I take one moment more just to talk to you about your plain duty? O God, bear Thou in upon us tonight the realization of this thought: we are left here to speak to dying men and women and children at every possible place and in every possible way concerning the saving grace of Jesus Christ.

Shall I talk to you about such duty? You Christians are to remember that teaching school is incidental; practicing medicine is incidental; pleading law is incidental; being a farmer is incidental—mere incidents in the life that you are left here to live. The supreme thing for which you live is to point men to Christ.

Shall I talk to you about your responsibility? That is, indeed, a solemn question: "Am I my brother's keeper?" The answer must be that I am his keeper to the last limit of my ability to help him, but by just letting him alone by simple neglect, I may become my brother's spiritual murderer.

Yonder is a man, let us suppose, dying on the streets of Dallas tonight. You will see him as you go home. He is sick or drunk. It is a cold and stormy night. The snow and sleet are falling fast. The man is helpless. He lies in the gutter, unconscious, it may be, of his awful danger. You look upon him, then pass him by. Leave him to that awful fate, and in the morning he will be dead. In the sight of Heaven, his blood will be required at your hands. You have no right to leave your brother to such a fate as that.

Here is a neighbor or a child or a brother or a friend in spiritual night, and he does not realize it. He is condemned under the law of God, and he does not apprehend it. He may be in eternity tomorrow, and he does not take it to heart. He is without God, without hope, without light, without life, without grace and without salvation, and you know it. Leaving him alone to die in his sins, with such knowledge in your possession, means that, going down the dusty way of death, his blood may be required at your hands.

Do you wish for God to revive you and this church and His people here just as He wishes to? Do you men and women here tonight wish Him to send you that quickening of conscience, that renewal of strength, that restoring of the joy of salvation that will help you to do what He asks at your hands? Do you wish a revival here just like He wishes it? What say your hearts? Answer honestly, and we are ready to be dismissed.

Every man and woman here who answers back from the heart, "Before God, I do tonight go on record, with His eye upon me and in the sight of men, that I wish Him to come during these quiet meetings and absolutely have His way with me and with these meetings," will now, in this solemn moment, quietly signify such wish by standing.

(During the solemn pause many quietly rose.) The preacher added: "Behold us, Lord, as our solemn wish is now recorded in Thy sight and in each other's sight. From our hearts we would most fervently pray, 'Wilt thou not revive us again: that thy people may rejoice in thee?' "

(From the book, WE WOULD SEE JESUS, by Fleming H. Revell Company. Used by permission.)

HYMAN JEDIDIAH APPELMAN
1902-1983

ABOUT THE MAN:

Dr. Appelman was born in Russia and was reared and trained in the Jewish faith. He could speak many languages. The family moved to America in 1914. Dr. Appelman graduated with honors from Northwestern University and from DePaul University where he was one of the highest in the class and was awarded a scholarship. He received his license to practice law from DePaul Law School and was a trial lawyer in Chicago 1921-25.

At age 28 he was converted. His Jewish family, then living in Chicago, disowned him. His father said to him, **"When your sides come together from hunger and you come crawling to my door, I will throw you a crust of bread as I would any other dog."**

Feeling a definite call to preach, he attended Southwestern Baptist Theological Seminary in Fort Worth 1930-33.

In 1933 he was elected to be one of the State Evangelists for Texas; he faithfully ministered for eight years in this capacity for the Southern Baptist Convention. Later he launched into larger meetings, both in Texas and outside, and soon was spending some time, year after year, in a foreign country. His meetings were large meetings, with hundreds, sometimes thousands, of conversions in each.

Dr. Appelman made eight or nine trips around the world and several trips to Russia as an evangelist.

His schedule left one breathless. It was hard to find a day in his long ministry of fifty-three years that he was not preaching somewhere. He averaged two weeks at home out of a year. That was the intenseness of a Jew! Of this Jew, at least! His prayer life, hard work and biblical preaching reminded one of the Apostle Paul.

Dr. Appelman was the author of some forty books.

V.

God's Plan for a Revival

HYMAN J. APPELMAN

Preached at the memorable Sword Conference on Evangelism
at Winona Lake, Indiana, in 1945

The subject assigned to me tonight suits me down to the ground, especially for a conference such as this. After all, it is concerned with the preparation of our own hearts and the hearts of those to whom we minister.

"God's Plan for a Revival"—there is no better plan than II Chronicles 7:14:

"If my people, which are called by my name, shall humble themselves, and pray, and seek my face, and turn from their wicked ways; then will I hear from heaven, and will forgive their sin, and will heal their land."

Here is God's plan for a revival.

WHAT DOES "REVIVAL" MEAN?

By way of introduction, let us think together, first, about the meaning of a revival. There are all kinds of ideas about what a revival is. The word is one of the most sinned against in all of the Christian vocabulary.

Here is a church that has not been doing anything. It has no baptisms. The pastor of that church comes to the association or the convention with a mighty slim annual report. The church hears about a man whom God has been using to win souls, so he is invited to conduct a revival in order that the church might have a good report to make at the end of the year.

People call that a revival. It is not!

Then, in some other place, the church has been doing pretty good work. But there are some old stumps, some old nesters that everybody has burned over, still left around in the community—middle-aged sinners, old, hardened cases. The saints hear of a man whom God is honoring with His power. They think that if he will but come, the dynamite of his personality, or whatever else it is that he has, will blast those stumps out and get them into the church.

I used to rejoice when an old man was converted. But now I had rather see one junior child converted than any five grown men. Gipsy Smith was right when he said, "When you win an old man, you have won a cipher; when you win a child, you have won a multiplication table."

I have read after the great preachers of this and other generations. The vast majority of them were converted when they were children, before they had a chance to go into the depths of sin.

Not even God can teach an old dog new tricks. He had to keep the Jews forty years in the wilderness before He had a generation that was pliable enough for what He wanted them to do in the Promised Land.

There are some other places where church and pastor are having a fuss. It doesn't take much to have a fuss in a church. Maybe the people don't like the pastor's necktie or his wife or some other fool thing. So there is a definite cleavage, a division. There is danger of the church's splitting. The pastor, not wanting to lose his job and some people in the church not wanting to lose the pastor nor have a split, invite an evangelist, thinking that by the acetylene torch of his power he will weld the two factions together, and the church will go on in the even, or uneven, tenor of its way.

Folks call that a revival.

But what is a revival?

A Revival, a Time of Testing

First, a revival is a time of testing, examination time, a time of balancing and weighing, a time of judgment. The revival is the testing of the evangelist. I am an evangelist! I am talking about myself first! I didn't want to be an evangelist but a pastor. If God would release me from the evangelistic field, I would rather be a pastor now. Dr. Hankins will remember the incident I am about to tell, and he will bear me out. He knows about it because I wrote to him.

A certain tremendous church wanted me to be their pastor. The pulpit committee met me at the station as I was on my way to New York and said, "We are going to call you Wednesday night."

I went into my Pullman thanking God, rejoicing that at last, after all these driving, lonely years, I was going to be with my wife and babies in the pastorate of a church I loved, among people whom I knew and loved. Oh, I was thanking God in gratitude, with tears starting down from my eyes and rolling down my cheeks.

But in that Pullman, racing through the night at express speed, I had a visit from Jesus.

He asked, "Son, why do you want to be a pastor?"

I answered, "Lord, I'm tired. Lord, I'm blue. Lord, my nerves are frayed. My mind is ready to crack. I cannot stand much more. I am just tired. I want to be at home with my wife and children for awhile."

Jesus said, "Son, you have forgotten that I was away from Home thirty-three years, and I had to die to get back Home."

Do you know what I did? I put on my clothes and got out of that berth. When the train stopped at the next station, I sent a telegram to those people: DON'T CALL ME; I AM GOING TO KEEP ON WITH JESUS. It was a time of testing.

But here is what I started to say: if the evangelist is right with God, he is going to have some kind of a revival. Don't pass the buck to anybody else. Don't blame the Catholics. Don't blame the Federal Council of Churches. Don't blame the modernists or any of the rest of them. An evangelist is not going to have as great a revival as he would have if he could get the church on fire; but if he is right with God and living a clean life, if all of him is on the altar, God is going to give him a taste of revival wherever he goes. "The effectual fervent prayer of a righteous man availeth much" (Jas. 5:16). "My word . . . shall not return unto me void" (Isa. 55:11).

I learned a long time ago that when I stopped sweating so hard and toiling so burningly to make the other fellow do what I wanted him to do, and started trying to make myself do the right thing, my revivals were different.

I had a session with the Lord a couple of years ago. I used to scold. I used to stand up, nag and criticize. One night I came home from a meeting where I had scolded the people up one side and down the other, and I began praying, complaining to God.

The Lord said, "Hyman, what were you trying to do with those people?"

"Lord, I was trying to straighten them out."

"Son, let Me straighten them out."

I have let them almost alone ever since.

A revival is a time of the testing of both pastor and church.

When I went to the seminary at Fort Worth (God be praised for those three wonderful years; I would not take ten years of my life for them), my professors told me that one could not have a great ingathering in an evangelistic church because they were always having souls saved. And I believed it. But when I started out as an evangelist, I found that the more evangelistic the church, the easier to have a revival.

My friends, there is just one thing in any given church that can keep us from having a revival. If this microphone were Hell and this pulpit were a church, and if there were enough people in that church right with God, on the very brink of Hell we could have a revival. God would honor us. God would bless us. God would give us the victory!

Listen! Raising money is not a test. Hear me now! I am not the seventh son of a seventh son; I am the first son of a fifteenth child. The churches of America, especially the fundamentalist churches, are going to pay in heartache, in heartbreak, in loss of power, in loss of spiritual magnetism, because of the easiness with which they are raising money in this day and time. Too many of our people are salving their consciences by giving money instead of going after the lost.

Too many of our preachers, too many of our denominational leaders, are bragging about how much money they raise instead of how many souls they are winning to the Lord Jesus Christ. This is a time of testing.

A revival meeting is not only a time of testing for the evangelist and the church, but a time of the testing of God.

Anybody can raise money. Try it. You can build a building. You can draw crowds by almost any sort of a worldly program, by some kind of a social gospel, by an attractive ritual, by making it easy for people to join the church, by not requiring anything of them; but when the shouts of newborn souls begin to be heard in Zion, then people know that God is still on the throne and still answering prayer.

I defy you to show me out of your own experience and understanding any program, any activity in the church that can demonstrate the power of God as much as a real revival of religion, a real visitation of God's grace, a real outpouring of God's Spirit.

A Revival, a Time of Weeping

A revival is not only a time of testing, but it is a time of weeping. I have seen revival meetings without much advertising, but I have never seen a real revival without tears.

Let me again tell of an experience that Dr. Joe Henry Hankins and I had, not once but twice—once in that great church of his in Childress, Texas, and again in that matchless church in Little Rock, Arkansas, where he formerly was pastor. I never told him this before. I am confessing publicly to him and to God. He invited me to come to Childress to help him in a revival. I knew Childress, a town of about 7,500, on the south plains. He had been there for seven years. During that time he baptized more than nine hundred people. His church was packed all the time. He could beat me preaching anytime, and I knew it. So I didn't want to go. I wanted to go where I could have a harvest of souls.

Finally he persuaded me, and I went. We were supposed to hold a revival on the outside. It can rain with less judgment in Texas than in any other place in the world! It gets cold in the same way. This was in May when the weather should have been warm, but it was cold and raining. It rained Monday, Tuesday, Wednesday, Thursday, Friday, Saturday and Sunday. It poured down. By nighttime the benches would be so wet we couldn't meet outside. Sunday of the second week came, then Monday, Tuesday, Wednesday, Thursday. We had had some forty additions to the church.

Dr. Hankins stood up that Thursday night, put his hand on my shoulder, and said, "Before you dismiss the people I want to say something. We are going to have a prayer meeting across the street in the church. I want only those to come who are willing to stay until Jesus comes, if necessary."

I said to myself, *Brother Hankins, you have done shot your lead this time; you are not going to have many there.*

About thirty-five people came, including myself. We got down on our knees and prayed, got up and sang, got down on our knees and prayed again. It was three o'clock by my watch when Brother Hankins called on me to dismiss.

Before that revival was over, 126 people had come into the fellowship of the church.

I was preaching Sunday morning on "I Am Going to Heaven" when a woman in the congregation jumped up, began to clap her hands and shout, "Open the door, Lord, I'm coming in!" You can imagine what that did to the congregation.

It takes tears! It takes weeping. God knows there is plenty to weep about—our own condition, our own coldness, unconcern and indifference.

Dr. Bob Jones has been at this thing forty-six years. I am just forty-three years old [preached in 1945]. I am not as old as he has years in the ministry. He will say an "amen" to this: there are enough people right here in this crowd to start a Pentecost in America and the world if we will get right with God! Never mind talking about those folks out yonder; let's ask God to give *us* grace, to give *us* tears, the lamenting over *our* own sins.

A Revival, a Time of Reaping

A revival meeting is not only a time of testing, not only a time of weeping, but it is also a time of reaping. I told you that I get papers from all over this land. Some I subscribe to; some come free. When I read their reports, it is enough to make the demons in Hell blush with shame. They will report: "We had great crowds, marvelous singing, great preaching; eleven additions, eight for baptism, three by letter." That may be great in English, but it is mighty small potatoes in Jewish!

A great revival will result in a great ingathering of souls. There has never been any revival in the history of the world that did not result in the salvation of lost men and women. When the fire begins to burn, when God's people become magnetized—let me stop here and say something. We blame the unsaved for not coming to church. Why should they come? What is happening in our churches? We talk about the Catholics having a program. You come to your church on Sunday morning. (I have never been in your church, so I do not know a thing about it. I am just a shoemaker making shoes, but here they are, sizes five, six, seven, eight, nine, ten. If they fit you, put them on. If they don't fit you, let somebody else put them on.) You come into *your* church Sunday morning. The pastor has been racing around straightening out the intermediates, the juniors, the young people, the adults. About the time he gets ready to go into the pulpit, some dear sister pulls his coat and says, "Brother Pastor, Mrs. Tompkins said she is never going to step inside of this church again."

"What is the matter with Mrs. Tompkins?"

"Well, her little boy Johnny had his epizoodiks removed, and you were not there to hold his hand."

That is a good dose of inspiration, isn't it?

The ritual gets underway. It is the same all fifty-two Sundays of the year.

There is the Doxology.

The preacher pronounces the invocation.

The choir warbles the response.

The congregation stands up and sings a hymn—that is, about one person out of every three in the congregation sings.

After awhile the preacher leads in another prayer.

Then there is the time for announcements. You have a good bulletin—it costs money to print it—but the preacher doesn't believe the people can read, so he reads all the announcements.

Why should the unsaved people come? All day long, all week long, six days a week, they are going at top speed—at top speed in business, at top speed in sports, at top speed in politics, at top speed in radio, at top speed in literature. Then we expect them to come to church Sunday morning, be put in an ox cart, and expect them to have a good time.

A person would have to be of moronic intelligence to enjoy the average church service that I have attended in the time I have been a Christian. Oh, let us break away from the rut of the routine. For once, let us do things differently. Let the dead, dreary, dull drabness be thrown out the window. Let enthusiasm have the floor. Let initiative and sanctified invention have the right-of-way. Unshackle the Holy Spirit. Let the fire fall. Let something unusual happen. Then the crowds will come.

A Revival, a Time of Rejoicing

A revival is, furthermore, a time of rejoicing. Some of you have heard me say that. I have had lots of thrills in my life. I am forty-three, was born in Russia, and came to America when I was almost thirteen.

My, my, what thrills!

It was a thrill when I saw the Statue of Liberty.

It was a thrill when I learned to speak English.

It was a thrill when I was licensed to practice law.

It was a thrill when I was converted.

It was a thrill when I was ordained.
It was a thrill when I was married.
It was a thrill when my babies came.
It was a thrill when I held my first pastorate.
It was a thrill when I held my first revivals.
It was a thrill when I led my first soul to Christ.

But the thrill that I am living for, the thrill that I am working for, the thrill that I am preaching for, is when somebody comes down the aisle and says, "You win; I will take your Jesus as my Saviour." Boy! That is rejoicing!

If you have never led a soul to Christ, if you have never seen a hundred people converted, you don't know what it is all about! Listen—I say this honestly. It is the truth in Christ, my conscience bearing me witness with the Holy Spirit—God is going to have to get up mighty early in the morning and stay up mighty late at night and imagine lots of things before He will give me in Heaven more thrills than I have already had here upon this earth!

Oh, the joy of seeing souls saved! Oh, the joy of revivals! The sweep, the drive, the ecstasy, the Heaven-coming-down-to-earth, the fellowship of the Holy Spirit! There is nothing, even in the activities of the church, that can compare with a revival.

And now to the subject; that was just the introduction!

I. THE PURPOSE OF A REVIVAL

What is the purpose of a revival? What about the personnel of a revival? What about the plan, the program, the price for a revival?

I believe that the first purpose of a revival is to expose sin. Nothing will expose sin in the hearts of God's people as a revival. More people have quit drinking, more people have quit gambling, more people have quit smoking, more people have quit every kind of sin in the church and out of it, during a revival than at any other time. I am for Sam Morris and his temperance broadcasts with all my heart, with all my soul, with all my might. God give him strength to keep on preaching temperance. But revival will do more to bring temperance to America than any laws that Congress might pass.

A few preachers got together a little while ago and talked about something the government was doing. Some of the younger fellows were all fire and brimstone. They were saying, "We have to go to Washington.

We have to get our people to write letters," etc. An old preacher stood up to say, "Brethren, that is not the way I read it in my Book. A better place to go to than Washington is to God. He can make Washington behave faster than anybody else can."

A revival exposes sin. Oh, how desperately, how bitterly sin needs to be exposed in this country!

I came to America in 1914. In these years I have seen more different kinds of sin come into the United States than in all the history of this nation since the signing of the Declaration of Independence and the acceptance of the Constitution. I know whereof I speak. And the end is not yet!

We need a revival to expose sin. Nothing else will do it. Nothing else will help except the searchlight of the Holy Spirit in answer to the prayers of God's people.

We need a revival to enlist souls. Let me show you what I am talking about. You who were converted or joined the church during a revival, stand to your feet. We need no other defense of a revival than this. The majority of you are standing. Thank you. Be seated. This is the best, the choicest, the cleanest, the finest, the most consecrated crowd tonight in the United States.

My friends, a revival will do more to enlist souls than any other one thing.

How many times have I seen backslidden deacons, drifting stewards, cold elders, worldly trustees, barren Sunday school teachers, prayerless officers, come to the pastor, to the evangelist, to weep out their confession of sin bitterly, to ask God to give them another chance, to plead for work to do and for a witness to bear.

What shall I say about the enlisting of the souls of the unsaved, winning them for the Lord Jesus Christ? Come with me from one end of this country to the other. With the exception of four or five, or at most, ten churches, the Lord has given me the privilege of conducting revivals in every outstanding soul-winning work in America. The churches that are winning the lost are the ones that believe in evangelism, that conduct revivals, that major in revivals.

I will put Brother Hankins on the witness stand again. Put him out yonder in Little Rock, Arkansas. You say, "Well, anybody could do it in the South." Then why didn't anybody do it before he went there? For five years and two months he thundered out the Gospel of the Lord

Jesus Christ. God gave him almost twelve hundred souls for baptism and more than three thousand additions. Why? Because he believed in and practiced revivals. Twice a year, sometimes more than that, he had a revival.

You cannot have a revival Sunday by Sunday in the sense that I am talking about. You cannot have a harvest all the time. You must sow. You must chop. You must go out and plow up the weeds. You must fertilize the soil. You must saturate it with water, the water of your tears. You must have special seasons of revival rally to enlist souls.

O beloved, one of the reasons American churches are not keeping pace with the growth of the population in the United States as far as soul winning is concerned—I am not talking about membership but about new births—is that so many have turned their backs on this matter of revival.

The last purpose of a revival and the most important of all is to exalt Christ. I wish I had the ability to tell it to you as I feel it; I wish I had the tongue of a Chrysostom, the witchery of words of a Shakespeare, of a Milton; I wish I had the power of a Charles G. Finney; I wish I could lift my voice like a Whitefield—the chief purpose of a revival is to exalt the Lord Jesus Christ.

II. THE PERSONNEL OF A REVIVAL

Who are the people who go in to make up a revival? Let us name them. First, there is God the Father, God the Son, God the Holy Spirit.

Listen. I have read after preachers, have heard preachers tell and others tell about preachers who went through a revival and in a week, two weeks, three weeks, did not have a single move. My heart has ached and broken for them. My tears have flowed copiously as I thought of the agony in the hearts of such preachers.

But I say to you—and I am taking you as witnesses when I say this before God—I would rather spend the rest of my life without a single person walking down a single aisle under my ministry than to have millions come without the Holy Ghost. We have plenty of those kinds of members in our churches. We need born-again Christians. And the only One who can give them to us is the Holy Spirit.

They tell us about evangelists using outlandish methods. They tell us about evangelists falling into a rut. Beloved, I am not defending the evangelistic class—God is going to have to do that. At the end of time we shall see what we shall see. But nobody depends more on the Holy Spirit than an evangelist.

Listen! I can preach ten sermons as hard as I am preaching this one, and harder, if that is possible, and not be exhausted one-fifth as much by it as in giving the invitation one time. That is where the demons of Hell line up against you. That is where all your preaching, all your work, all your personality, all your ability, count for nothing. The Holy Spirit is the One who must convict. Thank God! Shout hallelujah to God! Rejoice in God!

I say to you without peradventure, beyond hesitation or doubt, the Holy Spirit is ready, willing, eager to use us to have the revivals for which we are praying.

The second person in the revival is the saint, the child of God, the Christian. Was it Wesley who said, "Give me two hundred men who fear nothing but sin, who love nothing but God, and we will turn this fair realm of England upside down for Christ"? There are more than a thousand people in this auditorium. Let this conference be marked by this one thing above all else: let each one of us determine that for ourselves and for our houses we will be on the firing line for Jesus in this matter of revivals.

The third person in a revival is the sinner—not only the Saviour, not only the saint, but the sinner. You say, "Preacher, we have you there. They will not come to church." That is too true.

I remember reading an article in a paper. If it is wrong, I sincerely hope Mrs. Billy Sunday, who is sitting here in the audience, will straighten me out. It was reported that the superlative Billy Sunday said at the end of his ministry that it was harder then to reach a fifteen-year-old boy than it was to win a seventy-year-old man when he first began preaching. Whether that is true or not, I am not prepared to say.

I have been preaching for a little more than fifteen years. It is getting harder and harder and harder (I am not minimizing the difficulty) to get the unsaved to come. But, beloved, they will come. They will come if we weep over them, break our hearts over them, agonize over them. I know whereof I speak. For twelve long weeks—these last twelve weeks—in Louisville, Cincinnati, Akron, Lansing, more than two thousand accepted the Lord Jesus Christ as their personal Saviour under the poor testimony of this little bit of a humble Jew preacher. Sure, we had to weep! Sure, we had to spend sleepless nights. Sure, we had to fast and pray. Sure, we went home crushed and broken again and again. Sure, some of us prayed for death rather than failure in winning the lost. But God answered prayer. They came and were saved.

III. GOD'S PLAN FOR A REVIVAL

The price, the program, the plan—God's plan for a revival. I don't know too much about this, but I speak to you out of what I have seen. There is a threefold plan. Three things must happen to us.

First, there must be a passionate devotion to the Lord Jesus Christ. There must be a personal passion for the Son of God, a passion for Christ, a falling in love with Jesus.

Tell me, do you not love Him? "For Jesus' sake" must be our motto. "For Jesus' sake" must be our theme. "For Jesus' sake" must be our challenge. "For Jesus' sake" must be our plea.

I am a Jew. You can tell by the way I talk and maybe by the way I use my hands. People curse me. They claim this and they say that. I go to them, plead with them in personal work and in public preaching. Thank God, for blood-stained Jesus' sake, for brokenhearted Jesus' sake, for the agony-souled Jesus' sake, the more they curse me, the more I love them, the more I want them for the Son of God. I am not in this business for anybody or anything, except for the sake of Him who loved us and gave Himself for us.

We must spend much time with Jesus in order to fall in love with Him. He is lovely, loving, lovable. There is nothing undesirable about Him. He has never failed us. I would like to see a revival in America because I love this country, and I know there is no hope for it outside revival. I would like to see a revival because there are multiplied millions of souls in America going to Hell.

But you know, the chief reason I want a revival in America is that it will wipe away some of the tears from the eyes of Jesus. It will take out a little of the smarting from His nail-pierced hands. It will assuage a bit of the agony of His broken heart. I want a revival for Jesus' sake.

Second, not only must there be a personal passion for Christ, but there must be an agonizing compassion, a purposeful compassion for the souls of men.

We have an evangelist down there in Texas by the name of B. B. Crimm whom God has used in a marvelous way—a Billy Sunday type. He just races up and down the platform, breaks chairs, and does things like that. He has a good time, and we have a good time watching him. When he sits down on a chair, begins to pat that pulpit and say, "Now I am preaching," brother, sister, nobody can do it better than he can! He is a fox hunter. He spends all night fox hunting and all day preaching for Jesus, having a good time. He can tell more dog stories than you can imagine.

He held a revival in 1929 in Lawton, Oklahoma. I was a Staff Sergeant in the Medical Department of the United States Army. I went to that revival every night. When he would talk about the loyalty of dogs, my eyes would just brim over with tears. I would wipe them away and look down because I didn't want to be embarrassed. I was a very young Christian and was ashamed of emotion. I would look around and see people all over that crowd and in the choir crying. I kept on watching them. I knew some of them.

There was Sunday School Teacher So-and-so sitting up there crying over a dead dog as if her heart would break, when I knew she would not draw a deep breath to win a lost soul to Jesus Christ! There was Deacon So-and-so sitting over there sobbing over a mangy dog that died in the chase, when I knew he would not put fingernail to fingernail to win a soul to Christ. Do you know what they call it in Jewish? Crocodile tears! Just plain old hypocrisy! Just plain old lying!

No, you need a compassion for souls that makes you willing to mark their way to the cross with your heart's blood, a compassion for souls that puts you in such torture, in such agony, in such anguish for those who are on the road to Hell that you say to God, "Anything, any cost, any amount, any prayers, any sacrifice, anything, Lord, only give me those souls!"

Who among us has not heard that matchless, classic illustration of the Presbyterian missionary who went out yonder to China with his wife and two-year-old boy? He worked like a mule day and night, night and day. He lasted a little more than ten years. He contracted tuberculosis but kept on working. Finally he had to go to bed. They put him on a litter, put him on board ship and sent him back to America. He was rushed across the country to one of the Carolinas to a mountain sanatorium. There he stayed for a little better than two years.

He was discharged. A little after his discharge, his denomination held its annual convention. He was asked to speak twice, on Thursday to give a report on China and on Friday night to finish the convention by preaching on foreign missions. He stood there before the great crowd on Thursday, told them the story of bleeding China until they swayed with emotion in front of him like a Texas wheat field swayed by a Texas breeze.

When he had finished, he moved forward. Raising his hands, he cried, "Brethren and sisters, send me back to China! Send me back to China!"

When the service was over, surrounding him they pled, "You can't go back. We need you here. There is a great church calling you to be its pastor. In awhile, we shall make you foreign missions secretary. Stay here. Your wife and boy and all of us need you."

"No, I have to go back to China," he responded.

Friday night came. Again he stood before the delegates and preached until they could hardly contain themselves. They sobbed out loud with the anguish of his communicated, burning concern and compassion.

When he got through, rocking, reeling, trembling with fatigue, he leaned on the side of the pulpit, raised his free hand and sobbed out, "Men and brethren, send me back to China. If you will not, I am going back anyway."

Once again they crowded around him to plead, "You can't go. We need you. We have a job for you. What about your wife and boy?"

He pushed them aside and said, "I have got to go!"

"Why? Why do you have to go?"

Pushing them all aside, he raised his voice until the auditorium echoed the groaning of his aching heart: "I have to go back because I cannot sleep nights for thinking about them!"

When enough of us get under a load like that, we will have a revival.

Then, not only must there be a personal passion for Christ and a purposeful compassion for the souls of men, but there must be a persistent intercession for a visitation of God's Holy Spirit, for an outpouring of God's mighty power.

O beloved, some people tell us that it is not right to pray for the Holy Spirit, that He is here in the world. But Luke 11:13 says, "If ye then, being evil, know how to give good gifts unto your children: how much more shall your heavenly Father give the Holy Spirit to them that ask him?"

I am not a good theologian, nor am I a good preacher. I am just doing the best I can. When I pray for the Holy Spirit, if I make a mistake the Lord will understand me. He knows I want His power, not to make money, not to gain name or fame. What would I do with it? I want to win souls, to be used of the Holy Spirit as a man uses a match, to set fire to this glorious land of ours, then to the ends of the earth.

A Bible conference is held each year in England. Some years ago a pastor from one of our great western churches was invited there to speak the last four nights, and to give the invitation. Souls were saved. In one sermon he told this story.

Years ago when he was a young fellow first starting out to preach, he came at the end of the year to the associational meeting, the annual workers' conference of his denomination. Report after report, sermon after sermon, song after song were given. Hearts were moved and thrilled.

The last afternoon, at three-thirty, the last speaker was to speak. But a few minutes before he was scheduled to appear, he foolishly helped to raise a car that had been stuck in the mud. It strained him so that he hurt himself and couldn't preach, couldn't even stand up. It was too late to have another speaker, so they decided to finish with a testimony meeting. Man after man, woman after woman, stood up and witnessed to the wonderful grace of God.

It came time to close. They were still rising from here, there, yonder, when from the very last row of that church there stood up and stepped out into the aisle a tall, slightly bent, superannuated preacher, a man way up in his seventies but still strong and fervent in the Lord.

He said, "Brother Moderator."

The moderator recognized him.

> Brother Moderator and you other brethren, I thought for awhile I would not say a word, but I can't keep from it. I want to tell you what God has done for me. Sitting here listening to your reports, my heart has burned within me. I want to tell you a story that some of you know, that will show you what God can do in answer to prayer.
>
> You know my wife [and he smiled down at his wife by his side] and I were married when I was twenty-four and she was just twenty-two. For a long time the Lord withheld the blessing of a child. Then a boy came, a bonnie boy, a beautiful boy, a blessed boy. We loved him, worshiped him, adored him, maybe too much.
>
> I was pastor of a very wealthy church. My boy was spoiled, I guess. When he got to be four he became ill of a nameless sickness that no doctor could diagnose. Our family physician called in some of the mightiest specialists in the country, but nothing could be done. The boy lay stretched out in bed, a wasting skeleton.

One Sunday afternoon the deacons came into that room. The chairman shyly, hesitantly said, "Brother Pastor, we had a meeting and are going to recommend to the church tonight that you be given a leave of absence indefinitely with full pay. We will take care of your supplies. Take your wife and boy and go anywhere you want to. Heal him, bring him back."

We had prayer. That night the deacons reported to the church, and the church voted in favor of the arrangement. An offering was taken amounting to a little better than two thousand dollars.

A day or two later my wife and I gathered up our effects and started out. For eight long months we traveled up and down the continent, trying to find a cure, but to no avail. We came back, put that little tiny skeleton to bed to die. The family physician came every day, sometimes twice a day. At times, he spent a good part of the day right there with the boy. But there just seemed to be nothing he could do.

One day the doctor walked into my study to say, "Brother Pastor, come with me into the lad's room. He is dying." We went in there to the bedside of my baby. I stood there holding the hand of my wife. What could I do? After awhile the doctor took his coat off, rolled up his sleeves, opened his valise, his little doctor's kit, took out a hypodermic needle. He put on rubber gloves. He filled the needle with some gray fluid. The doctor watched the patient. The boy began to get more and more pale. In a bit, he stiffened out and stopped breathing. The doctor plunged the needle into the boy's body. The boy opened his eyes, gritted his teeth, commenced breathing harshly again. The doctor watched him, his fingers still on the boy's pulse. Interminable minutes went past. The doctor gently put the boy's hand down, started rolling down his sleeves, buttoned them up, reached for his coat, put it on and said, "Brother Pastor, the boy is dead."

I turned to my wife, "Wife, light the oven. Get all the blankets and comforters you have. Heat them and bring them here."

I opened my coat and my shirt and tore my undershirt down. I picked up that little cooling body and pressed it against my hot, sweating body. My wife wrapped a heated blanket around us. It was almost impossible to stand it, but gritting my teeth I took it. When that one cooled off, my wife put another one about us. When that one cooled off, she put on still another one, and on, and on, and on. We kept it up for nine hours.

He stopped, smiled down at his wife. He stepped a little forward and raising his hands to God, said in a voice hoarse with emotion, "My boy has been preaching the Gospel for seventeen years."

It does not sound true! But I believe it! They do not tell lies at Keswick.

But this is what I have seen, and this is what I have experienced.

I have seen a church, a community, a city, stiff, cold in spiritual death. I have seen a group of God's people take that church, that community, that city to their burning hearts. I have seen them wrap that church, that community, that city with the white heat of their prayers. By God's grace, I have seen the church, the community, the city come to life in the Lord Jesus Christ.

Let us pay the price to have a revival.

CURTIS W. HUTSON
1934-1995

ABOUT THE MAN:

In 1961 a mail carrier and pastor of a very small church attended a Sword of the Lord Conference, got on fire, gave up his route and set out to build a great soul-winning work for God. Forrest Hills Baptist Church of Decatur, Georgia, grew from 40 people into a membership of 7,900. The last four years of his pastorate there, the Sunday school was recognized as the largest in Georgia.

After pastoring for 21 years, Dr. Hutson—the great soul winner that he was—became so burdened for the whole nation that he entered full-time evangelism, holding great citywide-areawide-cooperative revivals in some of America's greatest churches. As many as 625 precious souls trusted Christ in a single service. In one eight-day meeting, 1,502 salvation decisions were recorded.

As an evangelist, he was in great demand.

At the request of Dr. John R. Rice, Dr. Hutson became Associate Editor of THE SWORD OF THE LORD in 1978, serving in that capacity until the death of Dr. Rice before becoming Editor, President of Sword of the Lord Foundation, and Director of Sword of the Lord Conferences. He continued in these ministries until his death on March 5, 1995, literally changing the lives of thousands of preachers and laymen alike, as well as winning many more thousands to Christ.

Dr. Hutson was the author of many fine books and booklets.

VI.

Prescription for Revival
(The Burden of Proof Lies With Us!)

CURTIS HUTSON

R. A. Torrey was a great evangelist who followed in the footsteps of D. L. Moody. Dr. Torrey held great revivals. He went into buildings seating 7,000 to 8,000. Many vowed he would never fill the buildings, but in a few weeks they were packed and jammed, and people were arriving early to get a seat.

Dr. Torrey held great revivals, not only in this country but in Australia, England, and many other places throughout the world.

As pastor of the Church of the Open Door in California, he had what he called a perennial revival—that is, every service was a revival, with people being saved and baptized.

One of my philosophies has always been, *Learn from those who are doing it.*

If I were broke and wanted to learn to make a million dollars, I would talk to a fellow who made a million last year. I would certainly not waste time talking to one who went broke last year.

If I wanted to learn how to repair an automobile, I would find a man who had an automobile that would start when you pushed the starter and turned on the switch. I wouldn't talk with a fellow who had six jalopies in the yard and none running.

Learn from those who are doing it.

I enjoy playing golf. If I had an opportunity, I would like to play with Jack Nicklaus. I think my game would improve by being around him. That is a Bible principle: "He that walketh with wise men shall be wise: but a companion of fools shall be destroyed" (Prov. 13:20). *Learn from those who are doing it.*

It is an indisputable fact that R. A. Torrey was one of the greatest revivalists who ever lived. He gave this simple, three-point prescription as to how to have revival:

> First, let a few Christians get thoroughly right with God themselves. This is the prime essential. If this is not done, the rest I am going to say will come to nothing.
>
> Second, let them bind themselves together in prayer groups to pray for revival until God opens the heavens and comes down.
>
> Third, let them put themselves at the disposal of God, for Him to use them as He sees fit in the winning of others to Christ.
>
> That is all. This is sure to bring revival to any church or any community. I have given this prescription around the world. It has been taken by many churches and many communities, and in no instance has it ever failed, and it cannot fail.

If I were a member of this church and were serious about having revival, I would listen very carefully to Dr. Torrey's words: "I have given this prescription around the world. It has been taken by many churches and many communities, and in no instance has it ever failed." He puts his reputation on the block when he says, "It cannot fail."

I suggest that the burden of proof lies with us. If we do what Dr. Torrey says, and we don't have revival at this church, then, when we get to Heaven, we can say to Dr. Torrey, "Your prescription failed in one church."

But we won't ever know whether it will fail if we don't really try it. And we must try it exactly as he gave it.

The reason many things do not work is that the average congregation already has an idea of what they think will work and what they think will not work, and they accept only the part they have already agreed upon. If the pastor or evangelist happens to give something contrary to what they believe or think, they are not willing to try it.

Torrey cannot be responsible for whether you have revival unless you are willing to do everything he said to do. And his formula is very simple.

Don't be like the lady who said,

I didn't have potatoes,
So I substituted rice;
I didn't have paprika,
So I used another spice;
I didn't have tomato sauce;
I used tomato paste;
Not half a can—a whole can;

I don't believe in waste.
A friend gave me a recipe—
She said you couldn't beat it—
There must be something wrong with me;
I couldn't even eat it!

You can't substitute for what Torrey has given. You have to take the whole prescription.

I challenge you to listen to Torrey's prescription, then say, "Let's have revival!"

There is nothing better than old-fashioned revivals where half-asleep Christians wake up; where those who have lost their burden for souls get it back; where those who have quit tithing start again; where those who fail to attend church on Sunday night become faithful.

An old-fashioned revival where people get excited about the things of God—there is nothing better!

1. Let a Few Christians Get Thoroughly Right With God Themselves

We have an idea that it takes big crowds to have revival. Not so. Big fires are not built with wagonloads of lumber but with kindling wood. Great revivals begin with just a few Christians' getting thoroughly right with God.

You probably have the largest congregation in your area. But Torrey said you can have revival with just a few Christians! "Let a few Christians get thoroughly right with God themselves. This is the prime essential. If this is not done, the rest I am going to say will come to nothing."

It is like running all the bases when you hit a home run! You touched second, you touched third, and you touched home, only to be called out because you didn't touch first! You can't touch second and third and hope to have revival. You also have to touch first.

The hardest thing for any Christian is to get thoroughly right with God.

We do several things with our sins. One, we blame somebody else. Instead of saying, "I was wrong; I don't blame anybody else; it was all my fault," we say, "Well, I wouldn't have done it if. . . ."

When Adam, the first man to sin, was approached by God and asked, 'Why hast thou done this?' he said, "The woman whom thou gavest to be with me, she gave me of the tree, and I did eat." He not only blamed Eve for his sin; he blamed God.

If we quit church attendance, we blame it on somebody else. Did you know the happiest Christian in the world is he who will just be honest about his sins? The hardest three words you ever uttered were, "I have sinned." David said, "When I kept silence, my bones waxed old through my roaring all the day long" (Ps. 32:3). In other words, "When I kept my mouth shut about my sins, I was aging."

Some Christians are aging because they are keeping silent about their sins. I don't want you to confess to me nor to any other preacher. You tell it to Jesus and keep it between you and Him alone. Get it right with God!

My wife and I had been in a church on a Sunday morning. I had given her the car keys and everything else that jingled in my pockets.

After the service, we went out and got into the car. A young couple with us got in the back seat. I said to Gerri, "Where are the car keys?"

"I gave them to you."

"No, you didn't."

"Yes, I did."

"You know I always empty my pockets before church, and I gave the car keys to you."

"I know you did, and I gave them back to you after church," she said.

I said, "I wouldn't have forgotten between the door and the car. You lost them like you lost that ten-dollar bill one time." And I reminded her of everything she had ever lost—I have a good memory! I added, "Now you are trying to blame me for your mistake. Empty your purse. They are in there."

My wife emptied her purse on the front seat of the car—no car keys!

"I gave them to you. I know I did," she insisted.

"If you had given them to me, I would have them, and I don't have them!"

Since we could go nowhere without keys, I got out of the car and began to look around.

Then I made the worst mistake of my life—I looked down, and there were the keys in the car door where I had unlocked it to get in!

No way was I going to admit I was wrong in front of those people sitting in the back seat! So I took the keys out of the door and very quietly and carefully tried to get them into Gerri's purse when she wasn't looking! Had I succeeded, I would have said, "I don't have them," and had her open her purse again and then told her, "I told you they were there."

But God wouldn't let me do that. I couldn't hide them in her purse. Finally I had to start the car. She said, "Where did you get the keys?"

"It's none of your business where."

It is so easy to blame somebody else for our sins. People in the Bible excused their sins by blaming others—like Saul, who was told to slay utterly, but he saved the prize cattle and prize sheep. He also saved the king.

He brought them back into town, and the man of God said, "Have you done what God said?"

"Oh, yes! I obeyed God; I did everything He said to do."

About that time the sheep began to bleat, and the cattle began to low. Samuel asked, "What meaneth then this bleating of the sheep in mine ears, and the lowing of the oxen which I hear?"

Saul said, "Well, I can explain that. You see, I saved some prize cattle and some prize sheep to offer to God. What do you think about that?"

He was told, "To obey is better than sacrifice."

It is so easy to excuse our sins or blame someone else for them. Sometimes we even try to cover them up. But Proverbs 28:13 warns, "He that covereth his sins shall not prosper."

"I can hide them from the preacher! I can hide them from the church! I can hide them from my wife!"

Okay, maybe you can, but you cannot hide them from God!

The other morning I read the story of a bishop who early one morning walked out into the woods. It was wintertime, and there were no green leaves, no foliage—only dead trees. As he looked across the woods at the barren ground, he thought, *In a few months the leaves will begin to turn green, the grass will begin to grow, and the trees will blossom.* As he looked around at the deadness and thought of what would soon happen, he thought, *If that tree comes to life and the seed in the ground comes to life and the grass grows, God must be out here!* Then it dawned on him: *If God is here, then God must be everywhere!*

It changed his life. From that moment on, he lived with the thought in mind: *I am never out of the presence of God. God is everywhere!*

"The eyes of the Lord are in every place, beholding the evil and the good" (Prov. 15:3). You can't cover your sins, so don't try.

I think sometimes we have the idea that if we kneel and confess our sins, we are telling God something He doesn't already know. In other words, we are telling on ourselves. I'm not going to tell on myself. Let

God find out for Himself. But He already knows.

Last night there were a few thunderstorms between here [Savannah] and Atlanta. It was a little rough on the plane, and lightning was flashing in the distance on the left. It kept getting closer and brighter. I thought, *Well, I know that the pilot knows what he is doing, but, man, that looks awfully close to me! I feel uncomfortable.* Then I began to say, "Lord, have I done anything wrong? Are You trying to tell me something?"

I was scared. Everything I had ever done wrong seemed to flash across my mind. I thought, *Maybe God is going to kill me.* It was almost as if God spoke to me and said, "I don't need this plane if I want to get you. I can get you while you ride your horse in Murfreesboro. I can get you when you are in your little Honda that you think is so safe on the road. As a matter of fact, I can get you when you think you are the safest. When you are lying down sound asleep, I can stop your heart, and that will be the end of you!"

God can get us anywhere. He doesn't have to get us up in a plane to kill us! God can get us on the ground. He can get us anytime. We are never safe, if God wants us.

If He is trying to chastise you, God can get to you anywhere in the world! There is no need to hide your sins. The happiest Christians in the world are those who confess all their sins to God and level with Him.

D. L. Moody said, "If you want revival, then let every Christian here come forward, kneel and confess your sins!"

One pious member said, "I can't remember my sins."

Moody said, "Then guess at them."

He guessed them the very first try!

It would be well if we could all sing and mean it, as we look across the congregation at each other,

Nothing between my soul and the Saviour,
Naught of this world's delusive dream:
I have renounced all sinful pleasure,
Jesus is mine, there's nothing between.

Nothing between my soul and the Saviour,
So that His blessed face may be seen;
Nothing preventing the least of His favor,
Keep the way clear! Let nothing between.

Stay right with God.

I would be miserable coming here if I knew something were between me and the pastor. Every time I saw him, my conscience would bother me. I would have a tough time preaching.

It is good to know that there is no ice wall between me and anyone.

Some blame others for their sins. Some excuse their sins. Others try to cover their sins and keep them secret. The right thing to do with them is recorded in I John 1:9: "If we confess our sins, he is faithful and just to forgive us our sins, and to cleanse us from all unrighteousness."

Don't be like the lady who went to see the psychiatrist with two fried eggs on top of her head and a strip of bacon over each ear. When asked why she came, she answered, "I've come to see you about my brother."

I get in some prayer meetings where everybody is praying for everybody else. I have been in prayer meeting where all were praying for the preacher: "Lord, our preacher is wrong on this and wrong on that. We pray You will get him right."

When you pray, tell God about yourself. Tell Him, "Lord, I have sinned. I'm wrong. Forgive me, please."

It's not my brother, not my sister,
But it's me, O Lord....

Why not come down the aisle and say, "I don't know about anybody else, but for me and my house...we are going to get right with God! And if nobody else has revival, we are going to have revival!"

My first all-night prayer meeting was to pray for myself. I started one day listing my sins. I saw some things that looked pretty bad. When I would list one, I could think of three or four others. My list was three legal-sized sheets long.

Then I claimed I John 1:9, "If we confess our sins, he is faithful and just to forgive us our sins, and to cleanse us from all unrighteousness." I told the Lord, "Since You said it, it is guaranteed."

I don't have to wonder if it works. God said if I confess it, He forgives me and cleanses me! Glory to God!

I took the first sin on my list and confessed it, then told God, "I confess it because I want to be forgiven and cleansed. Now since I have confessed it, I know I'm forgiven and cleansed, and it doesn't even exist. Now I'm taking it off my list, Lord." I took my eraser and erased it and felt so good!

Then I took sin number two. I said, "Lord, I want to get rid of this one, too. I confess it as a dirty, rotten sin. I shouldn't have done it. I can't go back and undo it, but You can. You said if I confessed it, You would forgive and cleanse me. I have confessed it. Glory to God!

I'm now forgiven and cleansed. You said so, and You can't lie!" I erased that one.

It took me all night, but I can't tell you how good I felt the next morning! I had had a shower on the inside! Some of those things should have been taken care of a long time before.

In Isaiah 43:25 God said, "I, even I, am he that blotteth out thy transgressions for mine own sake, and will not remember thy sins."

I looked at those clean sheets. I knew at that moment that the sheets in Heaven were just as clean as my sheets. Talk about a good day! I had a good day! Talk about revival! I had revival—my own revival!

2. In Prayer Groups Pray for Revival Until God Opens the Heavens and Comes Down

The emphasis is on the word "until." I wish I could talk about persistent praying, but I give you this Bible lesson quickly.

Matthew 7:7 says, "Ask, and it shall be given you; seek, and ye shall find; knock, and it shall be opened unto you." How many of you ever asked for something and didn't get it? Many. What is wrong with that verse? "Ask, and it shall be given you." You asked and didn't get it. I asked and didn't get it.

You say, "Oh, God answered, but He said no."

He didn't say, "Ask, and I will tell you no." That is just an excuse for not getting an answer. His word to us is, "Ask, and it shall be given you."

Most of you don't understand that the word "ask" in this verse is in the continual sense. He that asketh, receiveth. To him that knocketh, it shall be opened. He that seeketh shall find. And I paraphrase it: He who keeps on asking, receives. He who keeps on seeking, finds. He who keeps on knocking, to him the door shall be opened.

Torrey didn't say, "Hold a prayer meeting and see what happens," but, "Let them pray until God opens the heavens and comes down."

He who keeps on praying, receives!

If you pray for something and keep praying and keep praying and keep praying, you will either get what you prayed for, or God will definitely change your prayer. Here is a Bible example.

Paul said, "For this thing I besought the Lord thrice, that it might depart from me" (II Cor. 12:8). Three times Paul asked the Lord to remove the thorn from his flesh. Can you hear him praying? "Now, Lord, this thorn in my flesh—I would like it removed. I can be a better preacher and hold better meetings if You will remove this thorn." It wasn't removed.

Paul prayed the second time and a third time; still it wasn't removed. After three times, God saw that Paul was going to keep on praying, that he meant to get it out, so God interrupted Paul. "Wait a minute, Paul. My grace is sufficient for you, and My strength is made perfect in your weakness."

Paul said, "Oh, I see." Then he changed his prayer to: "Most gladly therefore will I rather glory in my infirmities, that the power of Christ may rest upon me."

Paul never asked the fourth time for the thorn to be removed.

Too many of us pray a little, quick prayer, "Lord, give us a revival," and that is it. We are like the man drilling for oil. He couldn't strike oil, so finally he pulled out the drill and moved on.

Another came along behind him, put a drill in the same hole, drilled a few more feet and struck a gusher!

You have prayed for the salvation of sinners; now you have given up on them. Go back, take up where you left off and start begging God again.

Do you want revival? Pray. It doesn't mean coming here for a prayer meeting every night. You can pray with your family before you go to work. You can stop on your lunch hour and pray, "Lord, give us revival! You said if we asked, we would receive. So we will keep on asking and asking and pushing and pushing until this mountain starts to move; and all of this town will know it when it moves, Lord! We are not going to quit! We are going to move it!"

3. Put Yourselves at God's Disposal in Winning Others

Make yourself available to win the lost. God has no way to reach your neighbors except through you.

On New Year's Eve a young girl named Wanda Williams was out celebrating like everybody else. Her parents came home, checked her room, and she was still out—so they thought. Thinking she would be back sometime during the night, they fell asleep.

Early the next morning Mother fixed breakfast and called her, but she did not come. Dad went to her room, opened the door, went inside—no Wanda. The bed was undisturbed. He looked around the room and found this note on the dresser: "You will find me in the garage."

He rushed to the garage and found Wanda hanging by her neck. She had committed suicide. Under her feet was another note which read,

> Last year I was miserable, unhappy and dissatisfied with life. I prayed and told God that, if something didn't happen, I could not go into another year like that.
>
> It has been a year now. Nothing has happened. I'm still miserable, unhappy and dissatisfied. I will not live another year. I love you, Mother and Dad.

Didn't God care about Wanda? Sure He did. Didn't God hear her prayer? Sure He did. But God had no way to get to Wanda except through someone in her city. It was not that God didn't care; it was that He had no instrument through whom He could reach her. If someone had gotten to her with the Gospel, no doubt she would now be a happy, born-again believer and probably in a good, fundamental church. But she is dead and, as far as we know, in Hell. I am positive God tried to get someone to witness to Wanda, but no one heeded.

How many times have you felt led to speak to someone and didn't? A fellow told me last night of two incidents in the last few days where he should have witnessed to someone but didn't. That was God trying to get to that person or persons through His witness.

You are burdened about your neighbors. Right now you are thinking about those you would like to see saved. That is God trying to get to them through you. And if you are not available, He won't get to them.

Torrey said essentially, in summary, "Let a few Christians get thoroughly right with God—they need not be many; let them bind themselves together in prayer groups and pray until God opens the heavens and comes down; then let them put themselves at His disposal to use as He sees fit in the winning of others to Christ. That is all."

Torrey further said, "I have given this prescription in many countries and many churches around the world, and where it has been taken by a church or a community, it has never failed—and it cannot fail."

Now your Bible is open to Acts 1:14. I just recap two things with you. "These all continued with one accord. . . ." They were tuned up; they were in harmony. There was no discord among them. How were they all in one accord? They were all thoroughly right with God.

I play a guitar and banjo a little. My dad played a five-string banjo, and he and I used to tune the banjo and guitar together. He would say, "Hit your first string—bing-bing-bing-bing." He would hit the thumb string—ping-ping-ping-ping—trying to get in tune. We tuned up with each other. I thought that was the way everyone tuned all instruments.

The first time we had the piano and organ tuned in our church, wanting to help the guy, I said, "When you are ready to tune the piano, I will pitch the note on the organ so we will be sure to get them together."

He laughed. "Preacher, you may know something about preaching, but you don't know anything about tuning instruments."

I said, "I do. I play a guitar, and it is in tune."

He laughed again. "It is probably not standard pitch."

I didn't know what he was talking about. He pulled out a tuning fork, hit it and put it on top of the piano; and it made a sound. He smiled and said:

> I tuned the organ with this tuning fork. Now I forget about the organ and tune the piano with the tuning fork. When the organ is in tune with the fork and the piano is in tune with the fork, then the piano and organ are in tune with each other.
>
> If you tuned a hundred instruments with each other, by the time you got to the third or fourth instrument, they wouldn't be anywhere near the first one. But I can tune a thousand instruments in one big building with this fork, and when they are played, they will all be in harmony.

When born-again believers get thoroughly right with God and are tuned up with standard pitch, at church they will be all together. And if you are not all together, somebody is not on standard pitch. Now you don't need to copy anyone. Just get with the Tuning Fork.

"These all continued with one accord . . . ." They did what Torrey said—they got thoroughly right with God. The rest of the verse reads, ". . . in prayer and supplication." They all got tuned up; they banded together in prayer.

What else? Look at verse 4 of chapter 2: "And they were all filled with the Holy Ghost"—every one of them. Keep reading: ". . . and began to speak." How many spoke? Not just the evangelist, not just the pastor, not just the deacons. We say, "Boy! Three thousand saved on the day of Pentecost. Man! What a revival! That must have been some sermon Peter preached!" No, that must have been a bunch of soul winners working that crowd! It wasn't just Peter.

I wish you would talk so much this week that folks would think you had been vaccinated with a Victrola needle. I wish you would get to talking about Jesus and revival so much that people will say, "Man, his daddy was an auctioneer and his mother was a woman! Listen to him!" I mean, I wish you would get the gift of tongues and just talk about Jesus and talk about Jesus and talk about revival and get unsaved people saved! How many were talking at Pentecost? All of them!

Verse 7 says, "Are not all these which speak Galileans?" All of them! I can visualize all of them as they said, "What about you? Are you saved?"

When Peter gave the invitation, three thousand got saved! We can see that happen here. The burden of proof lies with us.

LEE ROBERSON
1909-

ABOUT THE MAN:

When one considers the far-reaching ministries of the Highland Park Baptist Church and pauses to reflect upon its total outreach, he has cause to believe that it is close to the New Testament pattern.

In the more than forty-one years—from 1942 when Dr. Lee Roberson first came to Highland Park until his retirement in April 1983—the ministry expanded to include Camp Joy, reaching some 3,000 children annually; World Wide Faith Missions, contributing to the support of over 350 missionaries; 50 branch churches in the greater Chattanooga area; Union Gospel Mission, which feeds and sleeps an average of 50 transient men daily; a Sunday school bus ministry, which covers 45 bus routes; a deaf ministry; "Gospel Dynamite," a live broadcast held daily over 2 radio stations, now in its 44th year; a church paper, THE EVANGELIST, being mailed free each month to over 73,000 readers; and Tennessee Temple University, Temple Baptist Theological Seminary, and Tennessee Temple Academy.

He is an author of many books.

He has preached to thousands, trained preachers, supported the mission cause. Dr. John R. Rice called him "the Spurgeon of our generation."

Dr. Roberson has many fine books in print. These include *Touching Heaven, The Man in Cell No. 1, The Faith That Moves Mountains, Coming to Chattanooga—Soon, Ten Thousand Tears, Disturbing Questions. . .Solid Answers, The Gold Mine* and *Diamonds in the Rough.*

VII.

The Holy Spirit and Revival

LEE ROBERSON

"And when they had prayed, the place was shaken where they were assembled together; and they were all filled with the Holy Ghost, and they spake the word of God with boldness."—Acts 4:31.

I want to begin this message in a very simple way. I want the youngest Christian to know the Holy Spirit and what He does.

Our Bible points out the fact of the Trinity—Father, Son and Holy Spirit. At the baptism of Jesus, we find the Trinity. Jesus was baptized, the Spirit of God descended upon Him, and a voice spoke from Heaven, "This is my beloved Son, in whom I am well pleased." When Jesus gave the Great Commission, we find mention of the Trinity. "Go ye therefore, and teach all nations, baptizing them in the name of the Father, and of the Son, and of the Holy Ghost" (Matt. 28:19).

All Christians know about God the Father. We know how to pray, "Our Father which art in heaven." Children are taught from their earliest days, "God is love."

Christians know about the Son. They know about Christ who was born of a virgin, lived among men, died on the cross, arose from the dead, and ascended on high. The average Sunday school child can give these facts which we have given about Christ.

But when coming to the Holy Spirit, many people hesitate. They know nothing of Him, or they know so little they feel embarrassed.

First, know about Him. Jesus gave the promise of the Holy Spirit. He said:

"And I will pray the Father, and he shall give you another Comforter, that he may abide with you for ever;

"Even the Spirit of truth; whom the world cannot receive, because

it seeth him not, neither knoweth him: but ye know him; for he dwelleth with you, and shall be in you."—John 14:16, 17.

Our Saviour tells us that the Holy Spirit abides with us. He comes in to dwell in our hearts when we believe on Christ. He is present to teach us all things ". . . and bring all things to your remembrance, whatsoever I have said unto you" (John 14:26).

Second, be conscious of Him. He indwells you. He is with you always. Do not be mystified by this fact. Simply recognize it and accept it—the Holy Spirit abides in your heart.

Now, this means that we must not grieve Him by wrongdoing. Ephesians 4:30-32 gives us the teaching on this:

"And grieve not the holy Spirit of God, whereby ye are sealed unto the day of redemption.

"Let all bitterness, and wrath, and anger, and clamour, and evil speaking, be put away from you, with all malice:

"And be ye kind one to another, tenderhearted, forgiving one another, even as God for Christ's sake hath forgiven you."

We must not grieve the indwelling Holy Spirit. Certain acts of life are unpleasant to Him. He will reprove us for them and will seek to correct us. May we give heed to His presence.

Third, depend upon Him. Let the Holy Spirit work through you. Be a clear channel for Him. This means that all Christians need the filling of the Holy Spirit. Paul tells us in Ephesians 5:18, "And be not drunk with wine, wherein is excess; but be filled with the Spirit."

The fullness of the Spirit cannot be accomplished unless there is emptiness of self and willingness for Him to take over and fill us.

Now, when we are filled with the Holy Spirit, we will bear the fruit of the Spirit. Let us read five verses in Galatians 5:22-26:

"But the fruit of the Spirit is love, joy, peace, longsuffering, gentleness, goodness, faith,

"Meekness, temperance: against such there is no law.

"And they that are Christ's have crucified the flesh with the affections and lusts.

"If we live in the Spirit, let us also walk in the Spirit.

"Let us not be desirous of vain glory, provoking one another, envying one another."

With this as an introduction, let me give the outline for my message.

I. THE HOLY SPIRIT AND CHRISTIAN LIVING

I repeat, the Holy Spirit comes in to abide when we believe in Jesus Christ. Now, it should be the aim and desire of every Christian to be filled with the Holy Spirit.

We are exhorted by the Word to live as Christian adults. We are not to be baby Christians. Paul spoke to the church in Corinth and said, "And I, brethren, could not speak unto you as unto spiritual, but as unto carnal, even as unto babes in Christ" (I Cor. 3:1).

To bear the name of "baby Christian" is to dishonor the Lord.

The sorry lives of Christians are ever before us. We question, "Are they saved?"

Someone said, "It's an unhappy occupation to try to act like a Christian when you are not."

This message concerns the Holy Spirit and revival—revival cannot come to a lost soul. The man without Christ needs salvation; but revival can come to the Christian.

Then what do we mean by the Holy Spirit and revival? We mean a great turning to Christ on the part of Christians. We mean the separation of the Christian from the world and the dedication of the Christian to the holy business of serving Christ.

When they sought out men to be the first deacons in the church at Jerusalem, they looked for men of honest report, "full of the Holy Ghost and wisdom." They wanted men who were living for Christ and whose lives were dedicated to His cause. A Spirit-filled life is a God-honoring, Christ-magnifying, Spirit-led life. From such a life rivers of living water will flow. From such a life, sweet manifestations of Christian character will come. The early saints were separated saints. They were saints who practiced purity in all matters of life. They adorned the Gospel by their conduct.

II. THE HOLY SPIRIT AND PRAYER

The book of Acts has so much to say about the matter of prayer. For example, "And they continued stedfastly in the apostles' doctrine and fellowship, and in breaking of bread, and in prayers" (Acts 2:42).

When we recognize the indwelling Guest—the Holy Spirit—we will desire to pray.

In Acts 2 Peter and John went up together into the temple at the hour of prayer. In Acts 4 we read that when they prayed, the place was shaken where they were assembled together, and they were all filled with the Holy Spirit. When Stephen was stoned to death, he died looking up toward God and praying.

When Saul of Tarsus was saved, the next thing we find said about him is, "Behold, he prayeth." In Acts 10 Peter was on the housetop praying.

When Peter was kept in prison, the saints of God met together in prayer for his release.

In Acts 13 the disciples were in prayer, then the Holy Spirit said, "Separate me Barnabas and Saul for the work whereunto I have called them."

It was at the place of prayer that Lydia was saved. It was also when Paul and Silas prayed that deliverance came to them. The jail was shaken, and their bonds were loosed.

Prayer may not be inviting to some people, but it will be inviting and will be desired when the Holy Spirit fills us and controls us.

In recent days we have been reading about many churches and the strange things that they are doing. For example, some time ago Duke Ellington, a jazz leader, directed a jazz concert in a church in San Francisco.

The night after Christmas Duke Ellington and his friends had a concert at New York's fashionable Fifth Avenue Presbyterian Church. Duke Ellington played, Lena Horne sang, a tap dancer gave a number. Duke Ellington is not a professing Christian. He does not belong to any church.

We have come to a very sad place when our work has to be done by unbelievers to the accompaniment of jazz. This is a long way from the old-fashioned prayer meeting, a long way from a simple waiting on God for divine direction in your life.

Dr. R. A. Torrey used to tell a very strange and interesting story of a faithful Scotch minister who was traveling through Scotland and stopped one night at an inn. The innkeeper came to him and asked him if he would conduct family worship. He replied that he would if the innkeeper would bring to the worship all the guests in the house and all the servants. This the innkeeper agreed to do.

When they were gathered in the big room for the service, the minister turned to the innkeeper and said, "Are all the servants here?"

"Yes," replied the innkeeper.

"All?" insisted the minister.

"Well, not all—all but one. There is one girl who works in the kitchen, washing the pots and kettles, who is so dirty that she is not fit to come to the meeting."

The minister replied, "We will not go on with the service until she comes." And he insisted until the innkeeper went for this servant and brought her in.

This faithful man of God became greatly interested in this poor, neglected creature, and when the others were leaving the room he asked her if she would not stay for a few minutes. And when everyone had gone, he said to her, "I want to teach you a prayer for you to offer: 'Lord, show me myself.' Will you offer it every day?" She replied that she would.

The next day the minister left but in a short time came back again and asked the innkeeper about this girl. The innkeeper replied, "She is spoiled. She is not good at all. She is weeping all the time, weeping day and night and can hardly attend to her work."

The minister asked to see her again, and when she came in the minister said, "Now, I want to teach you another prayer: 'Lord, show me Thyself.' Now pray that prayer every day."

The Scotch minister left and a few years afterward was preaching one Lord's day in a church in Glasgow. At the close of the service a neat, trim-looking young woman came up to him and said, "Do you recognize me?"

He replied, "No, I do not."

She said, "Do you recall holding a service in an inn and speaking to one of the servants afterward and teaching her to pray the prayer, 'Lord, show me myself,' and afterward teaching her to pray the other prayer, 'Lord, show me Thyself'?"

"Oh, yes," he said, "I remember that."

"Well," she said, "I am that girl, and when you taught me that first prayer and went away, I asked God to show me myself. He gave me such a view of my vileness and my sin that I was overwhelmed with grief and could scarcely sleep or work by day for thinking of my sins. Then, when you came back and taught me the second prayer, 'Lord, show me Thyself,' God gave me such a view of Himself, of His love, and of Jesus Christ's dying on the cross for me, that all the burden of my sin rolled away, and I became a happy Christian."

Sinner friend, you need to pray these two prayers unto God: "Lord, show me myself," and "Lord, show me Thyself." Christians, we need it also. Ask the Holy Spirit to reveal our needs and to impress upon us the value of simple trust in Him and complete dedication of our all to His will.

III. THE HOLY SPIRIT AND WITNESSING

Jesus said, "But ye shall receive power, after that the Holy Ghost is come upon you: and ye shall be witnesses unto me" (Acts 1:8).

When the Holy Spirit controls our lives, then we will be witnesses. We will be channels of blessing. The Holy Spirit will work through us to others.

You are a channel. You are a witness!

How beautifully this is given to us in Acts 10. We have the story of Cornelius, the man who desired to know more of God and of salvation. The angel of the Lord spoke to Cornelius but did not tell him how to be saved. He told him to send men to Joppa and to call for one named Simon, whose surname was Peter. It was Peter, not an angel, who was commissioned to give the message of salvation.

When Peter gave his account of his ministry to the Gentiles, he gave these words:

"And the Spirit bade me go with them, nothing doubting. Moreover these six brethren accompanied me, and we entered into the man's house:

"And he shewed us how he had seen an angel in his house, which stood and said unto him, Send men to Joppa, and call for Simon, whose surname is Peter;

"Who shall tell thee words, whereby thou and all thy house shall be saved.

"And as I began to speak, the Holy Ghost fell on them, as on us at the beginning."—Acts 11:12-15.

In plain words, not even an angel could show Cornelius the way of eternal life. It must be a saved man, a Spirit-filled man, as Simon Peter.

The Holy Spirit has no way of getting to a lost man but through you and me. Are you a clear channel so that God can work through you? Are you living such a life that you are a witness for the Saviour?

IV. THE HOLY SPIRIT AND POWER

Jesus said, "But ye shall receive power" (Acts 1:8). "And with great power gave the apostles witness of the resurrection of the Lord Jesus: and great grace was upon them all" (Acts 4:33).

The Holy Spirit is synonymous with power. We need overcoming power. The world is too much for us. Satan's power is ever against us.

We need power to speak out for our Saviour. This power does not come through machines or education, but this power comes through the Holy Spirit. Now, allow me to review just a moment.

First, we are saved by the blood. We are not saved by any works of righteousness of our own. We are saved entirely by His grace. "For by grace are ye saved through faith."

Second, we are indwelt by the Holy Spirit. ". . . he dwelleth with you, and shall be in you."

Third, we are cleansed by the Spirit and for the Spirit. The Holy Spirit fills only the cleansed heart.

Fourth, we are filled with the Spirit. This means empowering for living and witnessing.

Being filled with the Spirit is exemplified in the case of Stephen. He spake with such power of the Spirit that the people gnashed upon him with their teeth and cried out with their voices, stopping their ears, and running upon him with one accord.

Paul summed up his ministry by saying, "My speech and my preaching was not with enticing words of man's wisdom, but in demonstration of the Spirit and of power."

The power of the early saints is witnessed by the results of their preaching. At Pentecost about three thousand were saved. A short time after, five thousand and more were saved. When Paul preached, they said of him that he turned the world upside down. The whole city of Ephesus was so stirred by the ministry of Paul that many believed and confessed and showed their deeds.

Amazing things happen when the Holy Spirit takes over. There is the story of the old Methodist preacher who had been called by his parishioners "Old Man Drysticks." He was so dry and unattractive that his people were preparing a petition, asking for his removal. The old minister found out what was going on under the surface and, with broken heart, he sought the Saviour's face. All night he cried and prayed unto God, confessing his sins, seeking the enduement of power. The next Sunday as he preached, the fire fell. His people were amazed. A new grip came into his sermons. A new response came from his pleas. A revival broke out. From night to night souls were saved, and many were added to the church.

The old man who had been called "Old Man Drysticks" became a live wire from Heaven. They did not want to get rid of this man, but they wanted him to be reappointed to the church.

May God give us the filling of the Holy Spirit.

The Holy Spirit and revival! Revivals are personal. Revivals concern you and the Lord. Revivals concern your heart condition. A revival will kill jealousy, envy and fault-finding.

Revivals are practical. Revivals straighten out a lot of strange ideas. Revivals will bring about correct behavior in financial matters. Revivals will correct your actions toward others and will cause you to live pure and clean lives.

Revivals are powerful! The Holy Spirit makes it so. They are powerful enough to change a man's life completely.

A revival is powerful enough to change a home completely. We have seen this over and over again.

Revivals are powerful enough to change a young person's social activities.

Revivals are powerful enough to call a young man out of the world and to lead him to follow Christ to the ends of the earth.

My plea is for every Christian to let the Holy Spirit have the right of way. I speak this to parents, to young people, to children—all who are indwelt by the Holy Spirit. May we let Him have His way with us.

Finally, I give my appeal to the sinner. My lost friend, I am praying that conviction may come upon you—the conviction that you are lost and Hell-bound and that only Jesus can save you.

A chaplain approached a wounded soldier on a battlefield with the question, "What can I do for you?"

The soldier said, "I don't need anything done for me. I need someone who can undo."

Yes, getting someone to undo our sins is the most important thing of our lives. Sin is as old as the first rebellious thought. It is as old as the first rebellious act. Sin damns. "The soul that sinneth, it shall die."

Sin cannot be ignored. Sin is like cancer, tuberculosis, or heart disease. It does not leave you of its own accord. Sin must not be ignored. Face the fact of your sin. Repent of sin. Believe on the Lord Jesus Christ. This is the word that Paul gave to the jailer in Philippi when he cried,

"Sirs, what must I do to be saved?" Paul and Silas answered, "Believe on the Lord Jesus Christ, and thou shalt be saved, and thy house." It was done for them. It will be done for you. Come to Christ. Receive Him as your Saviour.

CHARLES GRANDISON FINNEY
1792-1875

ABOUT THE MAN:

Charles Finney was born in Connecticut in the most ordinary of circumstances to a family and life that gave little hint of the great things God had in store for him. He was a schoolteacher and then a lawyer before his conversion at age 29.

Finney was filled with the Holy Spirit on the same day he was saved and immediately began witnessing to friends and family members. More than twenty people were saved in the 24 hours following Finney's conversion.

Finney's personal evangelism soon became public evangelism as he began to travel and preach in extended revival meetings. He considered revival to be a natural result of following the instructions God had laid out in His Word.

During Finney's fifty years of preaching, more than 500,000 were saved. He wrote many books, the most enduring of which are *The Autobiography of Charles Finney* and *Lectures on Revival of Religion*.

After ill health forced him to stop traveling in meetings, he accepted the pastorate of a church in New York City. From 1852 until 1866 he served as president of Oberlin College in Ohio.

Finney was a powerful, Spirit-filled soul winner who was mightily used of God as an instrument to bring revival to cities and towns across the eastern United States.

VIII.

When Revival Is to Be Expected

CHARLES G. FINNEY

"Wilt thou not revive us again: that thy people may rejoice in thee?"— Ps. 85:6.

This psalm seems to have been written soon after the return of the people of Israel from the Babylonish captivity, from the language at the commencement of it. The psalmist felt that God had been very favorable to the people, and while contemplating the goodness of the Lord in bringing them back from the land where they had been carried away captive, and while looking at the prospects before them, he breaks out into a prayer for a revival of religion. "Wilt thou not revive us again: that thy people may rejoice in thee?" Since God in His providence had reestablished the ordinances of His house among them, he prays that there may be also a revival of religion, to crown the works.

The topics to which I wish to call your attention tonight, are: When a revival of religion is needed; The importance of a revival when it is needed; When a revival of religion may be expected.

I. WHEN IS A REVIVAL OF RELIGION NEEDED?

A. When there is a want of brotherly love and Christian confidence among professors of religion, then there is a loud call for God to revive His work. When Christians have sunk down into a low and backslidden state, they neither have, nor ought to have, nor is there reason to have, the same love and confidence toward each other as when they are all alive, active and living holy lives. The love of benevolence may be the same, but not the love of complacency.

God loves all men with the love of benevolence, but He does not feel the love of complacency toward any but those who live holy. Christians do not and cannot love each other with the love of complacency, except in proportion to their holiness.

If Christian love is the love of the image of Christ in His people, then it can be exercised only where that image really or apparently exists. A person must reflect the image of Christ and show the spirit of Christ before other Christians can love him with the love of complacency.

It is in vain to call on Christians to love one another with the love of complacency, as Christians, when they are sunk down in stupidity. They see nothing in each other to produce this love. It is next to impossible that they should feel otherwise toward each other than they do toward sinners. Merely knowing that they belong to the church, or seeing them occasionally at the communion table, will not produce Christian love, unless they see the image of Christ.

B. When there are dissensions, jealousies and evil speakings among professors of religion, then there is great need of a revival. These things show that Christians have gotten far from God, and it is time to think earnestly of a revival. Religion cannot prosper with such things in the church, and nothing can put an end to them like a revival.

C. When there is a worldly spirit in the church, then it shows that they are far from God and that there is great need of a revival of religion. It is manifest that the church is sunk down into a low and backslidden state when you see Christians conform to the world in dress, equipage, parties, seeking worldly amusements, reading novels and other books such as the world reads.

D. When the church finds its members falling into gross and scandalous sins, then it is time for the church to wake up and cry to God for a revival of religion. When such things are taking place as give the enemies of religion an occasion for reproach, it is time for the church to ask of God, "What will become of Thy great name?"

E. When there is a spirit of controversy in the church or in the land, a revival is needful. The spirit of religion is not the spirit of controversy. There can be no prosperity in religion where the spirit of controversy prevails.

F. When the wicked triumph over the church and revile them, it is time to seek for a revival of religion.

G. When sinners are careless, stupid and sinking into Hell unconcerned, it is time the church should bestir itself.

It is as much the duty of the church to awake as it is of the firemen to awake when a fire breaks out in the night in a great city. The church ought to put out the fires of Hell which are laying hold of the wicked.

Sleep! Should the firemen sleep and let the whole city burn down; what would be thought of such firemen? And yet their guilt would not compare with the guilt of Christians who sleep while sinners around them are sinking into the fires of Hell.

II. THE IMPORTANCE OF A REVIVAL OF RELIGION IN SUCH CIRCUMSTANCES

A. A revival of religion is the only possible thing that can wipe away the reproach which covers the church and restore religion to the place it ought to have in the estimation of the public. Without a revival, this reproach will cover the church more and more, until it is overwhelmed with universal contempt.

You may do anything else you please, and you can change the aspects of society in some respects, but you will do no real good; you only make it worse without a revival of religion.

You may go and build a splendid new house of worship and line your seats with damask, put up a costly pulpit and get a magnificent organ and everything of that kind, to make a show and dash; and in that way you may procure a sort of respect for religion among the wicked, but it does no good in reality. It rather does hurt. It misleads them as to the real nature of religion; and as to converting them, it carries them farther away from salvation.

Look wherever they have surrounded the altar of Christianity with splendor, and you will find that the impression produced is contrary to the true nature of religion. There must be a waking up of energy on the part of Christians and an outpouring of God's Spirit, or the world will laugh at the church.

B. Nothing but a revival of religion will restore Christian love and confidence among church members. Nothing else can restore it, and nothing else *ought* to restore it.

There is no other way to wake up that love of Christians for one another which is sometimes felt when they have such love as they cannot express. You cannot have such love without confidence; and you cannot restore confidence without such evidence of piety as is seen in a revival.

If a *minister* finds he has lost in any degree the confidence of his people, he ought to labor for a revival as the only means of regaining their confidence. I do not mean that this should be his *motive* in laboring for revival, but that a revival through his instrumentality, and ordinarily nothing else, will restore to him the confidence of the praying part of his people.

If an elder or private member of the church finds his brethren cold toward him, there is but one way to remedy it. It is by being revived himself and pouring out from his life the splendor of the image of Christ. This spirit will catch and spread in the church, confidence will be renewed, and brotherly love will prevail again.

C. At such a time, a revival of religion is indispensable to avert the judgments of God from the church. This would be strange preaching if revivals were only miracles and if the church has no more agency in producing them than it has in making a thunderstorm.

To say to the church that unless there is a revival you may expect judgments, would then be as ridiculous as to say, If you do not have a thunderstorm, you may expect judgments.

The fact is, *Christians* are more to blame for not being revived than *sinners* are for not being converted. If they are not awakened, they may assuredly know that God will visit them with His judgments.

How often God visited the Jewish church with judgments because they would not repent and be revived at the call of His prophets! How often have we seen churches, and even whole denominations, cursed with a curse because they would not wake up and seek the Lord and pray, "Wilt thou not revive us again: that thy people may rejoice in thee?"!

D. Nothing but a revival of religion can preserve such a church from annihilation. A church declining in this way cannot continue to exist without a revival. If it receives new members, they will, for the most part, be made up of ungodly persons.

Without revivals there will not ordinarily be as many persons converted as will die off in a year. There have been churches in this country where the members have died off, and there were no revivals to convert others in their place, till the church has run out of members and the organization has been dissolved.

A minister told me that he once labored as a missionary in Virginia on the ground where such a man as Samuel Davies once flashed and shone like a flaming torch; and that Davies' church was so reduced as to have but one male member. The church had gotten proud and was all run out.

I have heard of a church in Pennsylvania that was formerly flourishing, but when it neglected revivals, it became so reduced that the pastor had to send to a neighboring church for a ruling elder when he administered the communion.

E. Nothing but a revival of religion can prevent the means of grace from doing a great injury to the ungodly. Without a revival, they will grow harder and harder under preaching, and will experience a more horrible damnation than they would if they had never heard the Gospel.

The Gospel is the "savour of death unto death" if it is not made a "savour of life unto life."

F. There is no other way in which a church can be sanctified, grow in grace, and be fitted for Heaven.

What is growing in grace? Is it hearing sermons and getting some new *notions* about religion? No—no such thing. The Christian who does this, and nothing more, is getting worse and worse, more and more hardened, and every week it is more difficult to rouse him to duty.

III. WHEN REVIVAL OF RELIGION MAY BE EXPECTED

A. A revival may be expected when the providence of God indicates that a revival is at hand. The indications of God's providence are sometimes so plain as to amount to a revelation of His will. There is a conspiring of events to open the way, a preparation of circumstances to favor a revival, so that those who are looking for it can see that a revival is at hand just as plainly as if it had been revealed from Heaven.

Cases have occurred in this country where the providential manifestations were so plain that those who are careful observers felt no hesitation in saying that God was coming to pour out His Spirit and grant a revival of religion.

There are various ways for God to indicate His will to a people—sometimes by giving them peculiar means, sometimes by peculiar and alarming events, sometimes by remarkably favoring the employment of means, by the weather, health and so on.

B. A revival may be expected when the wickedness of the wicked grieves and humbles and distresses Christians. Sometimes Christians do not seem to mind anything about the wickedness around them. Or if they talk about it, it is in a cold, callous and unfeeling way, as if they despaired of a reformation; they are disposed to scold sinners—not to feel the compassion of the Son of God for them.

But sometimes the conduct of the wicked drives Christians to prayer, breaks them down and makes them sorrowful and tenderhearted so they can weep day and night, and instead of scolding and reproaching them, they pray earnestly for them. Then you may expect a revival. Indeed this is a revival already begun.

Sometimes the wicked will get up an opposition to religion. When this drives Christians to their knees in prayer to God, with strong crying and tears, you may be certain there is going to be a revival.

The prevalence of wickedness is no evidence at all that there is not going to be a revival. That is often God's time to work. 'When the enemy cometh in like a flood, the Spirit of the Lord lifts up a standard against him.'

Often the first indication of a revival is the Devil's getting up something new in opposition. It will invariably have one of two effects—either drive Christians to God or drive them farther away from God to some carnal policy or other practice that will only make things worse. Frequently the most outrageous wickedness of the ungodly is followed by a revival.

If Christians are made to feel that they have no hope but in God, and if they have sufficient feeling left to care for the honor of God and the salvation of the souls of the impenitent, there will certainly be a revival.

Let Hell boil over if it will and spew out as many devils as there are stones in the pavements, if it only drives Christians to God in prayer—they cannot hinder a revival.

Let Satan get up a row and sound his horn as loud as he pleases; if Christians will only be humbled and pray, they shall soon see God's mighty arm in a revival of religion.

I have known instances where a revival has broken in upon the ranks of the enemy almost as suddenly as a clap of thunder and scattered them—taken the very ringleaders as trophies and broken up their party in an instant.

C. A revival may be expected when Christians have a spirit of prayer for a revival—that is, when they pray as if their hearts were set upon a revival.

Sometimes Christians are not engaged in prayer for a revival, not even when they are warm in prayer. Their minds are upon something else; they are praying for something else—the salvation of the heathen and the like—and not for a revival among themselves. But when they feel the want of a revival, they pray for it; they feel for their own families and neighborhoods and pray for them as if they could not be denied.

What constitutes a spirit of prayer? Is it many prayers and warm words? No. Prayer is the state of the heart. The spirit of prayer is a state of continual desire and anxiety of mind for the salvation of sinners. It is something that weighs them down.

It is the same, so far as the philosophy of the mind is concerned, as when a man is anxious for some worldly interest. A Christian who has this spirit of prayer feels anxious for souls. It is the subject of his thoughts all the time and makes him look and act as if he had a load on his mind. He thinks of it by day and dreams of it by night. This is properly praying without ceasing. The man's prayers seem to flow like water from his heart—"O Lord, revive thy work."

Sometimes this feeling is very deep; persons have been bowed down so that they could neither stand nor sit. I can name men in this state, of firm nerves, who stand high in character, who have been absolutely crushed with grief for the state of sinners. They have had an actual travail of soul for sinners till they were as helpless as children.

The feeling is not always so great as this, but such things are much more common than is supposed. In the great revivals in 1826, they were common. This is by no means enthusiasm. It is just what Paul felt when he said, "My little children, of whom I travail in birth."

I heard of a person in this state who prayed for sinners and finally got into such a state of mind that she could not live without prayer. She could not rest day nor night unless there was somebody praying. Then she would be at ease; but if they ceased, she would shriek in agony till there was prayer again.

This continued for two days until she prevailed in prayer and her soul was relieved.

This travail of soul is that deep agony which persons feel when they lay hold on God for such a blessing and will not let go till they receive it.

I do not mean to be understood that it is essential to a spirit of prayer that the distress should be as great as this. But this deep, continual, earnest desire for the salvation of sinners is what constitutes the spirit of prayer for a revival. It is a revival begun so far as this spirit of prayer extends.

When this feeling exists in a church, unless the Spirit is grieved away by sin, there will inevitably be a revival of Christians generally, and it will involve the conversion of sinners to God. This anxiety and distress increases till the revival commences.

One clergyman told me of a revival among his people which commenced with a zealous and devoted woman in the church. She became anxious about sinners and began praying for them; she prayed, and her distress increased. Finally she came to her minister and talked with him and asked him to appoint an "anxious" meeting, for she felt that one was needed. The minister put her off, for he felt none of the anxiety.

The next week she came again and besought him to appoint an "anxious" meeting; she knew there would be somebody to come, for she felt as if God were going to pour out His Spirit. He put her off again.

Finally she said to him, "If you do not appoint an 'anxious meeting,' I shall die, for there is certainly going to be a revival."

The next Sunday he appointed a meeting and said that if there were any who wished to converse with him about the salvation of their souls, he would meet them on such an evening. He did not know of one, but when he went to the place, to his astonishment he found a large number of anxious inquirers.

Now do not you think that woman knew there was going to be a revival? Call it what you please—a new revelation or an old revelation or anything else; I say it was the Spirit of God that taught that praying woman there was going to be a revival. "The secret of the Lord" was with her, and she knew it. She knew God had been in her heart and filled it so full that she could no longer contain it.

Sometimes ministers have had this distress about their congregations so that they felt as if they could not live unless they could see a revival. Sometimes elders and deacons or private members of the church, men or women, have the spirit of prayer for a revival of religion so that they will hold on and prevail with God till He pours out His Spirit.

The first ray of light that broke in upon the midnight which rested on the churches in Oneida County, in the fall of 1825, was from a woman in feeble health who, I believe, had never been in a powerful revival. Her soul was exercised about sinners. She was in an agony for the land. She did not know what ailed her, but she kept praying more and more, till it seemed as if her agony would destroy her body.

At length she became full of joy and exclaimed, "God has come! God has come! There is no mistake about it; the work is begun and is going over all the region."

Sure enough, the work began, and almost all her family were converted; and the work spread all over that part of the country.

Now, do you think that woman was deceived? I tell you no. She knew she had prevailed with God in prayer. She had travailed in birth for souls, and she knew it. This was but one instance in many that I knew in that region.

Generally, there are but few professors of religion who know anything about this spirit of prayer which prevails with God. I have been amazed to see such accounts as are often published about revivals, as if the revival had come without any cause—nobody knew why or wherefore. I have sometimes inquired into such cases when it had been given out that nobody knew anything about it until one Sunday they saw in the face of the congregation that God was there—or they saw it in their conference room or prayer meeting—and were astonished at the mysterious sovereignty of God in bringing in a revival without any apparent connection with means.

Now mark my words. Go and inquire among the obscure members of the church, and you will always find that somebody had been praying for a revival and was expecting it—some man or woman had been agonizing in prayer for the salvation of sinners until he or she gained the blessing. It may have found the minister and the body of the church fast asleep, and they woke up all of a sudden, like a man just rubbing his eyes open and running round the room pushing things over and wondering where all this excitement came from. But though few knew it, you may be sure there has been somebody on the watchtower constant in prayer till the blessing came.

Generally, a revival is more or less extensive as there are more or less persons who have the spirit of prayer; but I will not dwell on this subject any further at present.

D. A revival may be expected when the attention of ministers is especially directed to this particular object and when their preaching and other efforts are aimed particularly at the conversion of sinners.

Most of the time the labors of ministers are, it would seem, directed to other objects. They seem to preach and labor with no particular design to effect the *immediate* conversion of sinners, and then it need not be expected that there will be a revival under their preaching.

There never will be a revival till *somebody* makes particular efforts to that end. When the attention of a minister is directed to the state of the families in his congregation, and his heart is full of feeling of the necessity of a revival, and when he puts forth the proper efforts for that end, then you may be prepared to expect a revival.

The connection between the right methods for a revival and a revival is as philosophically sure as between the right methods to raise grain and a crop of wheat. I believe, in fact, it is more certain, and there are fewer instances of failure. The effect is more certain to follow. The paramount importance of spiritual things makes it reasonable that it should be so.

Take the Bible, the nature of the case, and the history of the church all together, and you will find fewer failures in the method for a revival than in farming or any other worldly business. In worldly business there are sometimes cases where counteracting causes annihilate all a man can do. In raising grain, for instance, there are cases which are beyond the control of man, such as drought, hard winter, worms, and so on. In laboring to promote a revival, things may occur to counteract it, something or other turning up to divert public attention from religion, which may baffle every effort. I believe there are fewer such cases in the moral than in the natural world.

I have seldom seen an individual fail when he used the methods for promoting a revival in earnest in the manner pointed out in the Word of God. I believe a man may enter on the work of promoting a revival with as reasonable an expectation of success as he can enter on any other work with an expectation of success, with the same expectation as the farmer has of a crop when he sows his grain. I have sometimes seen this tried and succeed under the most forbidding circumstances that can be conceived.

The great revival in Rochester began under the most disadvantageous circumstances that could be imagined. It seemed as though Satan had interposed every possible obstacle to a revival.

The three churches were at variance: one had no minister; one was divided and about to dismiss their minister. An elder of the third church had brought a charge of unchristian conduct against the pastor of the first church, and they were going to have a trial before the presbytery.

After the work began, one of the first things to happen was, the great stone church gave way and created a panic. Then one of the churches dismissed their minister right in the midst of it. Another church nearly broke down. Many other things occurred, so that it seemed as if the Devil was determined to divert public attention from the subject of religion.

But there were a few remarkable cases of the spirit of prayer, which assured us that God was there, and we went on. The more Satan opposed, the Spirit of the Lord lifted up the standard higher and higher, till finally a wave of salvation rolled over the place.

E. A revival may be expected when Christians begin to confess their sins to one another. At other times, they confess in a general manner, as if they were only half in earnest. They may do it in eloquent language, but it does not mean anything; but when there is an ingenuous breaking down and a pouring out of the heart in making a confession of their sins, the floodgates will soon burst open, and salvation will flow over the place.

F. A revival may be expected whenever Christians are found willing to make the sacrifice necessary to carry it on. They must be willing to sacrifice their feelings, their business, their time, to help forward the work.

Ministers must be willing to lay out their strength and to jeopardize their health and life. They must be willing to offend the impenitent by plain and faithful dealing and perhaps offend many members of the church who will not come up to the work. They must take a decided stand with the revival, let the consequences be what they may. They must be prepared to go on with the work, even though they might lose the affections of all the impenitent and of all the cold part of the church. The minister must be prepared, if it is the will of God, to be driven away from the place. He must be determined to go straightforward and leave the entire event with God.

I knew a minister who had a young man laboring with him in a revival. The young man preached pretty plain, and the wicked did not like him. They said, "We like *our* minister, and we wish to have him preach."

They finally complained so much that the minister told the young man, "Mr. Such-a-one, who gives so much towards my support, says so and so. Mr. A. says so, and Mr. B. says so. They think it will break up the society if you continue to preach; so I think you had better not preach anymore."

The young man went away, but the Spirit of God immediately withdrew from the place, and the revival stopped short.

The minister, by yielding to the wicked desires of the wicked, drove him away. He was afraid the Devil would drive *him* away from his people, and by undertaking to satisfy the Devil, he offended God.

God so ordered events that in a short time he had to leave his people after all. When he undertook to go between the Devil and God, God dismissed him.

The people also must be willing to have a revival, let the sacrifice be what it may. It will not do for them to say, "We are willing to attend so many meetings, but we cannot attend any more," or "We are willing to have a revival if it will not disturb our arrangements about our business or prevent our making money."

I tell you, such people will never have a revival till they are willing to do anything and sacrifice anything that God indicates to be their duty.

Christian merchants must feel willing to lock up their stores for six months, if it is necessary to carry on a revival. I do not mean to say any such thing is called for or that it is their duty to do so, but if there should be such a state of feeling as to call for it, then it would be their duty, and they ought to be willing to do it if God calls. He can easily burn down their stores if they do not.

In fact, I should not be sorry to see such a revival in New York as would make every merchant in the city lock up his store till spring and say he had sold enough goods he would now give up his whole time to lead sinners to Christ.

G. A revival may be expected when ministers and professors are willing to have God promote it by what instruments He pleases.

Sometimes ministers are not willing to have a revival unless *they* can have the management of it or unless *their* agency can be conspicuous in promoting it. They wish to prescribe to God what He shall direct and bless and what men He shall put forward. They will have no new measures. They cannot have any of this new-light preaching or of these *evangelists* who go about the country preaching. They have a great deal to say about God's being sovereign and that He will have revivals come in His own way and time, but then He must choose to have it just in their way, or they will have nothing to do with it.

Such men will sleep on till they are awakened by the judgment trumpet, without a revival, unless they are willing that God should come in His own way—unless they are willing to have anything or anybody employed that will do the most good.

H. A revival may be expected when the foregoing things occur. A revival, to the same extent, already exists. In truth, a revival should be *expected* whenever it is *needed*.

If we need to be revived, it is our duty to be revived. If it is duty it is possible, and we should set about being revived ourselves and, relying on the promise of Christ to be with us in making disciples always and everywhere, we ought to labor to revive Christians and convert sinners with confident expectation of success. Therefore, whenever the church needs reviving, they ought and may expect to be revived and to see sinners converted to Christ.

When those things are seen which are named under the foregoing heads, let Christians and ministers be encouraged and know that a good work is already begun. Follow it up.

Remarks

1. Brethren, you can tell from our subject whether you need a revival here or not in your church and in your city and whether you are going to have one or not. Elders of the church—men, women, any of you, and all of you—what do you say?

Do you need a revival?

Do you expect to have one?

Have you any reason to expect one?

You need not make any mistake about it, for you know—or can know if you will—whether you have any reason to look for a revival here.

2. You see why you have not a revival. It is only because you do not want one, because you are not praying for it nor anxious for it nor putting forth efforts for it.

I appeal to your own consciences: Are you making these efforts now to promote a revival? You know, brethren, what the truth is. Will you stand up and say that you have made the effort for a revival and been disappointed—that you have cried to God, "Wilt thou not revive us?" and God would not do it?

3. Do you wish for a revival? Will you have one? If God should ask you this moment, by an audible voice from Heaven, "Do you want a revival?" would you dare to say "Yes"? If He said, "Are you willing to make the sacrifices?" would you answer, "Yes"? If He asked, "When

shall it begin?" would you answer, "Let it begin tonight—let it begin here—let it begin in my heart NOW"? Would you dare to say so to God if you should hear His voice tonight?

(From LECTURES ON REVIVALS OF RELIGION by Charles G. Finney. Published by Fleming H. Revell Company.)

HUGH F. PYLE
1918-

ABOUT THE MAN:

Before his call into the ministry, Hugh Pyle had been in the newspaper field, associated with the *Tampa Tribune*.

Born in Portsmouth, Virginia, Pyle was called to preach in 1940. At age 22 he married Esther Webber, was ordained a Baptist preacher and began pastoring two country churches near Tampa. After awhile he accepted a call to the First Baptist Church, Graveland, then Pensacola; and later, Panama City, all in Florida.

Between the two latter pastorates, Pyle accepted a position with Dr. John R. Rice and the Sword of the Lord. There he enjoyed a very fruitful ministry; but when his children entered into their teenage years, Hugh returned to the pastorate.

Central Baptist Church, Panama City, was without a doubt Pyle's most productive pastorate. In 15½ years the membership grew to 1,600. He founded a Christian day school which eventually enrolled nearly 1,000 students. There he conducted a daily broadcast for 14 years. In addition to the above, Pyle made time to conduct revival campaigns, Bible conferences, speak in summer camps and write booklets and articles.

In 1973 he resigned his fruitful Panama City pastorate to go on the road again as an evangelist.

Pyle campaigns are planned to meet needs. Before each service he dramatizes a Bible story especially designed for the children; his sermons are sin-exposing and repentance-producing and challenge and charge Christians to obey God in baptism, spiritual living, soul winning, strong Christian homes—to live sold-out lives for Christ! At the conclusion of each service, he conducts a brief session called "Good Ship Courtship," tailored for teenagers.

Hugh Pyle, his wife and their children practice what he preaches in his campaigns! All three children are happily and fruitfully serving the Lord today!

His sermons are regularly read in THE SWORD OF THE LORD. He has published several books and booklets—24 titles at the last count are now in circulation, most published by Sword of the Lord Publishers. Many of his books have to do with the home, marriage and family life. He has frequently been a prize winner in evangelistic sermon contests.

Dr. Hugh Pyle is desperately desirous of seeing an old-time revival from God sweep our land. It is a worthy desire and prayer of a worthy preacher who has his eyes, ears and heart tuned in on a nation's needs!

IX.

Can We Still Have Successful Revival Meetings?

Do We No Longer Need the Evangelist?

HUGH PYLE

Remember revival meetings? What has happened to us? Why have many pastors stopped holding revivals in their churches? What are we afraid of? Has God withdrawn the gift of the evangelist? What are the alternatives?

Some mighty good evangelists have left the revival trail and taken pastorates. Some are now in secular work, feeling it is the only way they can support their families. Did God make a mistake when, along with pastors and teachers, He "gave . . . evangelists" (Eph. 4:11) to the church "for the perfecting of the saints, for the work of the ministry, for the edifying of the body of Christ" (Eph.4:12)?

Judging from the verses that follow, it is evident that God knew we needed evangelists as well as pastors so that we might "all come in the unity of the faith, and of the knowledge of the Son of God, unto a perfect man . . . That we henceforth be no more children, tossed to and fro, and carried about with every wind of doctrine" (vss. 13, 14).

Let us consider this extremely important matter under four different headings: (1) Why Some Have Quit Having Revivals; (2) What Revivals Can Do for You and Your Church; (3) Why We Need to Use the Evangelist; and (4) How to Have a Successful Revival Crusade.

I. WHY SOME HAVE QUIT HAVING REVIVALS

Of course all have not quit, by any means! But in my travels across the continent I've been asking questions of pastors to see what is happening and why. Many of them tell me that neighboring pastors never visit their crusades anymore and that, indeed, a number of them are no longer having meetings in their own churches.

Here are some of the reasons they give:

1. "Crowds won't come like they used to." Since, in some crusades, people have not flocked to the meeting house upon the announcement of a "revival," they conclude that folks are just not interested anymore.

Crowds are smaller than they had on Sunday, and the pastor is sometimes embarrassed that his people do not show up on the evenings of the campaign.

2. "We have too many other things going on in the church now. Folks are just too busy for a week-long crusade."

3. "It costs too much to bring in a full-time man. We just can't afford it."

4. "Evangelists have been given a bad name—you know, the big TV scandals, etc."

5. "People don't want that strong preaching anymore."

6. "Results are too meager in recent meetings."

7. "The competition is too keen, too many other things going on, what with TV, ball games, etc."

8. Some say, "Some pastors themselves are too lazy, too worldly or too proud to want revival."

Let's take these excuses for not having revival crusades and examine them one by one:

1. "Crowds won't come." Oh, but in many places they **do** come still to special meetings. **We** just have to work harder, prepare better, publicize more, organize properly and pray as we've never prayed before. When we get to the last segment of this message on "How to Have a Successful Revival Crusade," you'll see what we're talking about!

2. "Too many other things going on." True, we've let ourselves get into a frenzy of activity in our churches as well as in our families and work schedules. So the pastor must train his leaders and teachers that soul winning and revival are the most important things the church has to do. All other activities culminate in that which is most important—the revival of God's people into Christlike living and the reaching of the lost. The other things we do in the church are just means to this end. (Maybe that will help us eliminate some of the unnecessary activities!)

Nowadays the pastor may need to start many weeks ahead of the crusade to get the entire church pointed toward revival. Some suggestions will follow under "How to. . . ."

3. "It costs too much." But everything else has gone up, too. You're paying more for literature, electricity, salaries and janitor supplies than you ever did before. It's impossible to put a price on a soul. Anyway, if you handle it the right way the people will take care of the expenses of the crusade without hurting the church at all! You'll see!

4. "Evangelists have been given a bad name." Just because a few charlatans have been exposed in immorality or found out to be money-grabbing phonies is no reason to reject the true men of God who have answered God's call to evangelize the lost and revive the church! The exposure of the counterfeit only proves the existence of the real thing! People know better. They can tell the difference between the true and the false. That's just a cop-out!

5. "People don't want strong preaching anymore." Who says they don't? I'm in churches all the time that revel in strong preaching. I also constantly encounter people who are looking for a church where they can find strong preaching. I've just come from a new church in metro-Atlanta. It has grown from a handful to over one hundred in a few short months. Many of these people are driving a great distance through maddening traffic to sound out this new church where the Bible is preached in its purity and the great old traditional hymns are sung. They have already bought property and must build immediately.

For the most part these are "yuppies," the upper middle class professional people, who are looking for a real church. They came every night to the meeting, and the pastor counted over thirty families who signed visitors' cards in this one week! Strong preaching ("speaking the truth in love") is exactly what they're looking for!

6. "Results are too meager." I know that in an evangelistic campaign we hope to see many saved. No one longed for that more than I did when I was a pastor. But some of the best meetings that really did my church the most good were revivals or Bible conferences where the saints got worked over and we did not have any great ingathering of souls. If we ever see real revival in a church, the souls inevitably will be reached sooner or later because that is the natural result of revival.

7. "The competition is too keen, other things going on," etc. Some of us look around and see the charismatics and the liberals with their entertainment centers, rock music and other excesses, and we get intimidated by this. We know, too, that television is a great charmer and that, along with ball games, school activities and pleasure seeking of all sorts, it is sometimes discouraging to the faithful pastor who is plodding along trying to build a work for God.

Still, there have always been other distractions. It has never been easy to really do business for God in the face of satanic and worldly opposition. It just means we have to try harder, pray much and use every proper and legitimate means of reaching the people. We may not always be the biggest, but we can be the **best** if we obey God and determine to do God's work in God's way.

8. If some pastors are too lazy or too worldly to still have revivals, then those pastors need to repent and get back to their calling. Certainly a man who is not living a godly life and sincerely seeking souls for Christ is, himself, the one most in need of revival! ". . . as with the people, so with the priest" (Isa. 24:2). "I am against the prophets, saith the Lord, that steal my words every one from his neighbour" (Jer. 23:30).

A pastor should not have a defeatist attitude about using the evangelist and revivalist his church so greatly needs.

II. WHAT REVIVALS CAN DO FOR YOU AND YOUR CHURCH

A revival is not just an evangelistic campaign. Neither is it an unexplained, sovereign miracle. It is not something man can produce; neither is it something God sends without the help and cooperation of men.

Revival is a release of heavenly power; it is an awakening of joy, work and power. It is a conviction that leads to cleansing. It is "clearing the way for God," as the old revivalists termed it. It will remove the "rubbish" (Neh. 4:10) so that the wall of God can be built.

Business people have periodic sales to stimulate business and bring people back into their stores again. No wonder Jesus said the children of this world are wiser in their generation than the children of light (Luke 16:8). Can't we have sense enough to know that a periodic "sale" will be good business for the church?

Some criticize revivals, saying they do not last. Billy Sunday said, "Neither does a bath last, but you need to take one now and then!" Is soap a failure just because you have to use it over and over again?

America (and every other country I know of) desperately needs revival. We can come up out of the swamp again. "Sin is a reproach to any people" (Prov. 14:34). Our land can be "healed" (II Chron. 7:14);

but it starts when God's people humble themselves, pray, seek God's face and turn from their wicked ways—which is just what real revival is calculated to make us do!

Revival should make us conscious of sin again and burden us that it breaks the heart of God. Revival will bring the church to repentance. Lives will be changed. The church will be edified, God will be glorified, Christians will find great joy in serving God, and souls will be saved!

Read again the masterful books on revival by Charles G. Finney. Revel in the journals of the Welsh revival. Dig up your old copies of THE SWORD OF THE LORD and read of revivals that swept Christian colleges in America. Read Dr. John Rice's *We Can Have Revival Now*. We still can! Get the book, *The Revival We Need*, by Oswald J. Smith. Read John Wesley and George Whitefield. Also read again the Bible accounts of great revivals under Asa, Nehemiah, Jonah, Peter, Paul and Jesus, among others. The God of revival still lives!

Cry with David, "It is time for thee, Lord, to work." And with Isaiah, "Oh. . . that thou wouldest come down . . .!" Say with Habakkuk, "O Lord, revive thy work in the midst of the years" (Hab. 3:2). Almost every revival has begun in a small place with just a few who really got under a burden to seek God's face until revival came. Why not purpose that it will begin at your place?

Now will this happen if you call up an evangelist and set a date for a revival meeting in your church?

Possibly not. And I will confess (as most honest evangelists will) that we do not see nearly as many heart-warming, soul-stirring, sin-killing, Christ-exalting, crowd-moving, long-lasting revivals as we did twenty, thirty and forty years ago. But we still do see some. And we see a measure of blessing in others. We still see the mercy drops, and we plead for the showers of blessing.

Some of those old-time revivals lasted a month, two months or more—I mean, they came every night for that long! Some modern-day Christians act like they are utterly astounded at the suggestion that they attend every night for one week (which shows how badly we need revival)!

When I was an evangelist in the fifties, most of my meetings were scheduled for fifteen days (three Sundays) or for twelve days (Wednesday through two Sundays). Some would settle for an eight-day meeting so that you could begin and end on a Sunday.

When I went back into evangelism in 1973, most invitations were for one week at most, usually Monday through Sunday or Sunday through Friday. Once in awhile a pastor would urge me to try to be with him for the full eight days, Sunday through Sunday. Now the daring pastors ask an evangelist for six days, Sunday through Friday. Most of them feel it better to ask for a four-day meeting, Sunday through Wednesday; some want just a weekend meeting; and many want a one-day (Sunday) revival! Wouldn't we all like to see revival come to our churches in one day!

Well, one day is better than nothing. But don't expect to be able to do in one day, or even in four days, what the old-timers saw God do in two weeks or a month! But whatever you do, don't give up on using the God-called evangelist and having special meetings in your church.

If you are going to have just a Sunday rally with your evangelist or a four-day meeting, then it needs to be planned, promoted, powered and prayed for like no other meeting you've ever had.

If the church you now pastor has not been used to having week-long revival meetings, you will need to educate them about what real revival is and why it is so desperately needed.

If I were a pastor again, I would plan to have at least one full-week revival each year. Then I'd want to bring in good men for four days on other occasions, either for a revival emphasis, an evangelistic thrust or a Bible conference, depending on the need and circumstances in my church and the type man I was using at the time. There are great men, of course, who can do your church some real good in one day. Then perhaps you can line one up for a revival at a future date. In addition to this, I would have a missions conference each year, stressing both home and foreign missions.

What can these revivals do for your church?

1. They will help to keep the people strong. The sheep need to hear other voices from God as well as that of the pastor. In Ephesians 4 where God speaks of His gift of the evangelist to the New Testament church, He reminds us that, along with pastors and teachers, the evangelist will help them grow "unto the measure of the stature of the fulness of Christ: That we henceforth be no more children, tossed to and fro, and carried about with every wind of doctrine, by the sleight of men, and cunning craftiness, whereby they lie in wait to deceive" (vss. 13, 14).

Obviously, there are many evil forces and seductive voices attempting to lure the people away from God and from good, fundamental churches. The God-called evangelist will help to keep them safe and in line, making "increase of the body unto the edifying of itself in love" (Eph. 4:16).

2. The evangelist backs up what the pastor says! If a pastor has been preaching good, scriptural messages to his people, he needs some reinforcement every now and then; and it is good for the people to know he is not the only "nut" around. Here is a well-known, experienced man of God who says just what your pastor has been saying, only he says it in a different way. This helps to drive it home!

3. The revival helps reach the lost. There are people won in revivals who never darken the door of the church in normal Sunday services. Just as a big sale will bring in new customers to a retail store, so the special meetings will draw people to the church who have not been before, or who have seldom come. Even if that customer is "only looking" and doesn't buy at the time, it is very likely that, if he likes what he sees, he will return as a customer at some later date. The same is true with special meetings in the church.

Christians are stimulated and inspired to bring others during revival meetings, and they have some added leverage that they do not have for regular Sunday services for prying some of those lost friends and loved ones loose from their modernistic churches.

4. Revivals give you needed prospects to work on long after the meetings are over. Not only lost people but backsliders, weak saints and nonaffiliated Christians may very likely get interested in your church as a result of a visit made while you were having a revival.

5. Revivals and Bible conferences publicize your church so that the entire community knows something is going on at your place. Unless your church has a big, imposing auditorium on a main thoroughfare, the city may never even know you're there if you do not have special meetings advertised in the local papers and on radio and television.

Some people who are invited to or see your ads about your revival may be tied up that week, but they, nevertheless, will remember church the next time something is going on, or they may get in the hospital and realize that they need somebody to pray for them. The fact that your church has been publicized may very well prompt them to call on you for help.

6. More importantly, a revival activates your members. They will think

much more about surrender, service and soul winning during several days of strong preaching than they will just by coming on Sunday. When I was a pastor, many of our members got burdened for souls for the first time under the fiery preaching of an evangelist, or for the first time they saw the need for consecrated living. The evangelist may not have really given them anything that I had not already said, but suddenly with a new voice God brought it home to their hearts. They were revived and were much better members from then on.

7. Revivals will help the church financially. If people get stirred up to do right and to live strong Christian lives, they are bound to loosen up and give more to the support of the church when it is all over. The very fact that they are challenged to give during the campaign will bring blessing to them. "Give, and it shall be given unto you." As God increases their bounty, they will have more to give in the days ahead.

Besides this, the church that has been generous with God's servants, whether they be evangelists or missionaries, will enjoy the blessing of God upon them; for we reap what we sow!

8. Your people will appreciate their own pastor more after the crusade is over. Many of our own people have thanked me for having brought to town some good preacher they had always wanted to hear.

If some of their loved ones or friends found the Lord in the revival, they will always be grateful to you. And no matter how good the visiting man may have been, most people are glad that now they can enjoy their own pastor again.

9. You will be a better man after the revival! So many pastors have admitted to me that they needed the meeting for themselves and that it had been a great blessing to them. Young pastors have asked for counsel about things that would help them in their ministry. And pastors need the fellowship of a visiting preacher now and then. We can share our experiences, burdens and blessings. It is a blessing, too, for the pastor to have a week sometimes when he doesn't have to get fresh messages but can have his own soul fed by the visiting man of God.

III. WHY WE NEED TO USE THE EVANGELIST

A pastor often just brings in a neighboring pastor or some personal friend to conduct his special meetings. Pastors have been known to just "swap pulpits" and call this their evangelistic effort for the year.

But the visiting pastor has a different calling. He may or may not have a burden for souls.

1. The first reason we should use the evangelist is that God says we should! It is the Lord who gave the evangelist as a gift to the church. God knows the pastor needs the kind of help the evangelist can give.

If churches do not use the God-called evangelist, we may be forcing him out of his ministry. He must have invitations to churches to survive and stay in the work God has called him to do.

2. A pastor needs the kind of help an evangelist can give him. His is a unique calling.

3. Society needs the impact of sin-fighting preachers in the community. If the church has no voice raised against sin, then such a voice will not be heard at all.

4. Saints need the encouragement and stirring of a good revival crusade. It helps keep our witness sharp.

5. Souls need to be saved. The evangelist has the experience, the zeal, the burden to lead the church to go after the lost.

6. Young preachers and would-be preachers need the example of a God-called evangelist in their church. I find in almost every church I minister to young boys (and sometimes older young men) who are thinking about the ministry and need to have their hearts inspired and fired up for God. The plan of God for these young people may be frustrated if the church does not use the God-called evangelist.

IV. HOW TO HAVE A SUCCESSFUL REVIVAL CRUSADE

Churches can still have good revival meetings with crowds attending, Christians revived and souls converted to Christ. It is still happening. Some evangelists are still keeping a full schedule. Many churches, too, are conducting Bible conferences, prophetic conferences and family life meetings with great blessing. Some seasoned evangelists have special talent and experience in these kinds of meetings.

Others are especially adept at working with children or youth. Still others have a great burden for missions. I have often been asked to be the evening Bible speaker at missionary conferences. If you feel a full week of preaching on missions, prophecy or the family would be a bit much for your people, then why not start off with a four-day meeting, Sunday through Wednesday?

It would be wonderful to see two-week revivals (or longer) come back again, perhaps even month-long meetings. When the church gets sick enough of what sin is doing to our civilization, perhaps we will bring them back. When someone gets such a burden for prayer that great conviction sweeps the church again, there may be no limit to what God will do for us in bringing revival in our time.

Meanwhile, experience proves that we can still have good meetings and much blessing in the one-week revival crusade.

Here are some pertinent suggestions on how to have successful meetings:

1. *Pray* for God's man. Think about just what your church needs most and then trust God to lead you to the one God would have come. Sometimes a church needs the seasoned help of an old veteran in the ministry, but don't sell the younger men short, either. If a man is Spirit-filled and genuine, his age may not make that much difference. On the other hand, you may have the kind of situation that calls for experience.

Make sure he is a spiritual man who knows what's going on today. You don't want a will-o'-the-wisp who flutters along with the wind of popularity. Our people need not so much a preacher who has caught the spirit of the age as one who determines to *correct* the spirit of the age. We need uncompromising dedication to the truth of the Book!

I want to hear a preacher who sits at the feet of the Christ of Calvary. Many of the men whose sermons you've read in THE SWORD would be a good place to start.

When you find an evangelist who is on your heart, it would be good to go hear him preach if possible. If not, you can talk to fellow pastors who have used him and others who have heard him preach. Seek God's face about it, and He will surely lead you.

2. *Prepare* as if it were your last effort on earth! Get all of the material the evangelist has about himself, and start preparing your people for the big week. Meet with your teachers, deacons and staff members and get them excited about the upcoming meeting. Soak all of your preparations in prayer. Begin to de-emphasize other things several weeks ahead of the crusade so everything will point to revival.

3. *Plan* your attack on Satan's fortresses. Alert your people as to what your plans are. Enlist them in reaching the careless, the discouraged and the backslidden members of your flock. Start some telephone enlistment efforts. Train your personal workers. Get your choir and singing groups working on revival music. Have a refresher course with your ushers. Make a big thing of it from the very start.

A thorough census of your entire area would be most helpful. There will be untold prospects to work on. Try hard to lay the burden on your people to win at least one family to the Lord and to your church during the crusade. Others can win at least one individual. They should have several they are working on. Then if one fails to come they can still be victorious with others.

4. *Preach* sermons that will prepare your people. Show them how souls can be won. Give good illustrations of revivals and what will happen if God really gets into the thing. Saturate your own soul with messages on revival and by reading the journals and messages of great evangelists.

5. *Publicize* the upcoming meeting in various ways. We have to do more these days to capture the attention of people than we did a few years back. The money invested in good revival advertising is well spent.

Be sure to read very carefully the material and information letters sent to you by your evangelist. He may have some very good ideas that will help you publicize your campaign.

Revival cards are more impressive than handbills and much easier to use and carry around. If they are slick, well-printed cards that can fit into a man's pocket or a lady's purse, you will have your people giving out a lot more of them. If you have the funds to also print some larger cards to put in store windows or to nail up on poles, that is good, too. The more the people see your advertising, the more impressed they will be, and the more likely to come to your meetings.

Newspaper advertising is important. If you are not familiar with writing ads, make friends with someone in the advertising department and tell him (or her) that you want something different from (and superior to) the average run-of-the-mill church page ad. There are good books on advertising your church, too. Note the difference between a free news story in the paper and a paid advertisement. You can use both to your advantage.

An attractive sign out front and/or a colorful banner up over the street advertising your meeting is good also. You can't use too much advertising of the right kind.

Radio and TV spots are good and can often be placed free of charge if you carry a well-written, double-spaced, typed copy of your information to the studios well ahead of the time you want the announcements made. If you can afford some paid TV spots in addition, you may need to use the help of a professional in writing them and presenting them.

In your advertising use pertinent information about your evangelist. Don't exaggerate but do make the invitation as appealing as possible. If you have an outstanding music man coming, too, or other featured members of the revival team, it is good to emphasize this in your ads.

6. *Put off* other things. In some meetings you get the idea that there are so many things going on that the revival is just a necessary evil that is being endured for a few days. While we rejoice in the good Christian school movement, it is a fact that, in churches where a busy school is operating, the activities of the church (including even revivals) have to sort of fit into the present curriculum. At least it seems that way in some cases.

The pastor should be in charge of and on top of all that goes on in the church facilities and on church property. School officials should understand that the revival takes precedence over all other matters during the crusade. School chapel services should feature the evangelist, of course. Some schoolteachers offer special incentives to students to have them in the night services. Some even offer special credit points for attendance. Contests can be held with the classes competing for attendance in the revival, and a proper reward can be given.

Some pastors instruct their teachers not to give homework during the crusade. Others, perhaps to a better advantage, state that homework can be omitted or postponed for students who are present in the night services. Needless to say, this makes for more students in the revival!

A special school night is helpful, using some of the students on the program if possible, and giving points or some special award to the class with the most school parents present that night. This should be planned well ahead of time.

Missionary meetings, deacons' meetings, youth activities, senior citizens' parties and all such should be tabled until after the revival. Better still, channel these things into making the revival a success. Instead of the usual Saturday night social for the teens on the eve of the revival, why not challenge them to see how many youth they can reach in a special effort to enlist them for the revival? A "Bring-a-Friend" theme could work well here. At least, have them going door to door with the revival cards, lining up prospects.

It is best to keep announcements about future things in the church very brief or better still, wait until the last night of the crusade to mention future things so that all emphasis for the week will be upon the revival at hand.

7. *Promote* attendance in every sensible way possible. "Pack-the-Pew" or "Host-and-Hostess" plans may be good for bringing in people each night. I dramatize stories for boys and girls each night in my meetings, but other things can be done to make children a part of the crusade—a special prayer meeting for them, a kids' songfest, booster club or a contest to see who brings the most visitors.

Special nights can be incorporated into the crusade. Sunday school night, family night, fellow workers' night and other such efforts are good if worked right and promoted well ahead of time. Bus workers should be working well ahead of time to have their riders lined up, with a special determination to get the unsaved parents of the bus children there. (Note, it is best to limit the nighttime revival riders to children aged over seven or eight to eliminate noise and confusion which might defeat our own purpose.)

Promote great revival singing and quality special music. The choir should be present every night even if they do not sing a special every night.

8. *Promptly* begin each service. Starting on time is important. Sometimes it is good to start the singing even a little ahead of time. Give the impression that this is so great we just can't wait to get underway. Dragging in and starting late is discouraging to members and visitors who have sacrificed to get there on time.

Keep things moving. Make announcements very brief if they have to be made at all. Don't sing all the verses of every hymn. Variety is the spice of life. Use lively gospel choruses. Use your best special music with songs that are appropriate for revival. You'd be amazed at some of the songs chosen for revival music by some song leaders. Keep the service lively. Limit the number of specials. Dismiss the service each night with optimism and enthusiasm. Don't hold the people more than a few seconds after the evangelist is through with them. Send them away in a happy frame of mind—or so under conviction they'll have to come back the next night!

Some pastors of smaller churches hesitate to bring in a full-time evangelist for fear they cannot handle it financially. You might be amazed at what your people will do in the way of giving if they really get a blessing in a revival. Anyway, a God-called man will come by faith and trust

God to supply his needs. Some evangelists travel now by motor home and thus eliminate plane fares, motel room costs, etc. I do not know any evangelist who would not cooperate with the pastor in seeking the lowest possible air fares. There are usually special deals (if you book the flights thirty days ahead) that make it possible for the evangelist to save money for the church.

Money for advertising and even for travel expense can often be raised ahead of time and thus make it possible for the church to do the right thing in giving for the support of the evangelist. The pastor should do all that he can to take care of God's servant who has come to help him. Most of them do, I believe.

So, dear pastor friend, don't give up on having good special meetings in your church. God will bless you for it.

Vary your week-long meetings with some four-day crusades or Bible conferences. Have an occasional big "Super Sunday" for which you should adequately prepare but on which you would not necessarily have to spend as much time and money. Keep your people excited and guessing about what you're going to do for them next. Have some music, prophetic or family meetings from time to time. And don't sell the young people short. They can be led to hunger after the things of God, too.

Yes, we can still have successful revival meetings. And who knows? The one in your church may turn out to be "the BIG one" that will ultimately save our nation.

TOM MALONE
1915-

ABOUT THE MAN:

Tom Malone was converted and called to preach at the same moment! At an old-fashioned bench, the preacher took his tear-stained Bible and showed Tom Malone how to be saved. He accepted Christ then and there. Arising from his knees in the Isbell Methodist Church near Russellville, Alabama, he shook the circuit pastor's hand; and this bashful nineteen-year-old farm boy announced: "I know the Lord wants me to be a preacher."

Backward, bashful and broke, Tom borrowed five dollars, took what he could in a cardboard suitcase and left for Cleveland, Tennessee. Immediately upon arrival at Bob Jones College, Malone heard a truth that totally dominated his life and labors for the Lord ever after—soul winning!

That day he won his first soul! The green-as-grass Tom, a new convert himself, knew nothing of soul-winning approaches or techniques. He simply asked the sinner, "Are you a Christian?" No. In a few minutes that young man became Malone's first convert.

Since that day, his experiences in personal evangelism have been countless.

Mark it down: Malone began soul winning his first week in Bible college. And he has never lost *the thirst* for it, *the thrill* in it, nor *the task* of it since. Pastoring churches, administrating schools, preaching across the nation have not deterred Tom Malone from this mainline ministry.

It is doubtful if young Malone ever dreamed of becoming the man he is today. He is now Doctor Tom Malone, is renowned in fundamental circles for his wise leadership and great preaching, is pastor of the large Emmanuel Baptist Church of Pontiac, Michigan, founder and president of Midwestern Baptist Schools, and is eagerly sought as speaker in large Bible conferences from coast to coast.

Dr. John R. Rice often said that Dr. Tom Malone may be the greatest gospel preacher in all the world today!

X.

Biblical Revival in Our Generation

TOM MALONE

(Sermon prepared for Fundamental Baptist Congress of North America, preached in Grand Rapids, Michigan, October 6, 1966)

"If my people, which are called by my name, shall humble themselves, and pray, and seek my face, and turn from their wicked ways; then will I hear from heaven, and will forgive their sin, and will heal their land."—II Chron. 7:14.

"Wilt thou not revive us again: that thy people may rejoice in thee?"—Ps. 85:6.

"O Lord, I have heard thy speech, and was afraid: O Lord, revive thy work in the midst of the years, in the midst of the years make known; in wrath remember mercy."—Hab. 3:2.

The word "revival" is not found in the Bible. However, "revive," "reviving" and "revived" are found some fifteen times, and they do not in every instance refer to "revival" as we are considering it at this time. When we come to an examination of the Word of God on "revival," we must ask the Holy Spirit to help us lay aside all preconceived opinions and all traditional practice. If we are to experience biblical revival in our generation, we must determine from God's inspired Word what a true, scriptural revival really is.

An example of the lack of knowledge of what a revival is, is the usual advertising attached to a special meeting:

REVIVAL WILL START ON SUNDAY, APRIL 3,
AND END ON SUNDAY, APRIL 10.

Now, who but God Himself knows if a real revival will begin on Sunday, April 3? If by His grace it did, what Christian, worthy of the name, would want such a wonderful thing to end on Sunday, April 10?

A revival is not just a special service or a crusade or an evangelistic campaign. A revival is a refreshing from God, a reviving of existing spiritual life, a fire from Heaven, a moving of God's Holy Ghost in and upon the lives of born-again people.

Modern-day revival efforts are often directed toward the unsaved, when, in reality, only the saved can be revived. However, it should be understood that when revival comes, the unsaved will be reached.

"Restore unto me the joy of thy salvation; and uphold me with thy free spirit. Then will I teach transgressors thy ways; and sinners shall be converted unto thee."—Ps. 51:12, 13.

"Then they that gladly received his word were baptized: and the same day there were added unto them about three thousand souls."—Acts 2:41.

We shall seek from the Bible the answers to such important and relevant questions as: Were there revivals in Bible times? Have there been biblical revivals in the history of the New Testament church? Can we have a scriptural revival today? Are the great campaigns today, involving thousands of people, a manifestation of God's power? Is there such a thing as a counterfeit revival?

God has the answer!

"If any of you lack wisdom, let him ask of God, that giveth to all men liberally, and upbraideth not; and it shall be given him."—Jas. 1:5.

"To the law and to the testimony: if they speak not according to this word, it is because there is no light in them."—Isa. 8:20.

I. GREAT REVIVALS IN BIBLE TIMES

First, let us see that there were real revivals in Bible times. Though the word or noun "revival" is not found in the passages with which we shall deal, nevertheless these passages describe revival as we know and want and hunger and weep for.

Jacob knew the meaning of revival. He, like many of the saints today, needed to know experientially a real revival from God. He had lived deceitfully and practiced subterfuge and, by cunning trickery, had twisted the birthright from his brother and misled his blind father. He had spent twenty years or more away from home and had prospered materially but not spiritually.

However, the day of reckoning arrived, as it always does, and he met again the people he had wronged. In the divine record concerning Jacob there is both a personal and a family revival. The personal experience is described in Genesis 32:24-30:

"And Jacob was left alone; and there wrestled a man with him until the breaking of the day. And when he saw that he prevailed not against him, he touched the hollow of his thigh; and the hollow of Jacob's thigh was out of joint, as he wrestled with him. And he said, Let me go, for the day breaketh. And he said, I will not let thee go, except thou bless me. And he said unto him, What is thy name? And he said, Jacob. And he said, Thy name shall be called no more Jacob, but Israel: for as a prince hast thou power with God and with men, and hast prevailed. And Jacob asked him, and said, Tell me, I pray thee, thy name. And he said, Wherefore is it that thou dost ask after my name? And he blessed him there. And Jacob called the name of the place Peniel: for I have seen God face to face, and my life is preserved."

We read, "And Jacob was left alone." Being alone with God is a vital step toward revival. It is a facing up to individual and personal sins. It is a face-to-face experience with God when the soul's needs are laid bare before Him.

Jacob also travailed with God: "And Jacob was left alone; and there wrestled a man with him until the breaking of the day." With sweat and tears, agony of soul and exertion of body, he wrestled with God. This must mean Jacob wanted something from God more than he wanted food or rest or the company of others.

This angel asked for release from Jacob, but Jacob refused. He would not let go because he wanted to prove to God that he would pay the price for power regardless of how high the cost.

Jacob was in a wrestling match most of his life:

1. He wrestled before his birth—Gen. 25:22.
2. He wrestled for his birthright—Gen. 25:33.
3. He wrestled for the blessing—Gen. 27:21-23.
4. He wrestled Laban for Rachel—Gen. 29.
5. He wrestled for power with God—Gen. 32:24.

He got what he went after, and we read of the glorious results of the experience in verse 28: "Thy name shall be called no more Jacob, but Israel: for as a prince hast thou power with God and with men, and hast prevailed." The angel said, ". . . hast thou power with God and with men." This is the right order: *power with God and then with men.*

Oh, for a personal experience today as Jacob had with God at the Jabbok ford!

Not only was Jacob revived, not only did he experience the power of God in his life, but his family had a revival, too. The account of this household revival is found in Genesis 35:2-5:

"Then Jacob said unto his household, and to all that were with him, Put away the strange gods that are among you, and be clean, and change your garments: And let us arise, and go up to Beth-el; and I will make there an altar unto God, who answered me in the day of my distress, and was with me in the way which I went. And they gave unto Jacob all the strange gods which were in their hand, and all their earrings which were in their ears; and Jacob hid them under the oak which was by Shechem. And they journeyed: and the terror of God was upon the cities that were round about them, and they did not pursue after the sons of Jacob."

Several things are outstanding here. First, a revival usually starts with one person or a small group. This one started with Jacob and spread to his whole family.

Also, we see that sin had to be dealt with before revival would come. Jacob said, "Put away the strange gods that are among you, and be clean, and change your garments." God demands separation, cleanliness of life and absolute surrender before a real, Heaven-sent revival can take place.

This revival was so real and so genuine that "the terror of God was upon the cities that were round about them." This family not only went back to Bethel—"house of God"—but they went back to El-Bethel—"God of the house of God."

Israel had a revival under the leadership of Samuel:

"And Samuel spake unto all the house of Israel, saying, If ye do return unto the Lord with all your hearts, then put away the strange gods and Ashtaroth from among you, and prepare your hearts unto the Lord, and serve him only: and he will deliver you out of the hand of the Philistines. Then the children of Israel did put away Baalim and Ashtaroth, and served the Lord only."—I Sam. 7:3, 4.

They were being overcome by their enemies, as is true in the church of Jesus Christ today in many instances. When they returned to the Lord, put away their strange gods and gave to the Lord the preeminence due Him, a great revival came.

Samuel cried unto the Lord for them and, as is almost always the case in the Word of God, one dedicated child of God was responsible for the revival being sent from Heaven.

Oh, that God would burden hearts today to pay the price, to face sin as it is, to weep before God day and night until revival comes in every Bible-believing church in America.

Revival came in Elijah's day. The fire fell! Our need in this crucial hour is for the fire of Heaven to fall upon the church. "Then the fire of the Lord fell and consumed the burnt-sacrifice, and the wood, and the stones, and the dust, and licked up the water that was in the trench" (I Kings 18:38).

A revival took place which honored the true God, brought heavy judgment upon false religion and set the hearts of God's people on fire. Elijah's prayer is a masterpiece; in sixty-three words he got God's attention and moved His mighty arm into action.

Who could deny that a mighty revival came on the day of Pentecost, as recorded in Acts 2? In this great revival a number of things took place that we need to have happen again.

There was the glorious, wonderful unity of the people. Some five times we read that they were "of one accord and in one place." Here is the mighty work of God when cowardly Christians were made bold to witness and to win the lost. In fact, a by-product of this revival was the thorough and sound conversion of some three thousand souls who gladly received God's Word and were baptized and added to the church. Yes, a mighty revival from God took place on the day of Pentecost.

We do not expect today that God will answer with visible, cloven tongues of fire and with an audible, mighty rushing wind—this was all in fulfillment of Bible prophecy—but we can expect that the same God who sent revival on the day of Pentecost can today stir cold, dead churches and give spiritual power, warmth, compassion and revival to the fundamental leaders in America and across the world. We can expect for God to stir His church once again, this living army, until we shall go across the face of the earth a blazing flame for His glory. We can expect to be filled with the Holy Spirit and empowered just as they were then.

Lord, do it again as You did in Bible days. Do it again as You have done on occasions in the history of the church. Lord, do it again! There must be a mighty, biblical revival in America today if the work of God is to be saved.

Who could deny that a biblical revival took place in the wicked city of Nineveh in Jonah's day? In this short book is the record of God's dealing with an individual. We repeat: revival usually begins with one man with whom God deals and who is willing to pay the price, such as in the case of Jonah.

After his experience in the belly of the fish for three days and three nights, God could get his attention, could talk to him, could deal with him, and did! God commissioned Jonah to preach His Word to wicked Nineveh. As a result of God's requirement, the great city repented in totality, and over a hundred thousand souls turned to God for the forgiveness of sin and for salvation.

That same kind of revival can happen again when God's people meet the requirements laid down in the Bible. Such a revival will come, but God has no "bargain basement" deal to offer in the matter of revival. Revival always comes when God's requirements are met. There must be a forsaking of sin, a repenting of wrong, a searching of heart and soul. There must be a complete surrender of body, mind and heart to God; then God begins to work, and revival comes.

Yes, a mighty, biblical revival took place in Nineveh in the days of Jonah.

Who could deny that a revival took place in the days of Nehemiah? A revival was certainly needed. God's people were in captivity. The walls of Jerusalem had been leveled to the ground, and the temple destroyed. The Lord's chosen people had been overrun, conquered and taken into captivity to Babylon and to other heathen countries. So a revival was needed.

The work of God was in disrepute and in defeat when He once again laid it on the heart of one man. Nehemiah went before the Lord with tears and waited before God in days of fasting, with a sad countenance because of the burden upon his soul. Then began the work of revival. The walls were to be rebuilt, the temple restored, and the work of God put back where it ought to be.

Nehemiah 4:2 says, "Will they revive the stones out of the heaps of the rubbish which are burned?" The answers are affirmative. A revival will come when God's requirements are met.

The book of Ezra is also connected with the work of God described in the book of Nehemiah. Ezra 9:8, 9 is a tremendous passage of Scripture:

"And now for a little space grace hath been shewed from the Lord our God, to leave us a remnant to escape, and to give us a nail in his holy place, that our God may lighten our eyes, and GIVE US A LITTLE REVIVING in our bondage. For we were bondmen; yet our God hath not forsaken us in our bondage, but hath extended mercy unto us in the sight of the kings of Persia, TO GIVE US A REVIVING, to set up the house of our God, and to repair the desolations thereof, and to give us a wall in Judah and in Jerusalem."

Here we read this great expression, ". . . to give us a reviving." What is needed today is a reviving from God, a scriptural, spiritual and Holy Ghost reviving.

II. THE NEED OF REVIVAL TODAY

Only the most blindly optimistic could ever deny that the church is in a bad state and in great need of a refreshing from God.

Let us list a few reasons why revival is badly needed in this generation.

First, it would be honest to say there are few Spirit-filled Christians when we consider the vast body of people who profess to be saved. Just how many of those are filled with the Spirit as the Bible plainly commands us to be?

In Ephesians 5:18 we read, "And be not drunk with wine, wherein is excess; but be filled with the Spirit." God's message to the church is, "Be filled with the Spirit."

Spirit-filled Christians have victory. Spirit-filled Christians overcome the world, the flesh, the Devil. Spirit-filled Christians bear fruit—that is, fruit of the Spirit. Spirit-filled Christians win lost souls to Christ. Spirit-filled Christians make contributions to the body of Christ.

You may be a Christian leader, a pastor, an evangelist, a deacon, a Sunday school teacher, an officer in your church, but may I ask you as honestly and humbly as I know how: Are you filled with the Spirit of God?

Several times in the book of Acts we read that the early Christians were filled with the Holy Ghost. That accounts more than anything else for the fire of God demonstrated in their daily living, for the many souls getting saved, for churches being established, for the Gospel being sent to the ends of the earth, for a worldwide evangelization program that God blessed and that swept thousands into His kingdom.

Second, the Bible plainly teaches that when revival comes, in spite of the travail and burden for souls, the weeping that comes in the midst of a great revival, Christians will have joy. The writer in the book of Psalms was probably thinking of this when he asked, "Wilt thou not revive us again: that thy people may rejoice in thee" (Ps. 85:6)?

Christians today have lost their joy. The early Christians had great grace and great joy within. When people saw the joy they had, the happiness they experienced, it was an attraction.

Today the opposite is true. People demonstrate the kind of Christianity that nobody wants when they are without joy. The reason is unconfessed, unrepented sin. David was praying about that in Psalm 51:12, 13: "Restore unto me the joy of thy salvation; and uphold me with thy free spirit. Then will I teach transgressors thy ways; and sinners shall be converted unto thee." He had to pray with weeping, remorse and a turning to God: "Restore unto me the joy of thy salvation."

Then we think of the few soul-winning churches in America today. Many of us run in a circle of friends and acquaintances who are either members or pastors or leaders in great soul-winning churches, and we forget that scattered across America are literally thousands of churches that call themselves fundamental, Bible-believing churches that are not winning souls to Jesus Christ. If these few churches baptize half a dozen converts a year, they feel they are doing well.

This is not Bible Christianity. This is not the kind of Christianity that fills all the city with its teaching and doctrine. This is not the kind of Christianity that gets people saved, baptized and added to the church daily. God's standard is a soul-winning ministry—constant, seven days a week, fifty-two weeks out of the year until Jesus comes. **The only reason it is not happening is that God's people are living below God's standard for revival.**

Another thing that shows there is a great need of revival today is the overemphasis on ritualism and formalism in many Bible-believing churches. Plain simplicity of worshiping God in spirit and truth has been forsaken for a fleshly, religious procedure of ritualism and formalism.

It is according to the letter, but it kills the spirit. This overemphasis on ritualism and formalism is not conducive to people's being born again, not conducive to Christians' being set on fire.

When I think of the worldwide progress and success of the cults that engulf literally millions of blinded souls whom Christians ought to win; when I think of the inroads of modernism in the schools, in the institutions of theological training and in the churches which once stood for the Faith; when I think of the capitulation of outstanding leaders in our lifetime and our generation, the capitulation of these leaders from fundamentalism to neo-orthodoxy, and even worse, to modernism and apostasy, I am convinced that what we need is another one of those old-fashioned, Heaven-sent, Holy Ghost revivals that get the job done.

Revival is needed in America today! God help us to pray like the psalmist prayed, "Wilt thou not revive us again: that thy people may rejoice in thee?" and pray like Habakkuk prayed when he said, "O Lord, revive thy work in the midst of the years, in the midst of the years make known; in wrath remember mercy."

Only God can send a revival. It can only come to God's people and on God's terms.

III. REVIVALS ARE DEFINITELY POSSIBLE IN OUR GENERATION

The Bible plainly teaches that a revival can happen anytime or anywhere an individual or a group of people, regardless of how small, meets God's requirements and claims His promises.

One of the great promises in the Bible concerning revivals is found in II Chronicles 7:14. Though the word "revival" is not found in this verse, it is certainly the greatest formula for a revival given in all the Bible: "If my people, which are called by my name, shall humble themselves, and pray, and seek my face, and turn from their wicked ways; then will I hear from heaven, and will forgive their sin, and will heal their land."

A great deal in this verse needs to be remembered today.

"If my people. . . ." When churches start planning revivals today, they start talking about the unsaved. That is important, but not first. God says,"If my people. . . ."

A revival is reviving of life that already exists. An unsaved man can be won to Christ, but only a Christian can be revived.

God says, "If my people, which are called by my name, shall" do four things.

These four things are not easy. Notice the first: a humbling of the Christian—the most difficult to do.

Jesus is a classic example of this. We read in Philippians 2:5-8:

"Let this mind be in you, which was also in Christ Jesus: Who, being in the form of God, thought it not robbery to be equal with God: But made himself of no reputation, and took upon him the form of a servant, and was made in the likeness of men: And being found in fashion as a man, he humbled himself, and became obedient unto death, even the death of the cross."

In this instance, humility is a matter of forgetting reputation and thinking of character. It is being willing to take the low place if necessary. It is becoming obedient unto God no matter what the cost. It is being willing to die unto self, to be crucified with Christ.

Humility is no light thing, and it is a characteristic quality not found in many believers, nor in many of the leaders of the work of God today.

Many of us boast of our accomplishments as if God would be impoverished if it were not for our efforts. The fact is, Jesus said in Matthew 23:12: "Whosoever shall exalt himself shall be abased; and he that shall humble himself shall be exalted."

Humility is a prerequisite for revival. If we are not willing to start where God started, we will not have what He wants to give.

If we would study the Scripture on the subject and begin to look for the practical application in our lives, we might be astonished.

"Likewise, ye younger, submit yourselves unto the elder. Yea, all of you be subject one to another, and be clothed with humility: for God resisteth the proud, and giveth grace to the humble. Humble yourselves therefore under the mighty hand of God, that he may exalt you in due time."—I Pet. 5:5, 6.

"If my people, which are called by my name, shall humble themselves" is number one! Humility—a swallowing of pride, a willingness to be embarrassed, to be dethroned, if necessary—is all a part and the beginning of a great revival.

The second requirement set forth in II Chronicles 7:14 is prayer: "If my people, which are called by my name, shall humble themselves and pray." There never has been and never will be a great, true, biblical revival without prayer.

The Bible says, "Whatsoever ye shall ask . . . ye shall receive." Many such promises are related to prayer. God has promised to answer prayer. Pray for a revival, then be assured of getting a revival. I have seen this happen on a small and localized scale, and I have seen it happen on a larger and longer scale.

I was a young man holding a revival in a little country school in northern Alabama where many of my people lived. Hundreds were coming. There was no sponsorship except the sponsorship of God. After I had been preaching a few mornings and evenings, a relative of mine stood with a white, ashen face and said, "There will be a great revival here, for I prayed all night last night." With tears streaming down her face, she added, "The promise came that a revival would take place, and our loved ones would be saved."

Scores of my own loved ones were converted. Some years later, upon the occasion of the death of my grandfather (who lived to be 91½ years of age), I recalled at his funeral that I did not know of a loved one (and his descendants numbered 109 living when he died) who had not been converted.

So revival comes in answer to prayer. I have seen it happen on a longer scale here in Emmanuel Baptist Church—salvation of souls, people being baptized and added to the church daily—as God's people have prayed.

Men of old prayed. It is said that Finney would unsaddle his horse, climb to the loft of the barn, throw the horse blanket about his shoulders and pray in the sub-zero weather until he perspired, as he travailed with God for revival.

The young David Brainerd knelt in the snow and prayed for the conversion of the Indians.

We need saints of God like those of old who will go to the secret place of the Most High and stay there until the victory comes.

The third part of this requirement is to seek the face of God. Notice Jeremiah 29:13: "And ye shall seek me, and find me, when ye shall search for me with all your heart." We find the personal pronoun "me" three times in this verse.

Many are not seeking the right thing. We may seek an increase in our membership or seek to have a good revival report, but God said,

"Ye shall seek me, and find me, when ye shall search for me with all your heart." This means getting to the place where you know God is pleased with you and His face is favorable toward you.

The fourth part set forth in II Chronicles 7:14 is, ". . . and turn from their wicked ways"—the forsaking of sins. It is elementary to say there is no revival without a facing of sin—personal sin in the lives of Christians.

Proverbs 1:23 says,"Turn you at my reproof: behold, I will pour out my spirit unto you, I will make known my words unto you." The first part of this verse is the forsaking of sin.

Proverbs 28:13 says, "He that covereth his sins shall not prosper: but whoso confesseth and forsaketh them shall have mercy." We need a forsaking of sin in the hearts of Christians in America.

Many will say,"Well, that was in the Old Testament days and other times in the history of the church when things were not as difficult, the day was not as dark, the people were not as hard." But the Bible says that all these promises are for us, all these blessing are for us, all these victories can be ours.

To those who say the promises of revival given in the Old Testament, for instance, are not meant for us, I refer you to Romans 15:4: "For whatsoever things were written aforetime were written for our learning, that we through patience and comfort of the scriptures might have hope."

Now God didn't say the promise in the Old Testament, in II Chronicles 7:14, is written *to* us, but He sure said it was written *for* us. Things which happened *to* the people of God in Old Testament days, happened *for* our benefit. So it can happen again. It can take place in our lives and in our generation. "Now all these things happened unto them for ensamples: and they are written for our admonition, upon whom the ends of the world are come" (I Cor. 10:11).

We can have revival today.

I remember years ago when we were building a little building and had begun the work of Emmanuel Baptist Church with fear and trembling, yet with hope and expectancy. We had launched out to start a fundamental, soul-winning, Bible-believing, independent work for God. In the building we purchased was a safe which, the realtors said, was included as part of the deal.

One day while there alone praying, I sat down in front of the safe and began to tinker with the lock. I tried various combinations to see if I could arrive at a formula which would open the door, but none of them worked. The big, heavy, iron door that guarded the inside of the safe was locked fast and secure.

I went to the telephone, called the realtor and asked if he would give me the combination to the door. He gave me four numbers. I sat down in front of the safe and began to turn the lock—first to the right, then to the left, then to the right, back to the left. This fourfold combination worked perfectly. When I turned the handle, the door opened.

The way to get the door and the windows of Heaven open is by using God's combination, by using God's formula. There is no other formula for revival. If we advertise, we get what advertising will produce. If we try God's way, we get what God can produce in the way of a great revival.

Many say, "Well, a revival might happen in some places, but it will never happen where I live. My place is too hard, too dry."

But God says in Psalm 107:35: "He turneth the wilderness into a standing water, and dry ground into watersprings." God can make a river in a dry place. He can send a revival to your place. Nothing is too hard for God!

Oh, that He would help us today to claim the promise of Isaiah 44:3: "I will pour water upon him that is thirsty, and floods upon the dry ground: I will pour my spirit upon thy seed, and my blessing upon thine offspring." How we need to have God create in us a thirst, then satisfy that thirst by pouring His floods of blessings from Heaven upon the dry ground.

Yes, we can have revival.

IV. IS THERE SUCH A THING AS A COUNTERFEIT REVIVAL?

The last thing I consider with you is this delicate but pertinent subject: Is there such a thing as a counterfeit revival; or is there such a thing that seems to be a revival but is actually not a revival? There is no doubt about it.

When we study who Satan is, what his characteristics are, what his program is, there can be no doubt that there are such things as counterfeit revivals. Isaiah 14:12-14 is a great basic passage about the Devil and his program in the religious world and in the spiritual realm:

"How art thou fallen from heaven, O Lucifer, son of the morning!

how art thou cut down to the ground, which didst weaken the nations! For thou hast said in thine heart, I will ascend into heaven, I will exalt my throne above the stars of God: I will sit also upon the mount of the congregation, in the sides of the north: I will ascend above the heights of the clouds; I will be like the most High."

We see here, first, that Lucifer is a fallen angel. He was known as a bright and shining one. He is a religious being, a spiritual being. He is not spiritual in the sense that we know it, but he is a spiritual being. The last statement recorded from his lips is this: "I will be like the most High." All through the Bible, Lucifer sought to carry that out.

He is an imitator. He imitates God. God is a Trinity. The Bible describes an evil trinity whose judgment and destruction climax in the book of Revelation. God has His Gospel—the Gospel of grace. Satan has his gospel—the gospel of works and self-righteousness. He has spread his gospel to the ends of the earth throughout the course of the centuries.

God has His church, that blood-bought church of which Christ is the Head; that majestic, spiritual body, not an organization but an organism. Satan has his church, the social church, the religious groups and cults. There are probably more churches headed by Satan today than there are Bible churches with Christ as the Head.

"I will be like the most High," Satan said, and he is able to transform himself "into an angel of light" (II Cor. 11:14).

Another basic passage on this operation is found in II Corinthians 11:13-15:

"For such are false apostles, deceitful workers, transforming themselves into the apostles of Christ. And no marvel; for Satan himself is transformed into an angel of light. Therefore it is no great thing if his ministers also be transformed as the ministers of righteousness; whose end shall be according to their works."

The angel of light says that a revival can come by getting everyone together, regardless of whether they believe the Bible, the deity of Christ, the blood atonement, the verbal inspiration—regardless of whether they believe these fundamental, cardinal doctrines of the Faith or not. This is Satan's effort to add a little more light than what God has taught on revival in His Word. "Satan himself is transformed into an angel of light."

Now, notice! "Therefore it is no great thing if his ministers also be transformed as the ministers of righteousness; whose end shall be according to their works." Much is called revival today, but when measured by the scriptural standard, it is actually not revival.

Revival brings about many things. Social reform is a result of revival; it does not lead the revival. Revival brings about the salvation, the conversion, the new birth; not just a decision or human commitment. It leads people to follow Christ in baptism, in identification with and an enlistment in a Bible-believing, Christ-honoring church. Satan said, "I will be like the most High." So, much of what is called revival today is merely an imitation of the real thing.

May God give us the right kind of refreshing and warming and stirring and moving from Heaven. *May the fire fall.* May God speak from Heaven. May there be a shaking in the mulberry trees. May there be a moving upon the waters. May there be a trembling beneath us. May revival come in our generation and in our hearts individually.

REUBEN ARCHER TORREY
1856-1928

ABOUT THE MAN:

Torrey grew up in a wealthy home, attended Yale University and Divinity School, and studied abroad. During his early student days at Yale, young Torrey became an agnostic and a heavy drinker. But even during the days of his "wild life," he was strangely aware of a conviction that someday he was to preach the Gospel. At the end of his senior year in college, he was saved.

While at Yale Divinity School, he came under the influence of D. L. Moody. Little did Moody know the mighty forces he was setting in motion in stirring young R. A. Torrey to service!

After Moody died, Torrey took on the worldwide revival campaigns in Australia, New Zealand, England and America.

Like many another giant for God, Torrey shone best, furthest and brightest as a personal soul winner. This one man led 100,000 to Christ in a revival that circled the globe!

Dr. Torrey's education was obtained in the best schools and universities of higher learning. Fearless, quick, imaginative and scholarly, he was a tough opponent to meet in debate. He was recognized as a great scholar, yet his ministry was marked by simplicity.

It was because of his outstanding scholastic ability and evangelistic fervor that Moody handpicked Torrey to become superintendent of his infant Moody Bible Institute. In 1912, Torrey became dean of BIOLA, where he served until 1924, pastoring the Church of the Open Door in Los Angeles from 1915 to 1924.

Torrey's books have probably reached more people indirectly and helped more people to understand the Bible and to have power to win souls, than the writings of any other man since the Apostle Paul, with the possible exceptions of Spurgeon and Rice. Torrey was a great Bible teacher, but most of all he was filled with the Holy Spirit.

He greatly influenced the life of Dr. John R. Rice.

XI.

Why God Used D. L. Moody

R. A. TORREY

INTRODUCTION

D. L. Moody died in the last days of the nineteenth century. Dr. R. A. Torrey was probably his closest associate and friend. Dr. Torrey was the first superintendent of the Moody Bible Institute and set up a curriculum for that Bible institute which has been a pattern for others like it.

When Moody died, Torrey soon took worldwide lead in great citywide campaigns in Australia, England and America. In 1923 Dr. Torrey was asked to speak at a great memorial service on "Why God Used D. L. Moody," and this is that remarkable address about that amazing man, probably the greatest man of his generation, as Dr. Torrey says.

The reader will notice that R. A. Torrey and D. L. Moody both used the phrase, "baptized with the Holy Ghost" just as it is used in Acts 1:5 about Pentecost. Later, because of some wildfire and false doctrine of people who used the phrase, "the baptism of the Holy Ghost," Plymouth Brethren said that that term should refer only to Pentecost and the origin of the church. Thus in retreating from the extremists, they took out of the Moody Bible Institute and other Bible institutes the teaching of D. L. Moody and R. A. Torrey, and took out the emphasis which those great men of God had put on the fullness of the Spirit or baptism with the Spirit. And so Dr. C. I. Scofield, in the note to the Scofield Bible, took the Plymouth Brethren position and forsook the position of Moody and Torrey which he originally held.

But Dr. Will H. Houghton, president of Moody Bible Institute, in an edition of this little book, *Why God Used D. L. Moody*, said, "But let no one quibble about an experience as important as the filling with the Spirit. In the little book Dr. Torrey quotes Mr. Moody as saying, in a discussion of this very matter, 'Oh, why will they split hairs? Why don't they see that this is just the one thing that they themselves need? They are good teachers, they are wonderful teachers, and I am so glad to have them here, but why will they not see that the baptism of the Holy Ghost is just the one touch that they themselves need?' " And Dr. Houghton further said, "The tragedy is that so many are technically correct and spiritually powerless."

God is looking for men whom He can mightily use in winning souls. We pray that many a reader of this sermon will earnestly decide to follow the pattern of D. L. Moody in the qualities which made him so God could use him with mighty power to win multitudes!

John R. Rice

WHY GOD USED D. L. MOODY
by R. A. TORREY

Eighty-six years ago (February 5, 1837), there was born of poor parents in a humble farmhouse in Northfield, Massachusetts, a little baby who was to become the greatest man, as I believe, of his generation or of his century—Dwight L. Moody. After our great generals, great statesmen, great scientists and great men of letters have passed away and been forgotten, and their work and its helpful influence have come to an end, the work of D. L. Moody will go on and its saving influence continue and increase, bringing blessing not only to every state in the Union but to every nation on earth. Yes, it will continue throughout the ages of eternity.

My subject is "Why God Used D. L. Moody," and I can think of no subject upon which I would rather speak. For I shall not seek to glorify Mr. Moody, but the God who by His grace, His entirely unmerited favor, used him so mightily, and the Christ who saved him by His atoning death and resurrection life, and the Holy Spirit who lived in him and wrought through him and who alone made him the mighty power that he was to this world. Furthermore: I hope to make it clear that the God who used D. L. Moody in his day is just as ready to use you and me, in this day, if we, on our part, do what D. L. Moody did, which was what made it possible for God to so abundantly use him.

The whole secret of why D. L. Moody was such a mightily used man you will find in Psalm 62:11: "God hath spoken once; twice have I heard this; that POWER BELONGETH UNTO GOD." I am glad it does. I am glad that power did not belong to D. L. Moody; I am glad that it did not belong to Charles G. Finney; I am glad that it did not belong to Martin Luther; I am glad that it did not belong to any other Christian man whom God has greatly used in this world's history. Power belongs to God. If D. L. Moody had any power, and he had great power, he got it from God.

But God does not give His power arbitrarily. It is true that He gives it to whomsoever He will, but He wills to give it on certain conditions, which are clearly revealed in His Word; D. L. Moody met those conditions, and God made him the most wonderful preacher of his generation—yes, I think the most wonderful man of his generation.

But how was it that D. L. Moody had that power of God so wonderfully manifested in his life? Pondering this question it seemed to me that there were seven things in the life of D. L. Moody that accounted for God's using him so largely as He did.

I. A FULLY-SURRENDERED MAN

The first thing that accounts for God's using D. L. Moody so mightily was that *he was a fully-surrendered man.* Every ounce of that two-hundred-and-eighty-pound body of his belonged to God; everything he was and everything he had, belonged wholly to God. Now, I am not saying that Mr. Moody was perfect; he was not. If I attempted to, I presume I could point out some defects in his character. It does not occur to me at this moment what they were; but I am confident that I could think of some, if I tried real hard. I have never yet met a perfect man, not one. I have known perfect men in the sense in which the Bible commands us to be perfect, i.e., men who are wholly God's, out and out for God, fully surrendered to God, with no will but God's will; but I have never known a man in whom I could not see some defects, some places where he might have been improved. No, Mr. Moody was not a faultless man. If he had any flaws in his character, and he had, I presume I was in a position to know them better than almost any other man, because of my very close association with him in the later years of his life; and furthermore, I suppose that in his latter days he opened his heart to me more fully than to anyone else in the world. I think he told me some things that he told no one else. I presume I knew whatever defects there were in his character as well as anybody. But while I recognized such flaws, nevertheless, I know that he was a man who belonged wholly to God.

The first month I was in Chicago, we were having a talk about something upon which we very widely differed, and Mr. Moody turned to me very frankly and very kindly and said in defense of his own position: "Torrey, if I believed that God wanted me to jump out of that window, I would jump." I believe he would. If he thought God wanted him to do anything he would do it. He belonged wholly, unreservedly, unqualifiedly, entirely, to God.

Henry Varley, a very intimate friend of Mr. Moody in the earlier days of his work, loved to tell how he once said to him: "It remains to be seen what God will do with a man who gives himself up wholly to Him." I am told that when Mr. Henry Varley said that, Mr. Moody said to himself: "Well, I will be that man." And I, for my part, do not think "it *remains* to be seen" what God will do with a man who gives himself up wholly to Him. I think it has been seen already in D. L. Moody. If you and I are to be used in our sphere as D. L. Moody was used in his, we must put all that we have and all that we are in the hands of God, for Him to use as He will, to send us where He will, for God to do with us what He will, and we, on our part, to do everything God bids us do. There are thousands and tens of thousands of men and women in Christian work, brilliant men and women, rarely gifted men and women, men and women who are making great sacrifices, men and women who have put all conscious sin out of their lives, yet who, nevertheless, have stopped short of absolute surrender to God, and therefore have stopped short of fullness of power. But Mr. Moody did not stop short of absolute surrender to God; he was a wholly-surrendered man, and if you and I are to be used, you and I must be wholly-surrendered men and women.

II. A MAN OF PRAYER

The second secret of the great power exhibited in Mr. Moody's life was that *Mr. Moody was in the deepest and most meaningful sense a man of prayer*. People oftentimes say to me: "Well, I went many miles to see and to hear D. L. Moody, and he certainly was a wonderful preacher." Yes, D. L. Moody certainly was a wonderful preacher; taking it all in all, the most wonderful preacher I have ever heard, and it was a great privilege to hear him preach as he alone could preach;

but out of a very intimate acquaintance with him I wish to testify that he was a far greater *pray-er* than he was preacher. Time and time again, he was confronted by obstacles that seemed insurmountable, but he always knew the way to surmount and to overcome all difficulties. He knew the way to bring to pass anything that needed to be brought to pass. He knew and believed in the deepest depths of his soul that "nothing was too hard for the Lord" and that prayer could do anything that God could do.

Oftentimes Mr. Moody would write me when he was about to undertake some new work, saying: "I am begining work in such and such a place on such and such a day; I wish you would get the students together for a day of fasting and prayer"; and often I have taken those letters and read them to the students in the lecture room and said: "Mr. Moody wants us to have a day of fasting and prayer, first for God's blessing on our own souls and work, and then for God's blessing on him and his work." Often we were gathered in the lecture room far into the night—sometimes till one, two, three, four or even five o'clock in the morning, crying to God, just because Mr. Moody urged us to wait upon God until we received His blessing. How many men and women I have known whose lives and characters have been transformed by those nights of prayer and who have wrought mighty things in many lands because of those nights of prayer!

One day Mr. Moody drove up to my house at Northfield and said: "Torrey, I want you to take a ride with me." I got into the carriage, and we drove out toward Lover's Lane, talking about some great and unexpected difficulties that had arisen in regard to the work in Northfield and Chicago and in connection with other work that was very dear to him. As we drove along, some black storm clouds lay ahead of us, and then suddenly, as we were talking, it began to rain. He drove the horse into a shed near the entrance to Lover's Lane to shelter the horse, and then laid the reins upon the dashboard and said: "Torrey, pray"; and then, as best I could, I prayed, while he in his heart joined me in prayer. And when my voice was silent he began to pray. Oh, I wish you could have heard that prayer! I shall never forget it, so simple, so trustful, so definite and so direct and so mighty. When the storm was over and we drove back to town, the obstacles had been surmounted, and the work of the schools and other work that was threatened went on as it had never gone on before, and it has gone on until this day.

As we drove back, Mr. Moody said to me: "Torrey, we will let the other men do the talking and the criticizing, and we will stick to the work that God has given us to do and let Him take care of the difficulties and answer the criticisms."

On one occasion Mr. Moody said to me in Chicago: "I have just found, to my surprise, that we are twenty thousand dollars behind in our finances for the work here and in Northfield, and we must have that twenty thousand dollars; I am going to get it by prayer." He did not tell a soul who had the ability to give a penny of the twenty thousand dollars' deficit, but looked right to God and said: "I need twenty thousand dollars for my work; send me that money in such a way that I will know it comes straight from Thee." And God heard that prayer. The money came in such a way that it was clear that it came from God in direct answer to prayer. Yes, D. L. Moody was a man who believed in the God who answers prayer, and not only believed in Him in a theoretical way but believed in Him in a practical way. He was a man who met every difficulty that stood in his way—by prayer. Everything he undertook was backed up by prayer, and in everything, his ultimate dependence was upon God.

III. A DEEP AND PRACTICAL STUDENT OF THE BIBLE

The third secret of Mr. Moody's power, or the third reason why God used D. L. Moody, was that *he was a deep and practical student of the Word of God.* Nowadays it is often said of D. L. Moody that he was not a student. I wish to say that he was a student; most emphatically he was a student. He was not a student of psychology; he was not a student of anthropology—I am very sure he would not have known what that word meant; he was not a student of biology; he was not a student of philosophy; he was not even a student of theology in the technical sense of the term; but he was a student, a profound and practical student of the one Book that is more worth studying than all other books in the world put together: he was a student of the Bible. Every day of his life, I have reason for believing, he arose very early in the morning to study the Word of God, way down to the close of his life. Mr. Moody used to rise about four o'clock in the morning to study the Bible. He would say to me: "If I am going to get in any study, I have got to get up before the other folks get up"; and he would shut himself up in a remote room in his house, alone with his God and his Bible.

I shall never forget the first night I spent in his home. He had invited me to take the superintendency of the Bible institute, and I had already begun my work; I was on my way to some city in the East to preside at the International Christian Workers' Convention. He wrote me, saying: "Just as soon as the Convention is over, come up to Northfield." He learned when I was likely to arrive and drove over to South Vernon to meet me. That night he had all the teachers from the Mount Hermon School and from the Northfield Seminary come together at the house to meet me and to talk over the problems of the two schools. We talked together far on into the night, and then, after the principals and teachers of the schools had gone home, Mr. Moody and I talked together about the problems a while longer. It was very late when I got to bed that night, but very early the next morning, about five o'clock, I heard a gentle tap on my door. Then I heard Mr. Moody's voice whispering: "Torrey, are you up?" I happened to be; I do not always get up at that early hour but I happened to be up that particular morning. He said: "I want you to go somewhere with me," and I went with him. Then I found out that he had already been up an hour or two in his room studying the Word of God.

Oh, you may talk about power; but if you neglect the one Book that God has given you as the one instrument through which He imparts and exercises His power, you will not have it. You may read many books and go to many conventions, and you may have your all-night prayer meetings to pray for the power of the Holy Ghost; but unless you keep in constant and close association with the one Book, the Bible, you will not have power. And if you ever had power, you will not maintain it except by the daily, earnest, intense study of that Book. *Ninety-nine Christians in every hundred are merely playing at Bible study; and therefore ninety-nine Christians in every hundred are mere weaklings, when they might be giants, both in their Christian life and in their service.*

It was largely because of his thorough knowledge of the Bible and his practical knowledge of the Bible that Mr. Moody drew such immense crowds. On "Chicago Day," in October, 1893, none of the theaters of Chicago dared to open because it was expected that everybody in Chicago would go on that day to the World's Fair; and, in point of fact, something like four hundred thousand people did pass through the gates of the Fair that day. Everybody in Chicago was expected to be at that end of the city on that day. But Mr. Moody said to me: "Torrey, engage the Central Music Hall and announce meetings from nine o'clock in the morning till six o'clock at night." "Why," I replied, "Mr. Moody, nobody will be at this end of Chicago on that day; not even the theaters dare to open; everybody is going down to Jackson Park to the Fair; we cannot get anybody out on this day." Mr. Moody replied: "You do as you are told"; and I did as I was told and engaged the Central Music Hall for continuous meetings from nine o'clock in the morning till six o'clock at night. But I did it with a heavy heart; I thought there would be poor audiences. I was on the program at noon that day. Being very busy in my office about the details of the campaign, I did not reach the Central Music Hall till almost noon. I thought I would have no trouble getting in. But when I got almost to the Hall I found to my amazement that not only was it packed but the vestibule was packed, and the steps were packed, and there was no getting anywhere near the door; and if I had not gone round and climbed in a back window they would have lost their speaker for that hour. But that would not have been of much importance, for the crowds had not gathered to hear me; it was the magic of Mr. Moody's name that had drawn them. And why did they long to hear Mr. Moody? Because they knew that while he was not versed in many of the philosophies and fads and fancies of the day, he did know the one Book that this old world most longs to know—the Bible.

I shall never forget Moody's last visit to Chicago. The ministers of Chicago had sent me to Cincinnati to invite him to come to Chicago and hold a meeting. In response to the invitation, Mr. Moody said to me: "If you will hire the Auditorium for weekday mornings and afternoons and have meetings at ten in the morning and three in the afternoon, I will go." I replied: "Mr. Moody, you know what a busy city Chicago is and how impossible it is for businessmen to get out at ten o'clock in the morning and three in the afternoon on working days. Will you not hold evening meetings and meetings on Sunday?" "No," he replied, "I am afraid if I did, I would interfere with the regular work of the churches."

I went back to Chicago and engaged the Auditorium, which at that time was the building having the largest seating capacity of any building in the city, seating in those days about seven thousand people; I announced weekday meetings, with Mr. Moody as the speaker, at ten o'clock in the mornings and three o'clock in the afternoons. At once protests began to pour in upon me. One of them came from Marshall Field, at that time the business king of Chicago. "Mr. Torrey," Mr. Field wrote, "we businessmen of Chicago wish to hear Mr. Moody, and you know perfectly well how impossible it is for us to get out at ten o'clock in the morning and three o'clock in the afternoon; have evening meetings." I received many letters of a similar purport and wrote to Mr. Moody, urging him to give us evening meetings. But Mr. Moody simply replied: "You do as you are told," and I did as I was told; that is the way I kept my job.

On the first morning of the meetings I went down to the Auditorium about half an hour before the appointed time, but I went with much fear and apprehension; I thought the Auditorium would be nowhere nearly full. When I reached there, to my amazement I found a queue of people four abreast extending from the Congress Street entrance to Wabash Avenue, then a block north on Wabash Avenue, then a break to let traffic through, and then another block, and so on. I went in through the back door, and there were many clamoring for entrance there. When the doors were opened at the appointed time, we had a cordon of twenty policemen to keep back the crowd; but the crowd was so great that it swept the cordon of policemen off their feet and packed eight thousand people into the building before we could get the doors shut. And I think there were as many left on the outside as there were in the building. I do not think that anyone else in the world could have drawn such a crowd at such a time.

Why? Because though Mr. Moody knew little about science or philosophy or literature in general, he did know the one Book that this old world is perishing to know and longing to know; and this old world will flock to hear men who know the Bible and preach the Bible as they will flock to hear nothing else on earth.

During all the months of the World's Fair in Chicago, no one could draw such crowds as Mr. Moody. Judging by the papers, one would have thought that the great religious event in Chicago at that time was the World's Congress of Religions. One very gifted man of letters in the East was invited to speak at this Congress. He saw in this invitation the opportunity of his life and prepared his paper, the exact title of which I do not now recall, but it was something along the line of "New Light on the Old Doctrines." He prepared the paper with great care, and then sent it around to his most trusted and gifted friends for criticisms. These men sent it back to him with such changes as they had to suggest. Then he rewrote the paper, incorporating as many of the suggestions and criticisms as seemed wise. Then he sent it around for further criticisms. Then he wrote the paper a third time and had it, as he trusted, perfect. He went on to Chicago to meet this coveted opportunity of speaking at the World's Congress of Religions. It was at eleven o'clock on a Saturday morning (if I remember correctly) that he was to speak. He stood outside the door of the platform waiting for the great moment to arrive, and as the clock struck eleven he walked onto the platform to face a magnificent audience of eleven women and two men! But there was not a building anywhere in Chicago that would accommodate the very same day the crowds that would flock to hear Mr. Moody at any hour of the day or night. Oh, men and women, if you wish to get an audience and wish to do that audience some good after you get them, study, *study*, STUDY the one Book, and preach, *preach*, PREACH the one Book, and teach, *teach*, TEACH the one Book, the Bible, the only Book that is God's Word and the only Book that has power to gather and hold and bless the crowds for any great length of time.

IV. A HUMBLE MAN

The fourth reason why God continuously, through so many years, used D. L. Moody was that *he was a humble man*. I think D. L. Moody was the humblest man I ever knew in all my life. He loved to quote the words of another; "Faith gets the most; love works the most; but *humility keeps the most*." He himself had the humility that keeps everything it gets. As I have already said, he was the most humble man I ever knew, i.e., the most humble man when we bear in mind the great things that he did and the praise that was lavished upon him. Oh, how he loved to put himself in the background and put other men in the foreground. How often he would stand on a platform with some of us little fellows seated behind him, and as he spoke he would say: "There are better men coming after me." As he said it, he would point back over his shoulder with his thumb to the "little fellows." I do not know how he could believe it, but he really *did* believe that the others that were coming after him were really better than he was. He made no pretense to a humility he did not possess. In his heart of hearts he constantly underestimated himself and overestimated others. He really believed that God would use other men in a larger measure than he had been used.

Mr. Moody loved to keep himself in the background. At his conventions at Northfield, or anywhere else, he would push the other men to the front and, if he could, have them do all the preaching—McGregor, Campbell Morgan, Andrew Murray, and the rest of them. The only way we could get him to take any part in the program was to get up in the convention and move that we hear D. L. Moody at the next meeting. He continually put himself out of sight.

Oh, how many a man has been full of promise and God has used him, and then the man thought that he was the whole thing and God was compelled to set him aside! I believe more promising workers have gone on the rocks through self-sufficiency and self-esteem than through any other cause. I can look back for forty years or more and think of many men who are now wrecks or derelicts who at one time the world thought were going to be something great. But they have disappeared entirely from the public view. Why? Because of overestimation of self. Oh, the men and women who have been put aside because they began to think that they were somebody, that they were "IT," and therefore God was compelled to set them aside.

I remember a man with whom I was closely associated in a great movement in this country. We were having a most successful convention in Buffalo, and he was greatly elated. As we walked down the street together to one of the meetings one day, he said to me: "Torrey, you and I are the most important men in Christian work in this country" or words to that effect. I replied: "John, I am sorry to hear you say that; for as I read my Bible I find man after man who had accomplished great things whom God had to set aside because of his sense of his own importance." And God set that man aside also from that time. I think he is still living, but no one ever hears of him or has heard of him for years.

God used D. L. Moody, I think, beyond any man of his day; but it made no difference how much God used him, he never was puffed up. One day, speaking to me of a great New York preacher, now dead, Mr. Moody said: "He once did a very foolish thing, the most foolish thing that I ever knew a man, ordinarily so wise as he was, to do. He came up to me at the close of a little talk I had given and said: 'Young man, you have made a great address tonight.'" Then Mr. Moody continued: "How foolish of him to have said that! It almost turned my head." But, thank God, it did *not* turn his head, and even when pretty much all the ministers in England, Scotland and Ireland, and many of the English bishops were ready to follow D. L. Moody wherever he led, even then it never turned his head one bit. He would get down on his face before God, knowing he was human, and ask God to empty him of all self-sufficiency. And God did.

Oh, men and women! especially young men and young women, perhaps God is beginning to use you; very likely people are saying: "What a wonderful gift he has as a Bible teacher, what power he has as a preacher, for such a young man!" Listen: get down upon your face before God. I believe here lies one of the most dangerous snares of the Devil. When the Devil cannot discourage a man, he approaches him on another tack, which he knows is far worse in its results; he puffs him up by whispering in his ear: "You are the leading evangelist of the day. You are the man who will sweep everything before you. You are the coming man. You are the D. L. Moody of the day"; and if you listen to him, he will ruin you. The entire shore of the history of Christian workers is strewn with the wrecks of gallant vessels that were full of promise a few years ago, but these men became puffed up and were driven on the rocks by the wild winds of their own raging self-esteem.

V. HIS ENTIRE FREEDOM FROM THE LOVE OF MONEY

The fifth secret of D. L. Moody's continual power and usefulness was *his entire freedom from the love of money.* Mr. Moody might have been a wealthy man, but money had no charms for him. He loved to gather money for God's work; he refused to accumulate money for himself. He told me during the World's Fair that if he had taken for himself the royalties on the hymnbooks which he had published, they would have amounted, at that time, to a million dollars. But Mr. Moody refused to touch the money. He had a perfect right to take it, for he was responsible for the publication of the books, and it was his money that went into the publication of the first of them. Mr. Sankey had some hymns that he had taken with him to England, and he wished to have them published. He went to a publisher (I think Morgan & Scott), and they declined to publish them, because, as they said, Philip Phillips had recently been over and published a hymnbook and it had not done well. However, Mr. Moody had a little money, and he said that he would put it into the publication of these hymns in cheap form; and he did. The hymns had a most remarkable and unexpected sale; they were then published in book form, and large profits accrued. The financial results were offered to Mr. Moody, but he refused to touch them. "But," it was urged on him, "the money belongs to you"; but he would not touch it. Mr. Fleming H. Revell was at the time treasurer of the Chicago Avenue Church, commonly known as the Moody Tabernacle. Only the basement of this new church building had been completed, funds having been exhausted. Hearing of the hymnbook situation Mr. Revell suggested, in a letter to friends in London, that the money be given for completion of this building, and it was. Afterwards, so much money came in that it was given, by the committee into whose hands Mr. Moody put the matter, to various Christian enterprises.

In a certain city to which Mr. Moody went in the latter years of his life, and where I went with him, it was publicly announced that Mr. Moody would accept no money whatever for his services. Now, in point of fact, Mr. Moody was dependent, in a measure, upon what was given him at various services; but when this announcement was made, Mr. Moody said nothing and left that city without a penny's compensation for the hard work he did there; and, I think, he paid his own hotel bill. And yet a minister in that very city came out with an article in a paper, which I read, in which he told a fairy tale of the financial demands that Mr. Moody made upon them, which story I knew personally to be absolutely untrue. Millions of dollars passed into Mr. Moody's hands, *but they passed through*; they did not stick to his fingers.

This is the point at which many an evangelist makes shipwreck, and his great work comes to an untimely end. The love of money on the part of some evangelists has done more to discredit evangelistic work in our day, and to lay many an evangelist on the shelf, than almost any other cause. While I was away on my recent tour I was told by one of the most reliable ministers in one of our eastern cities of a campaign conducted by one who has been greatly used in the past. (Do not imagine, for a moment, that I am speaking of Billy Sunday, for I am not; this same minister spoke in the highest terms of Mr. Sunday and of a campaign which he conducted in a city where this minister was a pastor.) This evangelist of whom I now speak came to a city for a united evangelistic campaign and was supported by fifty-three churches. The minister who told me about the matter was himself chairman of the Finance Committee. The evangelist showed such a longing for money and so deliberately violated the agreement he had made before coming to the city and so insisted upon money being gathered for him in other ways than he had himself prescribed in the original contract, that this minister threatened to resign from the Finance Committee. He was, however, persuaded to remain to avoid a scandal. "As the total result of the three weeks' campaign, there were only twenty-four clear decisions," said my friend; "and after it was over, the ministers got together and by a vote with but one dissenting voice, they agreed to send a letter to this evangelist telling him frankly that they were done with him and with his methods of evangelism forever and that they felt it their duty to warn other cities against him and his methods and the results of his work." Let us lay the lesson to our hearts and take warning in time.

VI. HIS CONSUMING PASSION FOR THE SALVATION OF THE LOST

The sixth reason why God used D. L. Moody was *his consuming passion for the salvation of the lost.* Mr. Moody made the resolution, shortly after he himself was saved, that he would never let twenty-four hours pass over his head without speaking to at least one person about his soul. His was a very busy life, and sometimes he would forget his resolution until the last hour; and sometimes he would get out of bed, dress, go out and talk to someone about his soul in order that he might not let one day pass without having definitely told at least one of his fellow-mortals about his need and the Saviour who could meet it.

One night Mr. Moody was going home from his place of business. It was very late, and it suddenly occurred to him that he had not spoken to one single person that day about accepting Christ. He said to himself: "Here's a day lost. I have not spoken to anyone today, and I shall not see anybody at this late hour." But as he walked up the street he saw a man standing under a lamppost. The man was a perfect stranger to him, though it turned out afterwards the man knew who Mr. Moody was. He stepped up to this stranger and said: "Are you a Christian?" The man replied: "That is none of your business, whether I am a

Christian or not. If you were not a sort of a preacher I would knock you into the gutter for your impertinence."

Mr. Moody said a few earnest words and passed on. The next day that man called upon one of Mr. Moody's prominent business friends and said to him: "That man Moody of yours over on the North Side is doing more harm than he is good. He has got zeal without knowledge. He stepped up to me last night, a perfect stranger, and insulted me. He asked me if I were a Christian, and I told him it was none of his business and if he were not a sort of a preacher I would knock him into the gutter for his impertinence. He is doing more harm than he is good. He has got zeal without knowledge." Mr. Moody's friend sent for him and said: "Moody, you are doing more harm than you are good; you've got zeal without knowledge: you insulted a friend of mine on the street last night. You went up to him, a perfect stranger, and asked him if he were a Christian, and he tells me if you had not been a sort of a preacher he would have knocked you into the gutter for your impertinence. You are doing more harm than you are good; you have got zeal without knowledge."

Mr. Moody went out of that man's office somewhat crestfallen. He wondered if he were not doing more harm than he was good, if he really *had* zeal without knowledge. (Let me say, in passing, it is far better to have zeal without knowledge than it is to have knowledge without zeal. Some men and women are as full of knowledge as an egg is of meat; they are so deeply versed in Bible truth that they can sit in criticism on the preachers and give the preachers pointers, but they have so little zeal that they do not lead one soul to Christ in a whole year.) Weeks passed by. One night Mr. Moody was in bed when he heard a tremendous pounding at his front door. He jumped out of bed and rushed to the door. He thought the house was on fire. He thought the man would break down the door. He opened the door and there stood this man. He said: "Mr. Moody, I have not had a good night's sleep since that night you spoke to me under the lamppost, and I have come around at this unearthly hour of the night for you to tell me what I have to do to be saved."

Mr. Moody took him in and told him what to do to be saved. Then he accepted Christ, and when the Civil War broke out, he went to the front and laid down his life fighting for his country.

Another night, Mr. Moody got home and had gone to bed before it occurred to him that he had not spoken to a soul that day about accepting Christ. *Well*, he said to himself, *it is no good getting up now; there will be nobody on the street at this hour of the night*. But he got up, dressed and went to the front door. It was pouring rain. *Oh*, he said, *there will be no one out in this pouring rain*. Just then he heard the patter of a man's feet as he came down the street, holding an umbrella over his head. Then Mr. Moody darted out and rushed up to the man and said: "May I share the shelter of your umbrella?" "Certainly," the man replied. Then Mr. Moody said: "Have you any shelter in the time of storm?" and preached Jesus to him. Oh, men and women, if we were as full of zeal for the salvation of souls as that, how long would it be before the whole country would be shaken by the power of a mighty, God-sent revival?

One day in Chicago—the day after the elder Carter Harrison was shot, when his body was lying in state in the City Hall—Mr. Moody and I were riding up Randolph Street together in a streetcar right alongside of the City Hall. The car could scarcely get through because of the enormous crowds waiting to get in and view the body of Mayor Harrison. As the car tried to push its way through the crowd, Mr. Moody turned to me and said: "Torrey, what does this mean?" "Why," I said, "Carter Harrison's body lies there in the City Hall, and these crowds are waiting to see it." Then he said: "This will never do, to let these crowds get away from us without preaching to them; we must talk to them. You go and hire Hooley's Opera House [which was just opposite the City Hall] for the whole day." I did so. The meetings began at nine o'clock in the morning, and we had one continuous service from that hour until six in the evening, to reach those crowds.

Mr. Moody was a man on fire for God. Not only was he always "on the job" himself, but he was always getting others to work as well. He once invited me down to Northfield to spend a month there with the schools, speaking first to one school and then crossing the river to the other. I was obliged to use the ferry a great deal; it was before the present bridge was built at that point. One day he said to me: "Torrey, did you know that that ferryman that ferries you across every day was unconverted?" He did not tell me to speak to him, but I knew what he meant. When some days later it was told him that the ferryman was saved, he was exceedingly happy.

Once, when walking down a certain street in Chicago, Mr. Moody stepped up to a man, a perfect stranger to him, and said: "Sir, are you a Christian?" "You mind your own business," was the reply. Mr. Moody replied: "This is my business." The man said, "Well, then, you must be Moody." Out in Chicago they used to call him in those early days "Crazy Moody" because day and night he was speaking to everybody he got a chance to speak to about being saved. One time he was going to Milwaukee, and in the seat that he had chosen sat a traveling man. Mr. Moody sat down beside him and immediately began to talk with him. "Where are you going?" Mr. Moody asked. When told the name of the town he said: "We will soon be there; we'll have to get down to business at once. Are you saved?" The man said that he was not, and Mr. Moody took out his Bible and there on the train showed him the way of salvation. Then he said: "Now, you must take Christ." The man did; he was converted right there on the train.

Most of you have heard, I presume, the story President Wilson used to tell about D. L. Moody. Ex-President Wilson said that he once went into a barber shop and took a chair next to the one in which D. L. Moody was sitting, though he did not know that Mr. Moody was there. He had not been in the chair very long before, as ex-President Wilson phrased it, he "knew there was a personality in the other chair," and he began to listen to the conversation going on; he heard Mr. Moody tell the barber about the Way of Life, and President Wilson said, "I have never forgotten that scene to this day." When Mr. Moody was gone, he asked the barber who he was; when he was told that it was D. L. Moody, President Wilson said: "It made an impression upon me I have not yet forgotten."

On one occasion in Chicago Mr. Moody saw a little girl standing on the street with a pail in her hand. He went up to her and invited her to his Sunday school, telling her what a pleasant place it was. She promised to go the following Sunday, but she did not do so. Mr. Moody watched for her for weeks, and then one day he saw her on the street again, at some distance from him. He started toward her, but she saw him too and started to run away. Mr. Moody followed her. Down she went one street, Mr. Moody after her; up she went another street, Mr. Moody after her; through an alley, Mr. Moody still following; out on another street, Mr. Moody after her; then she dashed into a saloon, and Mr. Moody dashed after her. She ran out the back door and up a flight of stairs, Mr. Moody still following; she dashed into a room,

Mr. Moody following; she threw herself under the bed, and Mr. Moody reached under the bed and pulled her out by the foot and led her to Christ.

He found that her mother was a widow who had once seen better circumstances but had gone down until now she was living over this saloon. She had several children. Mr. Moody led the mother and all the family to Christ. Several of the children were prominent members of the Moody Church until they moved away and afterwards became prominent in churches elsewhere. This particular child, whom he pulled from underneath the bed, was, when I was the pastor of the Moody Church, the wife of one of the most prominent officers in the church. Only two or three years ago, as I came out of a ticket office in Memphis, Tennessee, a fine-looking young man followed me. He said: "Are you not Dr. Torrey?" I said, "Yes." He said: "I am So-and-so." He was the son of this woman. He was then a traveling man and an officer in the church where he lived. When Mr. Moody pulled that little child out from under the bed by the foot, he was pulling a whole family into the kingdom of God, and eternity alone will reveal how many succeeding generations he was pulling into the kingdom of God.

D. L. Moody's consuming passion for souls was not for the souls of those who would be helpful to him in building up his work here or elsewhere; his love for souls knew no class limitations. He was no respecter of persons; it might be an earl or a duke, or it might be an ignorant boy on the street; it was all the same to him; there was a soul to save, and he did what lay in his power to save that soul. A friend once told me that the first time he ever heard of Mr. Moody was when Mr. Reynolds of Peoria told him that he once found Mr. Moody sitting in one of the squatters' shanties that used to be in that part of the city toward the lake, which was then called "The Sands," with a little boy on his knee, a tallow candle in one hand and a Bible in the other, and Mr. Moody was spelling out the words (for at that time the boy could not read very well) of certain verses of Scripture in an attempt to lead that ignorant boy to Christ. Oh, young men and women and all Christian workers, if you and I were on fire for souls like that, how long would it be before we had a revival? Suppose that tonight the fire of God falls and fills our hearts, a burning fire that will send us out all over the country and across the water to China, Japan, India and Africa, to tell lost souls the way of salvation!

VII. DEFINITELY ENDUED WITH POWER FROM ON HIGH

The seventh thing that was the secret of why God used D. L. Moody was that *he had a very definite enduement with power from on High, a very clear and definite baptism with the Holy Ghost.* Mr. Moody knew he had "the baptism with the Holy Ghost"; he had no doubt about it. In his early days he was a great go-getter; he had a tremendous desire to do something, but he had no real power. He worked largely in the energy of the flesh. But there were two humble Free Methodist women who used to come over to his meetings in the Y.M.C.A. One was "Auntie Cook" and the other, Mrs. Snow. (I think her name was not Snow at that time.) These two women would come to Mr. Moody at the close of his meetings and say: "We are praying for you." Finally, Mr. Moody became somewhat nettled and said to them one night: "Why are you praying for me? Why don't you pray for the unsaved?" They replied: "We are praying that you may get the power." Mr. Moody did not know what that meant, but he got to thinking about it and then went to these women and said: "I wish you would tell me what you mean"; and they told him about the definite baptism with the Holy Ghost. Then he asked that he might pray with them and not they merely pray for him.

Auntie Cook once told me of the intense fervor with which Mr. Moody prayed on that occasion. She told me in words that I scarcely dare repeat, though I have never forgotten them. And he not only prayed with them, but he also prayed alone. Not long after, one day on his way to England, he was walking up Wall Street in New York; (Mr. Moody very seldom told this, and I almost hesitate to tell it) and in the midst of the bustle and hurry of that city his prayer was answered; the power of God fell upon him as he walked up the street, and he had to hurry off to the house of a friend and ask that he might have a room by himself, and in that room he stayed alone for hours; and the Holy Ghost came upon him, filling his soul with such joy that at last he had to ask God to withhold His hand, lest he die on the spot from joy. He went out from that place with the power of the Holy Ghost upon him, and when he got to London (partly through the prayers of a bedridden saint in Mr. Lessey's church), the power of God wrought through him mightily in North London, and hundreds were added to the churches; and that was what led to his being invited over to the wonderful campaign that followed in later years.

Time and again Mr. Moody would come to me and say, "Torrey, I want you to preach on the baptism with the Holy Ghost." I do not know how many times he asked me to speak on that subject. Once, when I had been invited to preach in the Fifth Avenue Presbyterian Church, New York (invited at Mr. Moody's suggestion; had it not been for his suggestion the invitation would never have been extended to me), just before I started for New York, Mr. Moody drove up to my house and said, "Torrey, they want you to preach at the Fifth Avenue Presbyterian Church in New York. It is a great big church, cost a million dollars to build it." Then he continued: "Torrey, I just want to ask one thing of you. I want to tell you what to preach about. You will preach that sermon of yours on 'Ten Reasons Why I Believe the Bible to Be the Word of God' and your sermon on 'The Baptism With the Holy Ghost.'" Time and again, when a call came to me to go off to some church, he would come up to me and say: "Now, Torrey, be sure and preach on the baptism with the Holy Ghost." I do not know how many times he said that to me. Once I asked him: "Mr. Moody, don't you think I have any sermons but those two: 'Ten Reasons Why I Believe the Bible to Be the Word of God' and 'The Baptism With the Holy Ghost'?" "Never mind that," he replied, "you give them those two sermons."

Once he had some teachers at Northfield—fine men, all of them, but they did not believe in a definite baptism with the Holy Ghost for the individual. They believed that every child of God was baptized with the Holy Ghost, and they did not believe in any special baptism with the Holy Ghost for the individual. Mr. Moody came to me and said: "Torrey, will you come up to my house after the meeting tonight, and I will get those men to come; and I want you to talk this thing out with them." Of course, I very readily consented, and Mr. Moody and I talked for a long time, but they did not altogether see eye to eye with us. And when they went, Mr. Moody signaled me to remain for a few moments. Mr. Moody sat there with his chin on his breast, as he so often sat when he was in deep thought; then he looked up and said: "Oh, why will they split hairs? Why don't they see that this is just the one thing that they themselves need? They are good teachers, they are wonderful teachers, and I am so glad to have them here; but why will they not see that the baptism with the Holy Ghost is just the one touch that they themselves need?"

I shall never forget the eighth of July, 1894, to my dying day. It was the closing day of the Northfield Students' Conference—the gathering of the students from the eastern colleges. Mr. Moody had asked me to preach on Saturday night and Sunday morning on the baptism with the Holy Ghost. On Saturday night I had spoken about "The Baptism With the Holy Ghost: What It Is; What It Does; the Need of It and the Possibility of It." On Sunday morning I spoke on "The Baptism With the Holy Ghost: How to Get It." It was just exactly twelve o'clock when I finished my morning sermon, and I took out my watch and said: "Mr. Moody has invited us all to go up to the mountain at three o'clock this afternoon to pray for the power of the Holy Spirit. It is three hours to three o'clock. Some of you cannot wait three hours. You do not need to wait. Go to your rooms; go out into the woods; go to your tent; go anywhere where you can get alone with God and have this matter out with Him." At three o'clock we all gathered in front of Mr. Moody's mother's house (she was then still living) and then began to pass down the lane, through the gate, up on the mountainside. There were four hundred and fifty-six of us in all; I know the number because Paul Moody counted us as we passed through the gate.

After a while Mr. Moody said: "I don't think we need to go any further; let us sit down here." We sat down on stumps and logs and on the ground. Mr. Moody said: "Have any of you students anything to say?" I think about seventy-five of them arose, one after the other, and said: "Mr. Moody, I could not wait till three o'clock; I have been alone with God since the morning service, and I believe I have a right to say that I have been baptized with the Holy Spirit." When these testimonies were over, Mr. Moody said: "Young men, I can't see any reason why we shouldn't kneel down here right now and ask God that the Holy Ghost may fall upon us just as definitely as He fell upon the apostles on the Day of Pentecost. Let us pray." And we did pray there on the mountainside. As we had gone up the mountainside, heavy clouds had been gathering; and just as we began to pray, those clouds broke, and the raindrops began to fall through the overhanging pines. But there was another cloud that had been gathering over Northfield for ten days, a cloud big with the mercy and grace and power of God; and as we began to pray, our prayers seemed to pierce that cloud; and the Holy Ghost fell upon us. Men and women, that is what we all need—the baptism with the Holy Ghost.

JOHN R. RICE
1895-1980

ABOUT THE MAN:

Preacher. . .evangelist. . .revivalist. . .editor. . .counselor to thousands. . .friend to millions—that was Dr. John R. Rice, whose accomplishments were nothing short of miraculous. Known as "America's Dean of Evangelists," Dr. Rice made a mighty impact upon the nation's religious life for some sixty years, in great citywide campaigns and in Sword of the Lord Conferences.

At age nine, after hearing a sermon on "The Prodigal Son," John went forward to claim Christ as Saviour. In 1916, with only $9.35 in his pocket, he rode off on his cowpony toward Decatur Baptist College. He was now on the road to becoming a world-renowned evangelist, although he was then totally unaware of God's will for his life.

There was many a twist and turn before Rice rode through the open door into full-time preaching—the army, marriage, graduate work, more seminary, assistant pastor, pastor—then FINALLY, where God planned to use him most—in full-time evangelism.

Dr. Rice and his ministry were always colorful (born in Cooke County, in Texas, December 11, 1895, he was often called the "Will Rogers of the Pulpit" because of their likeness and mannerisms)—and controversial. CONTROVERSIAL—and correctly so—because of his intense stand against modernism and infidelity and his fight for the fundamentals.

Dr. Rice lived and died a man of convictions—intense convictions. But like many other strong fighters for the Faith, Rice was also marked with a sincere spirit of compassion. Those who knew him best knew a man who loved them. In preaching, in prayer, and in personal life, Rice wept over sinners and with saints. But there is more . . .

Less than seventy-one hours before the dawning of 1981, one of the most prolific pens in all Christendom was stilled. Dr. John R. Rice left behind a legacy in writing of more than 200 titles, with a combined circulation of over 61 million copies. And through October of 1981, a total of 24,058 precious souls reported trusting Christ through his ministries, not counting those saved in his crusades nor in foreign countries where his literature has been translated.

And who but God knows the influence of THE SWORD OF THE LORD magazine which he started and edited for forty-six years!

And while "Twentieth Century's Mightiest Pen"—and man—has been stilled, thank God, the fruit remains! Though dead, he continues to speak.

XII.

The Mantle of Elijah

JOHN R. RICE

Suppose we call this message "The Mantle of Elijah."

There is a fascinating story for us about Elisha and how he got the prophet's mantle. God has some rich blessings in the study of it for us today.

Elisha's call was to be a servant of Elijah. But at the time he knew that if God blessed him, if he were faithful and persistent, he could become the prophet of God in Elijah's place.

In that call God told Elijah to go by where Elisha ran a plantation. He was plowing with twelve yoke of oxen before him. Elijah passed by him and cast his mantle upon him. So far as we know, nothing else was said, nothing else was done. Elisha, the young man, ran after Elijah and said, "Let me, I pray thee, kiss my father and my mother, and then I will follow thee." So he killed a yoke of oxen, boiled their flesh with the instruments of the oxen and gave unto the people. Then he went after Elijah and ministered unto him. And from that time on he was called "Elisha the son of Shaphat, which poured water on the hands of Elijah." He was a servant, an errand boy who polished Elijah's shoes and carried his dinner pail. He got water to wash Elijah's hands—a servant of Elijah.

And now a great tragedy is coming. Elijah is going to Heaven. That is wonderful for Elijah, but what about the world? It is a time of great wickedness. Ahab is the king on the throne of Israel, and Jezebel, from the country of Sidon, is queen—both are wicked. The people are wandering away from God. Elijah, the voice of God, who one time said he was the only prophet left, is now going to Heaven. What will the people do?

Elisha said he would become the prophet of God, God's man in

Israel, with just as much power, with just as much authority, as Elijah. He would see as much demonstration of God's power in the hearts and lives of the people, and in miraculous happenings, as Elijah saw.

Now we come to the parting day. Everyone seems to know of it. The sons of the prophets and Elisha all know God is going to take Elijah to Heaven today in a whirlwind. We read the story in the Bible.

"And it came to pass, when the Lord would take up Elijah into heaven by a whirlwind, that Elijah went with Elisha from Gilgal. And Elijah said unto Elisha, Tarry here, I pray thee; for the Lord hath sent me to Beth-el. And Elisha said unto him, As the Lord liveth, and as thy soul liveth, I will not leave thee. So they went down to Beth-el. And the sons of the prophets that were at Beth-el came forth to Elisha, and said unto him, Knowest thou that the Lord will take away thy master from thy head to day? And he said, Yea, I know it; hold ye your peace. And Elijah said unto him, Elisha, tarry here, I pray thee; for the Lord hath sent me to Jericho. And he said, As the Lord liveth, and as thy soul liveth, I will not leave thee. So they came to Jericho. And the sons of the prophets that were at Jericho came to Elisha, and said unto him, Knowest thou that the Lord will take away thy master from thy head to day? And he answered, Yea, I know it; hold ye your peace. And Elijah said unto him, Tarry, I pray thee, here; for the Lord hath sent me to Jordan. And he said, As the Lord liveth, and as thy soul liveth, I will not leave thee. And they two went on. And fifty men of the sons of the prophets went, and stood to view afar off: and they two stood by Jordan. And Elijah took his mantle, and wrapped it together, and smote the waters, and they were divided hither and thither, so that they two went over on dry ground. And it came to pass, when they were gone over, that Elijah said unto Elisha, Ask what I shall do for thee, before I be taken away from thee. And Elisha said, I pray thee, let a double portion of thy spirit be upon me. And he said, Thou hast asked a hard thing: nevertheless, if thou see me when I am taken from thee, it shall be so unto thee; but if not, it shall not be so. And it came to pass, as they still went on, and talked, that, behold, there appeared a chariot of fire, and horses of fire, and parted them both asunder; and Elijah went up by a whirlwind into heaven. And Elisha saw it, and he cried, My father, my father, the chariot of Israel, and the horsemen thereof. And he saw him no more: and he took hold of his own clothes, and rent them in two pieces. He took up also the mantle of Elijah that

fell from him, and went back, and stood by the bank of Jordan; And he took the mantle of Elijah that fell from him, and smote the waters, and said, Where is the Lord God of Elijah? and when he also had smitten the waters, they parted hither and thither: and Elisha went over. And when the sons of the prophets which were to view at Jericho saw him, they said, The spirit of Elijah doth rest on Elisha. And they came to meet him, and bowed themselves to the ground before him."—II Kings 2:1-15.

I. TO FOLLOW ELIJAH, HAVE POWER LIKE HIS!

Consider with me the startling boldness of the request the young man Elisha makes. First, the man he wants to follow is Elijah, one of the two or three outstanding men in the Bible. In fact, it seems to be, with Moses as a possible rival, that Elijah was the one outstanding prophet of God in the Old Testament.

Several things about Elijah. He was given amazing power over nature. When Moses spoke, the ground opened and swallowed some men, and with a rod he smote a rock, and water flowed out. But those were temporary miracles. When Joshua spoke to the sun, *one time*, it stood still about the space of a day. But Elijah shut up Heaven for three and one-half years. He prayed earnestly that it might not rain, and it rained not for the space of three years and six months. Elijah even announced it to the king and said, "There shall not be dew nor rain these years, but according to my word."

Now I don't know that that kind of power was ever given any other man. I am reminded that the miracles of Elijah were very much like those of Jesus. Jesus could send rain or drought or stop a storm and control nature. So could Elijah by the power of God. Then Jesus could multiply loaves and fishes and make them enough. So could Elijah. It is amazing how God used this man and his startling power over nature, over men, over kings, to kill the priests of Baal, to tell the king what to do, or dispose of an army. The amazing power of this man!

Now Elisha said, "Let a double portion of thy spirit be upon me. I want to wear that mantle. I will wear it worthily. I want to be able to do miracles with nature, with fire, with drought, with war, and with floods, and to bring people to life." Elijah brought the widow's son to life. His raising the widow's son compares with Jesus' raising of Lazarus from the dead.

Not only did Elijah have amazing power and do miracles like Jesus, but he was also translated. Only two people down through the history of mankind were ever taken to Heaven without dying—Enoch "who walked with God" and Elijah. That privilege wasn't given to even the Apostle Paul or David or Moses. It was given only to Elijah after Enoch was taken to Heaven, translated. How wonderfully God honored this man Elijah!

When Jesus was on the Mount of Transfiguration, two great men, picturing all the Old Testament, picturing all the saints of the past, met Him. They were Moses and Elijah, brought back from Heaven to meet Jesus on the Mount of Transfiguration. What an honor! What a man of God was Elijah!

That isn't all. Elijah is a type of John the Baptist. He is pictured as one who would come as forerunner. Of John the Baptist it is said, "He shall go before him in the spirit and power of Elias." When the disciples asked, "Must Elijah come?" Jesus answered, "He has come already in the person of John the Baptist." Elijah was a type of John the Baptist.

Elijah is held up as a New Testament example. Whom shall I pattern after when I pray? In James 5 the Scripture says, "Elias [Elijah] was a man subject to like passions as we are, and he prayed earnestly that it might not rain: and it rained not on the earth by the space of three years and six months. And he prayed again, and the heaven gave rain, and the earth brought forth her fruit." Elijah is a New Testament model. You want to pray? Then look to Elijah. Pray like Elijah. Be persistent like Elijah.

Elijah is coming again. There will be two witnesses one day. It is clearly told that the Prophet Elijah shall come again. So I think that when the two witnesses come, Elijah will be one of those to come back to earth again.

Elisha, a young man, said, "I want just twice what you have. I want a double portion of the spirit that is on you." My, the boldness of this young man! He wanted to be a real prophet. That is a wonderful thing, isn't it?

II. "THOU HAST ASKED A HARD THING"

Notice also what the mantle pictured to Elisha. That day while plowing, when Elijah came and laid that mantle across his shoulders, he thought, *God help me to be worthy to wear the mantle of this man when You take him to Heaven; to do what he did and preach like he preached and rebuke sin as he did and have power as he had—God, give me that.* No doubt all these years that burned in his soul.

Now he said, "A double portion of Elijah's power." That is strange, isn't it? "A double portion." He didn't say, "If I can have only a little bit. . . ." We think we are modest when we say, "I am just a little one-horse preacher." We think we are modest and very pious when we say, "Of course, I can't be great like some people." God isn't looking for great people but for people who want a great God and who want God to reach out His mighty arm. God isn't embarrassed if somebody wants a miracle. God isn't embarrassed if somebody wants a drunkard or a harlot saved. God isn't embarrassed if someone asks for a million dollars for the Lord's work.

So Elisha said, "I want a double portion of thy spirit." I want you to think how presumptuous—no, not presumptuous—how BOLD and full of faith was that request.

Notice another thing. Elijah said to him, "Thou hast asked a hard thing." Why is it hard? It is not hard for God. It is hard for a man. Do you want the power of Pentecost? Yes, but you don't want to wait the ten days, do you? Do you want to be like these prophets of God?

Faith of our fathers! living still
In spite of dungeon, fire and sword:
Oh, how our hearts beat high with joy
Whene'er we hear that glorious word!
Faith of our fathers! holy faith!
We will be true to thee till death!

Our fathers, chained in prisons dark,
Were still in heart and conscience free:
How sweet would be their children's fate,
If they, like them, could die for thee!
Faith of our fathers! holy faith!
We will be true to thee till death!

Yes, how sweet it would be, we say. But nobody these days is looking for "the dungeon, fire and sword." Would anyone here like to get put in jail for God? Would anybody enjoy being hit in the head with a rock? If you preach as you ought, you might be. But we want the power without the cost. "Thou hast asked a hard thing," Elijah said. Do you want God to give you open doors? Do you want God to give you power? to give great blessings? "Thou hast asked a hard thing."

It is a hard thing, in the first place, because people are not willing to pay the price to wait on God. It is a hard thing in the second place for God to delegate His power to people who are not ready for it. Would you give to a three-year-old an open straight razor and tell him to go ahead and play with it? to do whatever he wants to? No! He will have to grow a good deal before you can trust him with a straight razor, before you can risk him with a very sharp pair of scissors, or before you risk him with electricity and cords.

It is a pretty hard thing to give Elisha a double portion of the power that is on Elijah. It is hard because men are not ready, and God wouldn't be honored unless somebody is ready to use it in power and faith and to the glory of God.

There is another thing. It is a hard thing because with this goes persecution. "Elisha, you want a double portion of this spirit?" "Yes." "Remember—Ahab has been trying to kill me for a long time. Remember—I had to run for my life. Remember—Jezebel swore she would cut off my head. When I cut off the heads of 450 prophets of Baal, people said I was high tempered and tough. And so you want this way? to be supported by widows and by ravens and be the off-scouring of the world and be hated and despised? If you want that, then that is a pretty hard thing."

To be an Elijah is a hard thing. To have the power is a hard thing because men are not ready for that. They don't want the dungeon, the fire, the sword, the reproach and shame that it takes to be an Elijah.

III. HOLY PERSISTENCE AND BOLDNESS OF ELISHA

See the persistence, the striking persistence. I almost said "presumption," but it is not that—it is the boldness and persistence of this man.

Elijah is going to Heaven today; so he said to Elisha, "Tarry here, I pray thee; for the Lord hath sent me to Bethel."

And Elisha answered, "As the Lord liveth, and as thy soul liveth, I will not leave thee."

So they went down to Bethel.

Then the sons of the prophets at Bethel said to Elisha, "Knowest thou that the Lord will take away thy master from thy head to day?"

To which Elisha replied, "Yea, I know it; hold ye your peace."

Then Elijah said to Elisha, "Tarry here, I pray thee; for the Lord hath sent me to Jericho."

But Elisha answered, "As the Lord liveth, and as thy soul liveth, I will not leave thee."

So they went to Jericho.

Then the sons of the prophets at Jericho said to Elisha, "Knowest thou that the Lord will take away thy master from thy head to day?"

And he answered, "Yea, I know it; hold ye your peace."

Again Elijah said to Elisha, "Tarry, I pray thee, here; for the Lord hath sent me to Jordan."

Elisha replied, "As the Lord liveth, and as thy soul liveth, I will not leave thee."

Then Elijah said to Elisha, "All right, you must want something."

"Yes, let a double portion of thy spirit be upon me."

So the two went down together to the Jordan River. Wasn't that persistence? Wasn't that insistence?

That is a strange thing. He is insisting on this power, a double portion of the power of God, and that persistence is not bad.

In Luke, chapter 11, verses 5 through 8, we have it again: "Which of you shall have a friend, and shall go unto him at midnight, and say unto him, Friend, lend me three loaves; For a friend of mine in his journey is come to me, and I have nothing to set before him? And he from within shall answer and say, Trouble me not: the door is now shut, and my children are with me in bed; I cannot rise and give thee. I say unto you, Though he will not rise and give him, because he is his friend, yet because of his importunity [because he keeps on begging and pleading and insisting and demanding so God will give it—the bread for sinners] he will rise and give him as many as he needeth." Then He goes on to say in verse 13, "If ye then, being evil, know how to give good gifts unto your children: how much more shall your heavenly Father give the Holy Spirit to them that ask him?" He said, "Ask, and it shall be given you; seek, and ye shall find; knock, and it shall be opened unto you" (vs. 9). Persistence and boldness in prayer are the way to have the power of the Holy Spirit.

We wonder why nobody has great power these days. They did at Pentecost, but they waited ten days and cried and prayed and pleaded. "These all continued with one accord in prayer and supplication, with the women, and Mary the mother of Jesus, and with his brethren" (Acts 1:14). That is the way D. L. Moody got power. That is the way any of us can have power. God forgive us if we do not seek the power of God by persistent prayer.

IV. MANY, LIKE THOSE SONS OF THE PROPHETS, DO NOT DETERMINE TO HAVE GOD'S POWER

Did you notice that all these other sons of the prophets knew that Elijah was going to Heaven? These other boys said, "Elisha, did you know your master, whom you run around with and wait on all the time, is going to Heaven today? You won't have anybody's hands to pour water on so they can wash nor anyone to run errands for."

He said, "I know it. I have something on my mind; hold your peace."

Elisha went with Elijah, but the other prophets didn't. Why didn't they?

They went on down to Jericho, and there some other sons of the prophets said, "Hey, do you know what is going to happen today? Elijah is going to Heaven today. Have you heard about it?"

"Well, shut your trap. Don't bother me; I have something on my mind. Hold your peace. I know it. I am going with him down there."

And the sons of the prophets stood afar off; they didn't go with him. They could have, but they didn't. They could have had power; they didn't have it, because they did not pay the price.

You say, "I guess it is not God's will to give me power." Well, that is because you are as those fifty sons of the prophets who stood aside, who didn't go with Elijah. They didn't crave that mantle; neither do you. People get in trouble who wear that mantle. Queen Jezebel is going to try to kill them. The prophets of Baal are against them. So the sons of the prophets said, "No, we don't want to wear that mantle—not that bad. Oh, if we could have it without its costing us anything." But they are not going yonder and be with this man. Yes, the other sons of the prophets *could* have had power.

A lot of people could have power, could work miracles, could have great answers to prayer, but they don't believe God; they are not willing to pay the price.

V. ELISHA'S ANSWER

Consider, will you, the promise, the answer that was given. My, what an answer! He got the answer. What was it? The mantle, the mantle of Elijah falls. That is the same mantle. Oh, he never, never could forget that day back yonder two years ago when Elijah came by and put that mantle on his shoulder, and he thought, *Oh, to wear the mantle of the prophet of God! I will give up this big plantation, these twelve yoke of oxen, all these servants and leave my father and mother.*

Oh, to have that mantle of the prophet of God!

Now when the chariot of fire comes, and the whirlwind begins to take up Elijah, he cries out, "My father, my father, the chariot of Israel, and the horsemen thereof." I have often thought that it may be that Elisha seized the fiery wheels of that chariot and held it and said,"God, You can't take Elijah until I get his mantle! I have asked for it; I have a right to it, and I am going to have it!" I think he could have just said, "I am not going to listen to the whirlwind or anything else until I get that mantle." God had to do it. God was obligated. That is the man God wants; so God lets the mantle fall. So he took up the mantle of Elijah to walk in the steps of Elijah.

It would be wonderful if every good Christian here would pick out somebody filled with the Spirit of God, some Bible character, and say, "I am going to walk in his tracks. I am going to have his mantle."

Oh, how I have been influenced by Elijah and by Paul particularly; then by men of more recent times—R. A. Torrey perhaps more than any other man—and D. L. Moody.

Timothy went with Paul and waited on him, and the power of God came on Timothy in Paul's stead somewhat.

Elisha has the mantle of Elijah now.

Notice this. He took his old garment.

"What are you planning to do?"

"Tear it up."

"Why?"

"I poured water on the hands of Elijah. I have run his errands, but now I am going to be the prophet myself; so I will tear up this old garment."

He tore it in two pieces and threw it aside. What does that mean? The same as when Jesus called to blind Bartimaeus by the roadside outside Jericho. Jesus was passing by, and Bartimaeus said, "Thou son of David, have mercy on me."

So of old blind Bartimaeus Jesus said, 'Command him to be called.'

And they called the blind man, saying, "Be of good comfort, rise; he calleth thee" (Mark 10:48, 49).

He got up, cast away his garment, rose, and came to Jesus.

What is the matter, Bartimaeus?

"I am through being a beggar. I won't need a beggar's garment now that I am able to see and work and make a living for my family."

He cast aside his beggar's garment.

Likewise, Elisha takes off the old garment and tears it in two. He is going to be the prophet of God.

That reminds me of B. H. Carroll. The night he was converted, he sat by his mother's bed, while she slept most of the night after she had rejoiced and praised God for answered prayer, and Dr. Carroll read *Pilgrim's Progress* through. As daylight came, and he was just finishing as Christian went into the Holy City, he said, "I knew then I would be a preacher. I would never be anything but a preacher of God."

So Elisha said, "I am going to be a prophet of God." And he set out to be.

Bill Rice was in a meeting close to Kansas City. He drove his car in to be serviced, and the fellow working on the car said, "Brother Rice, my name is so and so."

"I am glad to meet you," said Bill. "You are a Christian?"

"Oh yes," he said, "I am called to be an evangelist just like you. I am called of God as an evangelist."

Bill said, "Well, are you preaching?"

"No. I have a family, and there is no way to make a living without this work. But I am an evangelist just like you."

Bill replied, "No, you are not just like me. I was called too, and we starved, but we went to Moody Bible Institute. I gave up my job when I only had one or two revivals ahead of time. I gave my life to it. I am going to preach or starve. No, you are not like me unless you are out preaching like I am."

Elisha said, "I am going to be the prophet of God and put off the old garment, and I am going to wear the mantle of the man of God the rest of my days." Therefore he took it with him.

VI. O GOD, FOR SOMEONE TO SEE MIRACLES!

Notice another thing about the answer. He crossed the Jordan. I think he took up that mantle and said, "Just watch me! I am going back to that Jordan River and make the water stand up." I think maybe Elijah, who had crossed the Jordan with him a few minutes before, led him down there because he wanted Elisha to know, "If you are going to follow me, you have to have the power to work miracles. You cannot wear my mantle unless you can make this water stand up, unless you can multiply bread for a widow, unless you can raise the dead." For that reason Elijah had taken that same mantle and had struck the water, and the water stood aside; and they walked through.

Now Elisha has that mantle. So he rushes back to the Jordan River. The sons of the prophets are nearby watching. He takes that mantle, wraps it together, smites the water and says, "Where is the Lord God of Elijah?" I think the water was a little astonished. "We have a new boss telling us what to do. We knew what to expect from Elijah, but this fellow has it, too." So the water stands up so he can walk through, not in the mud, not through the water, but dry-shod, on dry ground.

If you are going to wear the mantle of Elijah, you have to work miracles; you have to have a miracle-working God; then God will help you, and you can do the things that need to be done. If you can't do that, then you can't have any mantle of a prophet.

O God, give us miracles! That is what Gideon said, 'If I am a mighty man of power and if the Lord be with us. . . where be all his miracles which our fathers told us of?' (Judg. 6:13). If God is with us, there ought to be miracles. Oh my, how we do need the miracles of God!

VII. ELISHA REALLY GOT A "DOUBLE PORTION"

Notice: he asked for a "double portion." Now the answer: he got the double portion!

This to me is very interesting, and I think very suggestive, so I call your attention to the miracles of these two different men as an indication that Elijah had miracles and Elisha had miracles, too. As Elijah had major miracles, Elisha had twice as many.

First, the miracles of Elijah. In I Kings 17 we read:

1. Verse 1: "There shall not be dew nor rain these years, but according to my word"—these three years it will not rain until he says so, neither rain nor dew—neither one.

2. Verse 6: "And the ravens brought him bread and flesh in the morning, and bread and flesh in the evening; and he drank of the brook." That is a miracle.

3. Verse 16, the widow: "And the barrel of meal wasted not, neither did the cruse of oil fail." Three for Elijah, according to the Word of the Lord.

4. In verse 22 he raised the child of the widow to life again.

5. In chapter 18, verse 38, fire fell from Heaven on Mount Carmel and burned up the wood and sacrifices.

6. In II Kings 1:10 fire comes down and destroys the captain and his fifty.

7. Verse 12: Fire comes down and destroys another captain and his fifty.

8. In the second chapter, verse 8, he crossed the Jordan, and the water stood up.

As number nine, in verse 11, there is the miraculous going to Heaven, the translation. But Elijah didn't do that. Eight major miracles.

Now here are the miracles of Elisha.

In the same chapter, II Kings 2, Elisha crossed the Jordan River; and the water stood up (vss. 13, 14), and in verses 21 and 22 the waters were healed that were cursed and the ground which was barren. Then in verse 24 a curse comes on those young people ("young men" is the meaning of the Hebrew word), and they were destroyed by two she bears.

In chapter 3, verse 20, water came for those kings and their armies in the valley—miracle number four.

In chapter 4, verse 6, the widow's oil was multiplied; in verse 17 the barren woman was given a son—miracles number five and six.

In chapter 4, verse 35, the boy was raised to life, and in verse 41 he cast meal into the pot, and the poisoned food was cured. Notice how these were just like the miracles of Elijah, but more.

In verses 42-44 he multiplied food to feed a hundred men with twenty barley biscuits and some unhusked corn—number nine.

In chapter 5, verse 14, Naaman dipped seven times in the Jordan and was cured of his leprosy—number ten.

In verse 27 the leprosy then came on the servant Gehazi, making eleven.

In chapter 6, verse 6, the iron did swim; the axe came back and floated.

And in verse 17 God opened the eyes of the young man at Dothan, and he saw the angels of God and chariots of the Lord. Then in verses 18 and 19 the soldiers were struck with blindness—number fifteen.

And chapter 7, verse 20, as the prophecy was fulfilled, a young man—the lord who kept the gate—because he didn't believe God, was trampled upon and died according to the word of Elisha—number sixteen.

And now there was a miracle when Elisha died. After he was dead they let down a dead man in the same cave and touched the bones of Elisha, and he rose to life. But that was after his death.

Eight major miracles by Elijah; sixteen major miracles by Elisha. He asked for and received a double portion of God's Spirit. Isn't that amazing!

VIII. WHERE IS THE LORD GOD OF ELIJAH TODAY?

Now let us consider today that question, "Where is the Lord God of Elijah?" I want you to get some lessons from this wonderful passage of Scripture.

First, a miracle-working God is available for today. God wants miracles. This world is in no worse condition now than it was with Ahab and Jezebel on the throne, Israel worshiping Baal, and the people about to be taken into captivity. America is no worse than that. We just need a miracle-working God. Let us say, we need people who will call on a miracle-working God. We need Elijah, and Elisha who called, "Where is the Lord God of Elijah?"

Then second, let us say that the miracle we need above everything else is the fullness of the Spirit. All these other wonderful things came out of the fact that the blessed Spirit of God was on Elisha. That was the answer about Elijah because the Lord says about John the Baptist that 'he would go in the spirit and power of Elijah.' Though he didn't work miracles as Elijah, John the Baptist had the same spirit and power. Oh, what we need is to be filled with the Spirit. The indwelling of the Spirit is a New Testament experience that began with the resurrection of Christ, but the power, enduement, the anointing, the pouring out of the Spirit and being filled with the Spirit is in the New Testament and in the Old Testament the same. We need to be endued with power from on High. Elisha sought and waited and cried and prayed and wouldn't give up.

A third lesson for us is that we ought to be persistent in prayer. We ought to insist on God's blessing, ought never give up. That is particularly true about the power of God. Oh, "we have not because we ask not." We have little power because we ask so little. We have few conversions because we ask so little when we ought to ask more.

Another lesson: Who wants the mantle of Elijah? The Lord God of Elijah is still here. The trouble is, nobody is wearing the mantle of Elijah. Who wants to wear the mantle of Elijah?

D. L. Moody, country boy, shoe salesman, converted at seventeen, had only gone to about the fifth grade. But he heard someone say, "The world has never yet seen what God can do with one man wholly surrendered to the Lord." And Moody determined to be that man.

R. A. Torrey started out to follow Moody, to wait on Moody. He would get Moody's laundry done. Once a young Episcopal rector, James M. Gray, said, "I can't look after his dirty laundry." Dr. Torrey said, "I can and will. I will shine his shoes; I will wash his feet; I will do anything to keep Moody going." Consequently the mantle of Moody fell on R. A. Torrey.

Did God ever rebuke bold praying? Was there ever a time when God said, "You are asking too much, you want too much power, you want too much demonstration"? Did God say, "Moses, you ought not ask for the Red Sea to open"? Or did He say to Moses, "You ought not to expect water to come out of the rock"? Did God say, "Moses, you should not ask the ground to open and swallow up these enemies"? Did God ever say, "Moses, you can't expect Me to bring quails in to feed three million people"? Or, "Moses, I can't feed the people manna from heaven every day for forty years"? No. God never said, "You are asking too much."

Did God rebuke Joshua when he said, "Sun, stand still right over there until I win this battle"? Was God against that? No. Did God rebuke Elijah when he declared there would not be rain nor dew until he said so? Did God say, "You are taking too much responsibility"? Did the Lord say to Elijah, "Wait! I am running this universe Myself. Keep your hands off"? No! No! God says, "I am glad somebody cares to get things done right. I will give him the key to Heaven. He can have it." God never rebukes bold praying.

When Elijah, the man of God, sat upon that hill and the wicked king sent word, "Come down," was Elijah scared? No. Did God rebuke him? No. He said, "If I be a man of God, then let fire come down from heaven, and consume thee and thy fifty," and the "fire of God came down from heaven, and consumed him and his fifty"—just like that. That was the end of him. Did God rebuke Elijah for that? Was God angry because somebody asked too much?

George Mueller said, "I will build an orphans' home to care for twenty-three hundred or twenty-four hundred orphans and never ask any person for a dollar; I will just pray and ask God to put it in the hearts of people to send that money" (seven and a half million dollars were prayed down without ever taking a collection). Was God angry because Mueller set out to prove God and asked much? No! No! It is said that years before Mueller died—about the middle of his career—he affirmed that up to that time five thousand of his definite prayers had been answered on the day of asking! If only somebody would ask God!

During the World's Fair, when the crowd was at Jackson Park, D. L. Moody was in town for a few days. He said to Torrey, "Go downtown and rent the auditorium at the theater which seats four thousand." Torrey argued, "Mr. Moody, the crowds won't be in town."

Moody said, "Yes, get it for noon."

"But Mr. Moody, the only people who stay in town are business people; the others are out at the World's Fair on the lake front."

Moody said, "You do as you are told." Torrey said, "That is the way I kept my job—doing as I was told." (Torrey was superintendent of Moody Bible Institute at the time.)

Torrey went down and rented the theater. When he returned, Moody said, "Get ready to speak on the baptism of the Holy Ghost, the fullness of the Spirit." Torrey went downtown at noon, and when he got there, a policeman was at the door. Torrey asked, "What's the matter?"

The policeman answered, "You can't get in."

"Why?"

"The building is full."

"But I am supposed to preach here." And Torrey had to go to the back and slip in through a back door because the building was running over. D. L. Moody spent the money and had the faith and claimed it. Was God angry with Moody when he expected a big crowd?

Does God say you are asking too much when you want large meetings? Are you asking too much when you say, "I want a revival invitation in the mail tomorrow morning"?

A few days ago a Conservative Baptist pastor in Chicago Heights phoned me and said, "Dr. Rice, a Catholic woman was saved in our services. I gave her your book on prayer. She has been reading it. She came to me and said, 'Pastor, why can't we pray for my husband to be saved this weekend? I believe God wants him to be saved.'" The good pastor said to her, "I feel that way, too."

On Wednesday night they mentioned it to the congregation for prayer. Another preacher present said, "You can't tell God when to save people." Others said, "You can't be that definite and say you want it done right away."

The pastor called me to ask about it. I told him, "If God led you and the wife to pray that way, go ahead and pray for his conversion this weekend."

So the pastor and this woman prayed. He called me on Saturday.

After the Sunday services the pastor phoned me again and said, "The man was saved fifteen minutes to midnight on Sunday. His wife went home and won him to Christ. She is on shouting ground." He said further, "We had three others saved, and sixteen young people rededicated their lives. A real revival is on here at the church."

Then the woman herself called me and said, "Dr. Rice, I have only been saved four months. After reading your book I saw we could ask big things from God, so I asked for my husband to get saved this weekend, and he was saved fifteen minutes to midnight Sunday night! Thank God for your book on prayer, which taught me to ask."

Is God angry when we ask for a lot? No! He isn't angry when we ask much. God must be heartsick because nobody wants Elijah's mantle. Nobody wants to ask much. Nobody wants to stick his neck out. Nobody wants to be a fool. Nobody wants to be presumptuous. So we are nice, meek, weak Christians who never get much done while the world goes to Hell. People don't know there is a God of Elijah.

Oh, where is the Lord God of Elijah! May God raise up people who believe Him. May God raise up people to call on Him. May God raise up people who won't give up but who will say, "I am not going to leave You. I am going with You."

What do you want? "I want a double portion that You put on D. L. Moody, a double portion You put on Torrey and on Billy Sunday and on Sam Jones. I want the mantle of Elijah."

May God give it to us!

ROBERT C. GRAY, JR.
1926-

ABOUT THE MAN:

Dr. Gray is one of the Christian world's most humble, gracious and dedicated servants of God. He was pastor of Trinity Baptist Church in Jacksonville, Florida, for many years.

He founded Trinity Baptist College, a four-year college with its motto: TRAINING SPECIALISTS FOR THE MINISTRY.

Born in Tampa, Bob Gray received his training in the public schools there. After graduation from high school, he entered the United States Air Force. During World War II he served as a war correspondent for Air Force publications and covered the famous Nuremburg War Crimes Trials as his last assignment before discharge. It was during his tenure of service overseas that he felt a definite call to enter the gospel ministry.

In the early days of his ministry, Gray taught public school and is well known in academic circles. He received his A.B. degree from Stetson University, the Doctor of Divinity degree from Tennessee Temple University, and the Doctor of Laws degree from Garland College. He serves on the Cooperating Board of the Sword of the Lord and the Advisory Board for Tennessee Temple University.

In 1954 Dr. Gray was called to Trinity Baptist Church, where he remained until 1992. Under his dynamic leadership, the church grew from an average Sunday school attendance of 250 to around 4,000. He was a pioneer and leader in the bus ministry.

After preaching on missions for so many years, Dr. Gray felt God's call to go to the foreign field himself. In 1992 he left Trinity to begin a missionary career in Germany at the age of 66.

He is widely used in revival meetings and is a popular speaker in Bible conferences across the nation.

Dr. Gray looks back to a Sword of the Lord Conference at Lake Louise in Toccoa, Georgia, the summer of 1951 as being the time and place that his life and ministry were completely turned around.

He produced a book of sermons, *Love Letters in the Sand*, published by Sword of the Lord Publishers.

XIII.

What Happens When Revival Comes

ROBERT C. GRAY, JR.

(Preached at the National Sword of the Lord Conference on Revival and Soul Winning, Gospel Light Baptist Church, Walkertown, North Carolina, August 7, 1995)

"And all the people gathered themselves together as one man into the street that was before the water gate; and they spake unto Ezra the scribe to bring the book of the law of Moses, which the Lord had commanded to Israel.

"And Ezra the priest brought the law before the congregation both of men and women, and all that could hear with understanding, upon the first day of the seventh month.

"And he read therein before the street that was before the water gate from the morning until midday, before the men and the women, and those that could understand; and the ears of all the people were attentive unto the book of the law.

"And Ezra the scribe stood upon a pulpit of wood, which they had made for the purpose; and beside him stood Mattithiah, and Shema, and Anaiah, and Urijah, and Hilkiah, and Maaseiah, on his right hand; and on his left hand, Pedaiah, and Mishael, and Malchiah, and Hashum, and Hashbadana, Zechariah, and Meshullam."—Neh. 8:1-4.

(If you ever run out of names for little boys, here's a chapter to go to. Watch them blink their eyes when you check him in at the nursery!)

"And Ezra opened the book in the sight of all the people; (for he was above all the people;) and when he opened it, all the people stood up:

"And Ezra blessed the Lord, the great God. And all the people answered, Amen, Amen, with lifting up their hands: and they bowed their heads, and worshipped the Lord with their faces to the ground.

"Also Jeshua, and Bani, and Sherebiah, Jamin, Akkub, Shabbethai, Hodijah, Maaseiah, Kelita, Azariah, Jozabad, Hanan, Pelaiah, and the Levites, caused the people to understand the law: and the people stood in their place.

"So they read in the book in the law of God distinctly, and gave the sense, and caused them to understand the reading.

"And Nehemiah, which is the Tirshatha, and Ezra the priest the scribe, and the Levites that taught the people, said unto all the people, This day is holy unto the Lord your God; mourn not, nor weep. For all the people wept, when they heard the words of the law.

"Then he said unto them, Go your way, eat the fat, and drink the sweet, and send portions unto them for whom nothing is prepared: for this day is holy unto our Lord: neither be ye sorry; for the joy of the Lord is your strength.

"So the Levites stilled all the people, saying, Hold your peace, for the day is holy; neither be ye grieved.

"And all the people went their way to eat, and to drink, and to send portions, and to make great mirth, because they had understood the words that were declared unto them.

"And on the second day were gathered together the chief of the fathers of all the people, the priests, and the Levites, unto Ezra the scribe, even to understand the words of the law.

"And they found written in the law which the Lord had commanded by Moses, that the children of Israel should dwell in booths in the feast of the seventh month:

"And that they should publish and proclaim in all their cities, and in Jerusalem, saying, Go forth unto the mount, and fetch olive branches, and pine branches, and myrtle branches, and palm branches, and branches of thick trees, to make booths, as it is written.

"So the people went forth, and brought them, and made themselves booths, every one upon the roof of his house, and in their courts, and in the courts of the house of God, and in the street of the water gate, and in the street of the gate of Ephraim."—Vss. 5-16.

Scriptural revival has always begun after prayer and usually with a small minority. Think of the revivals down through church history that have swept entire nations, even continents; remember, each began in a prayer meeting, when a few dared to band together and cry out for the power of God.

Even so was it true in the days of the captivity, when the children of Israel had been compelled to go into slavery and enter Babylon. There, after many years, the Jews, being the entrepreneurs that they were, began to prosper and to find themselves at home in the land of their captivity. They chose to be at home, not only in the provinces of Babylon but likewise in the cities of Assyria.

When the heart of King Artaxerxes was touched by the Holy Spirit, God burdened him to call for a rally of just a few who might be willing to go back to Jerusalem, construct the walls, rebuild the Temple and establish once again the scriptural ordinances of the one true and holy God.

Thank God for this faithful remnant! And there always will be a faithful remnant if God can find those willing to pay the price and make the sacrifice that a holy God requires in order to have a revival.

So they came—Nehemiah and those who assisted him. Though he was under constant surveillance by Tobiah and Sanballat, and though he was opposed at every turn, the wall was rebuilt, and the foundation of the Temple was laid.

Now it is time for revival to come. On this occasion, Ezra the scribe is the human instrument whom God deigned to use to bring that revival to God's people.

What happens when revival comes to the people of God?

Notice, first, how it affects the preacher; second, how it affects the preaching of the preacher; third, its impact upon the people.

I. HOW REVIVAL AFFECTS THE PREACHER

It affects the preacher to the point that **he immediately recognizes the necessity of being scriptural in his presentation.** Look at verse 1:

"And all the people gathered themselves together as one man into the street that was before the water gate; and they spake unto Ezra the scribe to bring the book of the law of Moses which the Lord had commanded to Israel."

They were not there to view the artifacts of a previous civilization. Isn't it tragic that so many congregations on Sundays have to listen as their pastors extol the virtues of the archaeologists and talk about the artifacts that they have recovered to identify civilizations of the past? What a tragedy when people are compelled to sit and listen to a commentary on textual criticism from some so-called scholar! All we need to do to have revival is do it God's way. Go back to the Word of God and give the people the Book, written through the inspiration of the Holy Spirit.

The Apostle Paul, when writing to his young protégé, Timothy, said, "Preach the word"! He didn't say, "Give your opinion of the Bible." He didn't suggest that he deal with Grecian art and archaeology. He didn't suggest that he deal with some kind of an ancient Babylonian manuscript and question whether there was one Isaiah or two. He said, "Preach the word"!

Writing to the church at Philippi, that same apostle said, "Holding forth the word of life." Beloved, this is the Word of Life. This is what God's people need to hear. And this is what God's people must hear if we are to experience revival before Jesus comes.

Thank God, I've seen the power of this Book demonstrated over and over. Why would any man called of God to preach want to preach anything else but the Book?

Revival came because Ezra was committed to preaching the Book of God, to reading in the hearing of the people the Word of God. "So then faith cometh by hearing, and hearing by the word of God" (Rom. 10:17). That is how you got saved. Preacher, that is how you were called to preach. That is how you sustain your spiritual life. Jesus said, "Man shall not live by bread alone, but by every word that proceedeth out of the mouth of God" (Matt. 4:4).

That is another reason I believe in verbal inspiration. Jesus didn't say, "By every paragraph." He didn't say, "By the philosophical concepts in every chapter." He said, "The *words* that I speak unto you, they are spirit, and they are life" (John 6:63). Thank God, they are!

Many years ago when I was in high school, there was a young man a grade lower than I. He and I became bosom buddies. We wouldn't even date unless we could double date. If the girls weren't willing to go with both of us, neither one of us would go.

World War II came along. Both of us went into the military. I went into the Air Corps; he, into the Navy. I went to Europe; he went to the South Pacific.

Our lives were spared. We came home. Several other fellows who had graduated the same time we did, agreed to get together with us and have dinner. Some of the fellows had married; some were still single.

We agreed on a time to get together. We went to a very fashionable restaurant in our hometown of Tampa. I had been called to preach while in service during World War II.

Our orders were delivered to the table. All the others began to dive in and eat. I waited for someone to say something, but nobody did; so I got my knife and beat on the water glass to get their attention. The conversation stopped.

I said, "Fellows, I think we ought to thank God that He brought us all back home safely. Let's thank God for this food." I could tell I had hit a somewhat discordant note. But I didn't wait for their approval. We didn't vote on it. It wasn't a Baptist church. So I prayed.

As the conversation wore on, they began to imbibe alcoholic beverages. Soon some were getting a little crude and rude, and several vulgar. I then realized we didn't have much in common anymore.

I reached over, took my knife and tapped on the glass again. Again they got quiet. The fellow to whom I was closest in high school looked up to me and said, "Don't tell me you're going to pray again!" I said, "No, I just have something to share with you."

I told them how God had called me to preach and that I had surrendered my life for that purpose. I said, "I love every one of you, and I want you to know I'm praying that you will get saved. But I really think you would be more comfortable—and I know I would—if I just left at this point. We're through eating, and your activities and mine are just not of the same choice. If you'll excuse me, I'll go."

As I laid my napkin on the table and started out the door, my high school bosom buddy stood up, his face reddened, and he said, "Gray, you're letting religion make a fool out of you!"

He went his way, and I went mine.

I went away and prepared for the ministry. He went to the University of Florida and got a degree in business. The years passed. We didn't even see each other.

After a number of years had passed, I was invited by my pastor to hold a revival meeting in my home church in Tampa. I told my wife, "You know, I'd like to reach Bobby and Billy while we're here. I think I'll go down to Penney's and talk to him." I did, and invited him to the meeting.

He said, "I'm not interested in that, but we'd be glad to have you folks over for refreshments some night after your church service."

I couldn't get him to come to church, so I said, "Okay, we'll come."

On Tuesday night after the service, we drove to his house. We had soft drinks and a homemade cake. His wife and my wife talked at the dining room table, and he and I walked into the living room. I brought up the subject of his relationship to the Lord.

He began expounding all the philosophical teachings he had absorbed at the University of Florida. He told me only people who had blind faith and foolish imaginations believed all the material that was in the Bible. He no longer could accept that.

I reasoned with him from the Word of God. But the more we talked, the angrier he became. The Holy Spirit laid one verse on my heart—I John 5:12: "He that hath the Son hath life; and he that hath not the Son of God hath not life." After every rebuttal he made in our conversation, I felt led to quote that verse. I quoted it a dozen times at least. I could tell it was really getting to him.

Finally he became disgusted and said, "Look, can't you say anything else but 'He that hath the Son hath life; and he that hath not the Son of God hath not life'?"

I said, "No, because 'He that hath the Son hath life; and he that hath not the Son of God hath not life.' "

He said, "Well, if your mind is in that kind of a rut, you can just leave."

I said, "All right, we'll go."

I called my wife in; we thanked them for the refreshments and went home. My heart was broken. I shared the experience with my wife. In our room we got on our knees and prayed and committed it to God.

The last night of the meeting, as I started to read my text, I noticed the ushers were showing a couple a seat in the very back row. There he was! His wife had on these spiked high heels that looked like some kind of a felonious weapon. I thought, *Dear Lord, I wonder why in the world they came!*

I preached. We gave the invitation. After four or five had come down the aisle and received Christ and gotten saved, I looked up; and to my astonishment, he was literally running down the aisle and holding his wife's hand. She was having a difficult time walking, much less running, in those spiked heels!

Finally he got her about two-thirds of the way down the aisle, then broke away. The personal worker standing at the end of the aisle reached out to shake his hand, but he pushed it away. He had an angry look.

I thought, *My soul! He's going to come up and punch me in the nose right here in the pulpit!* I stood there and watched as he walked right up onto the platform, threw his arms around my neck and said, "He that hath the Son hath life; and he that hath not the Son of God hath not life." Then he added, "I want the Son! I want the Son!"

Brother, that's the power of the Word of God! I didn't deal with him at the altar. He and I squatted down behind the pulpit. We had our own little private soul-winning station back there. Praise God, he got saved! We both came up hugging, rejoicing and praising God!

To have revival, we must return to scriptural preaching, authoritative preaching, and give people a "Thus saith the Lord"—not recommendations, not suggestions.

It galls me to hear preachers say, "I suggest to you. . ." What ever happened to "Thus saith the Lord"?

America doesn't need recommendations. America doesn't need suggestions. Moses didn't come down from the mountain with ten recommendations or suggestions on tablets of stone. He came down with the Word of God written with the very finger of God.

The preacher was scriptural. Not only was he scriptural; second, **he was steadfast.** Look at verse 4: "And Ezra the scribe stood upon a pulpit of wood, which they had made for the purpose." Someone had planned on having preaching.

Oh, God forbid this "rap" business, this "meaningful dialogue," this New Age guru stuff where the preacher sits on the communion table and blows his breathless words into a microphone and sighs and dies and people say, "Isn't that meaningful communication?"!

What ever happened to old-fashioned, Bible-thumping preaching? This is a pulpit. This is where you do business against the Devil. This is God's arena. There is no giving and taking. You're giving the Devil everything you can.

Paul wrote to Timothy and said, "Be instant in season, out of season." Thank God for those who are steadfast!

You preachers get the same kind of junk mail I get. Gospel bookstores are presenting every new book, trying to reach the baby-boomers and the baby-busters. I'll tell you how to reach them—by preaching!

We need more steadfast preachers who remember Paul's words, "Be ye stedfast, unmoveable, always abounding in the work of the Lord, forasmuch as ye know that your labour is not in vain in the Lord" (I Cor. 15:58).

We need more preachers who are steadfast, true to God; more preachers who will preach against sin; more preachers who will call a nation again to repentance; more preachers who will afflict the comfortable and comfort the afflicted; more preachers who will once again cry aloud and spare not; preachers who are steadfast and doing God's work in God's way!

Not only were they scriptural and steadfast, but **they were spiritual.** Look at verse 10: "This day is holy unto our Lord: neither be ye sorry; for the joy of the Lord is your strength."

What is going on out there in the realm of religion? Why all these best-selling books on "ministerial burnout"; this kind of preaching: "I'm okay; you're okay"? Paul would have had a rough time with that. No, you're not okay, and I'm not okay. None of us is okay. That's the problem. A self-satisfied generation never senses the need of spiritual revival, never experiences the desire to turn back to God and do God's work in God's way.

The Bible says, "The joy of the Lord is your strength." What kind of anti-depressants are you taking? People say, "Well, I do this just to relax." You do? What ever happened to the joy of the Lord?

During the Vietnam era, I was preaching for Dr. Curtis McCarley up at Hendersonville. A young man out of that church, one for whom the people had prayed fervently and faithfully, had come home. He had a minor wound. His life was not in danger. It was his first time to be in church since returning home.

The young fellow in his uniform was singing the praises of God. Just before time for me to preach, Dr. McCarley called him by name and said, "It's such a joy to see you home! Would you stand and give us a word of testimony? All the people have been praying for you. We love you."

He stood and gave a wonderful, radiant testimony about God's protective care. He thanked the people in that great church for remembering him in prayer. People were weeping and rejoicing with that young man who had given so much in the service of his country.

Hardly had he been seated when an elderly gentleman stood and told us how God had healed him of cancer. Then another lady told how God had blessed her and healed her of her infirmity. Others began to testify. This went for almost an hour. Our hearts were blessed.

Then the pastor said, "Now, has anyone else had a blessing that you wish to share before the preaching?"

No one said anything for a few moments. Then a little lady, probably not even five feet in height and dressed meticulously, stood. She had on a little pillbox hat and a nice outfit. Gloves were on top of her pocketbook, and underneath her watch was a little lace hanky—the essence of everything feminine and petite.

She said in a very quiet voice, "Pastor!"

"Yes, ma'am," and he called her name.

"I haven't had God heal me of any particular infirmity; but is it all right if I just praise the Lord on general principles?" She pulled that little white hanky out from under that watchband and started waving it back and forth and in her little quiet voice said, "Whew! Whew! Whew! Glory to God!"

I learned that night to praise God on general principles! Hallelujah! "The joy of the Lord is your strength."

I get so weary when Baptists get more excited about a ball game than about the blessings of God. We go to church, and if anybody breathes deeply or has a little bit of chest congestion, the ushers ask him to leave: "You're disturbing the tranquility of the sanctuary." Bless God, learn to praise Him on general principles! Why? "The joy of the Lord is your strength."

When revival comes, the preacher preaches the Word of God, is steadfast and true in season and out of season, faithful; the preacher is spiritual; he radiates the glow of God in his soul; and the people discover "the joy of the Lord is your strength."

The next time Satan tries to lead you into the pit of depression, just remember that "the joy of the Lord is your strength." Praise Him for it! "Let every thing that hath breath praise the Lord," said the psalmist.

II. HOW REVIVAL AFFECTS THE PREACHING

In verse 6 there is **conviction**.

"And Ezra blessed the Lord, the great God. And all the people answered, Amen, Amen, with lifting up their hands: and they bowed their heads, and worshipped the Lord with their faces to the ground."

It's very interesting. If you say "amen" in church, you're considered somewhat rural. "Those people over there—they're sweet folks, but just sort of country." Well, bless God! I'll have you know that this is not an R.F.D. situation. When they heard the Word of God, the Bible says—not just some of the people, not just the deacons and the "Amen

Corner"—but "all the people answered, Amen, Amen." It didn't say one "*Amen*" but two "*Amens*."

Let someone come into the service; if he lifts one hand, we become suspicious; but woe unto us if he lifts two hands! We've let a little education and culture drive us from the scriptural pattern of expressing our joy when the blessings of God come down in the wake of revival.

"I don't see that in the Bible," you say. It's right in front of you. If that isn't enough proof, turn to I Timothy 2 where Paul says, "I will therefore that men pray every where, lifting up holy hands, without wrath and doubting."

Some of you who pastor the First Refrigerated Baptist Church will go back home and raise your hand. When you do, you will scare your people half to death! Better take it gradual, brother!

The Bible says there was conviction. To say "amen" means "I agree with that." If you want to put fire in your preacher's bones, don't sit there with holy lockjaw. Open your big mouths. When God's man preaches God's Word and you get a blessing, "Let the redeemd of the Lord say so."

"All the people answered, Amen, Amen, with lifting up their hands."

"I just never have felt that way," you say. But if Holy Ghost conviction grabs your soul, you'll feel that way.

Isn't it strange that what we do at a ball game or an athletic event is socially acceptable but when we do the same thing at church over some things that are vitally more important, people think we're fanatics? At a football game, do you sit there with a stoic expression on your face, with cheerleaders out there screaming for your attention and response, and say (quietly), "Advance, team, rapidly"? No way! But at church, you sit in the seat of the scornful and find fault with God's people who are doing exactly what the Bible said they did when revival came.

"And all the people answered, Amen, Amen."

How many have said to me, "Preacher, I go to sleep so easily in church. I'm so exhausted from working all week; so I might as well stay home because I don't hear a thing."

Go to the right kind of church, and you won't go to sleep. If you are sitting next to one of these dozers and the "*amens*" don't keep him awake, give him a left jab with the elbow in the ribs and say, "How about that one, brother?" Amen! Amen!

"Lifting up holy hands, without wrath and doubting."

When revival comes, the preaching will not only enable the people to experience conviction, but there will be **contrition.** "For all the people wept, when they heard the words of the law" (Neh. 8:9).

Where are the Christians who are weeping over approximately thirty million abortions in this country, plus the uncounted ones that are never reported?

I was a reporter for the Air Corps at the Nuremburg Trials at the close of World War II. I sat in the courtroom day after day and witnessed the awful, barbarous acts that were read about and shown on captured film, committed by the Nazis in the death camps. These barbarous acts of inhumanity were perpetrated against over six million Jews. And that seemed almost unthinkable! No wonder God brought Nazi Germany to her knees in defeat!

But how much longer can that God exercise patience with a nation that puts its official approval upon murdering the unborn to the rate already of over thirty million little babies who never got to see the light of day nor nurse at their mothers' bosoms because abortion is being used in America as a form of birth control? And born-again, Bible-believing Christians, through the paying of their taxes from hard-earned labor, have to help finance these murderous acts!

Where are the Christians today who weep over the drug scene in America? God, have mercy! Alcohol is sweeping this nation at an unbelievable pace.

Just before I resigned from Trinity Baptist Church in Jacksonville to go to the mission field, there was going to be a "Say-No-to-Drugs Parade." I was contacted by a lady in our city who said, "You're the president of your Christian academy. [We had almost 1400 students in our Christian school.] We'd like for them to be included in this parade. We'll bring T-shirts, and they can make their own banners. We will march throughout the city and declare that we are against drugs and that we should say no to drugs."

I said, "I'm sure you mean well, and I'm sure your intentions are honorable. But our academy will not participate because you are not completely against drugs."

She said, "What do you mean by that?"

I said, "The City Council still issues licenses to sell liquor. Every grocery store in the city sells beer. Are you going to include alcohol in your stand against drugs?"

She said, "No, because that's legal."

I replied, "It may be legal in man's sight, but it's not legal in God's sight. Let our kids carry banners that say, 'Beer, Wine, Whiskey and Gin All Belong in Hell Where They Began'; let us advertise in that parade that we're against EVERY form of drug abuse, and we will march with you."

"Oh no, that is not permitted."

I said, "Then count us out."

I'm sick of this bias. Even church people say, "People have a right to drink." Wait till some drunk plows into your family's car and takes a life; then you will get a different perspective on that problem.

The Bible says, "When they heard the words of the law . . . the people wept." America hasn't heard the Word of God. Our pulpits are barren and sterile, and we have very few soul-winning churches.

There is no revival because we don't have preaching that brings contrition in the hearts of the people over sin.

When revival comes, it affects the preaching and leads people to make a **commitment.** Look in verse 12: ". . . because they had understood the words that were declared unto them," they "went their way."

When people understand what this Book really says and they make a commitment to keep the words of that Book, it makes a difference in their lifestyles; it makes a difference in the life of the church; it makes a difference in the families of the church; it makes a difference in the lives of the people who comprise the nation.

I suppose I'll get in trouble, but I'm going to say it anyway: There is a movement sweeping the land, and many independent Baptists have been sucked into it. It is called Promise Keepers. I'll be the first to acknowledge that much of their doctrinal platform is moral and good, but it is an attempt on the part of the Devil to deceive Bible-believing people into an ecumenical arrangement that abrogates and negates the autonomy of the local New Testament church.

Now, listen! If you're a born-again Christian and you stood at a marriage altar and took your vow before God, you don't need to go to a stadium somewhere and pay $60 in order to renew that vow. Every day, when you look at your husband or you look at your wife, just give him or her a good, old-fashioned kiss; you've renewed the vow right then.

III. HOW REVIVAL AFFECTS THE PEOPLE

They were hungry for the Word of God.

"And he read therein before the street that was before the water gate from the morning until midday, before the men and the women, and those that could understand; and the ears of all the people were attentive unto the book of the law."—Vs. 3.

They were hungry.

Can you imagine standing for half a day, listening to the preaching of the Word of God? The first time I preached in Romania, they nearly killed me. I've never been noted for brevity; but those people think if you preach under two hours, you're not sure of your calling! In so many churches here in the States, it's so different. Nobody asks what time church starts anymore. Everybody wants to know, "What time do we get out?" Let a preacher go past 12:00 on Sunday morning, and in most churches, he's committed the unpardonable sin.

I feel so sorry for preachers who are intimidated by the clock, pastoring a church full of "clock-eyed" members. You never saw anybody in your life who called a TV station and said, "Now, listen, last night you kept me up till 10:00. If that happens again, I'm going to file a complaint with the FCC." Hypocrites!

"Well, what time is getting-out time?" When God says it's over.

I'd rather get burned with wildfire than freeze to death in the Polar Bear Baptist Church.

People were hungry for the Word of God.

When we have revival, there will be an interest in the Word of God—not programs but the Word of God.

Not only were the people hungry, **they were humble.** Notice verse 6: "They bowed their heads, and worshipped the Lord with their faces to the ground." Oh, when we see ourselves in the light of His glory and brilliance and holiness, there's no place left but on our faces before a holy God.

In Heaven the four and twenty elders lie prostrate before the One who sits on that majestic throne. I cannot imagine going into the presence of the glorified Christ without falling prostrate and thanking God for His holiness and His willingness to have mercy and compassion on unworthy sinners like we are.

"They . . . worshipped the Lord with their faces to the ground." They were humble.

Some of our greatest men of God don't know they're great. Thank God for preachers who realize we're nothing but by the grace of God.

Having a servant's heart is so important. Jesus said, ". . . when ye shall have done all those things which are commanded you, say, We are unprofitable servants: we have done that which was our duty to do."

We like to pride ourselves, "Bless God, I'm a member of an independent Baptist church. I tithe my income. We give to Faith Promise. I don't smoke, I don't chew, I don't run with the folks who do. Hallelujah! I'm isolated, separated, Simonized, petrified; yes sir, bless God!" **But are you humble?**

In the late 1800s there was a little girl named Eleanor Chestnut. Her mother died when she was nine, and her father abandoned the family. She was saved at an early age. She and her two brothers were separated by well-meaning relatives and were never allowed to live together. Each went his own separate way. She grew up terribly poor. But in her isolation and loneliness, she determined, with the help of God, to serve the Lord who loved her and gave Himself for her.

She resolved to go to a Christian Bible college. She worked her way through. In her senior year a medical missionary lectured in the chapel service. She was impressed by the Holy Spirit to pursue medicine. This was in an era when it was very uncommon for a woman to enter that profession. But enter it she did.

Finally, after struggle and crisis, she managed to get her medical degree.

She went to China. This was before the Communist Revolution. She felt a burden for the people of China, to win them to Jesus Christ.

There was a coolie in that village, the lowest caste in the caste system there. This coolie had an injured leg. Without amputation, he would die of blood poisoning from infection. She had none of the equipment necessary, and there was no hospital for hundreds of miles.

The people in the village came and gathered about her door and pled and begged that somehow she might try to save that coolie's life. In the eyes of the people in the government, he was just another peasant, just another worker and of no significant value. But to her he was a precious soul whom she hoped to win to the Lord Jesus Christ.

Finally she determined to help him. She took the last little bit of anesthesia that she had, placed him in a bathtub and amputated his leg. She was not a surgeon. She had never before done an amputation.

When she went to bind up the stump, she had not calculated properly on the measurement of the skin; and there was not enough left to cover the stump of the amputated leg. Without any more anesthesia available, she reached under her skirt, sliced a piece of meat off her inner thigh and hurriedly put it on the stump of his leg and sutured it. It took, and it grew.

She walked with a limp for days, and only a few of the servants had any idea why. She never told anybody. But God let her have the joy of leading that coolie to the Lord.

When I read that story, my heart ached. I thought, *Dear God, what an example of humility! What courage!*

In 1905 the communists began their oppression of the people. They began to move into villages and strike terror into hearts. One of the communist soldiers took the butt of his rifle and hit a young boy in the back of the head. Blood began to gush out. Quickly Eleanor took bandages she had made and rushed out into the street to put those bandages on his head.

While she was dressing his wound, the communist soldier took the butt of his rifle and crushed her skull, sending her into the presence of her Saviour whom she loved and whom she served.

You may never hear anything about Eleanor Chestnut; but in Heaven you will meet that humble lady whose very life was exemplary of the Bible spirit of humility.

"They. . .worshipped the Lord with their faces to the ground" (vs. 6).

God says in II Chronicles 7:14:

"If my people, which are called by my name, shall humble themselves, and pray, and seek my face, and turn from their wicked ways; then will I hear from heaven, and will forgive their sin, and will heal their land."

Not only were the people hungry and humble, but **they were holy.** Look at verse 15: "And that they should publish and proclaim in all their cities, and in Jerusalem." They had good news to share. They had information to pass on that others needed to know, from a God who loved them.

Two years ago I was with a team of preachers and laymen in the former Soviet Union. We had gone to the Ukrainian city of Dnepropetrovsk. In a rented hall seating 1600 people, God allowed me to preach the Gospel. Henry Benach, a converted Jew, gave his testimony. When we gave the invitation, 679 people walked the aisles of that rented coliseum to accept Christ as their personal Saviour.

The next city to which we were going was the Ukrainian city of Char'kov. Here we had a 2500-seat auditorium rented for just one night. For four days we passed out handbills and advertised the meeting.

I prayed and begged God, "Lord, if You can give us that many souls down in Dnepropetrovsk out of 1600, You could give us at least 1,000 out of a 2500-seat auditorium."

Praise God, the people came! We delayed the beginning of the service for fifteen minutes so we could get the people in. Not only was every seat taken, but people were standing in the back and crowding all around. We finally put a speaker in the lobby so all could hear.

Again, God let me preach the Gospel, the simple Gospel of Jesus Christ, the Word of God. The Holy Spirit did His work. We had pastors and personal workers, but it still took 3½ hours to deal with all the people who came forward.

When we got back to the hotel that night, I asked, "Henry, how many did we have?"

"You won't believe it. We had 999."

I said, "Praise God! That's wonderful." But I went to my room and said, "Lord, I asked You for 1,000."

I thanked Him for the 999, then went downstairs to drink a cup of coffee. One of the preachers came in. He reached in his pocket and said, "By the way, here are three more salvation slips I forgot to turn in."

God gave 1,002—'exceeding abundantly above all that we could ask or think.' Hallelujah!

We gave out Bibles to all those people. Three peasant women who got saved must have been in their seventies or eighties. We gave each of them a complete copy of the Russian Bible. Through the translator, these three women wanted to say something to me. One said, "When I was a little girl, somebody in our village had one page out of the New Testament. That's all the contact we had with the Bible, but we passed it around, and all the families got to read it—just one page. I always wondered about the rest of what it said. I can't believe now I have my own Bible!"

As she pressed it to her bosom, she began to weep, and I began to weep. I watched her kiss that Bible.

Thank God that revival came to a people who had been oppressed for over seventy years and denied the right and the opportunity to worship the true and the living God!

O God, let us pray with the psalmist, "Wilt thou not revive us again: that thy people may rejoice in thee" (Ps. 85:6)?

SHELTON SMITH
1942-

ABOUT THE MAN:

Born December 4, 1942, in rural Western Kentucky, Shelton L. Smith grew up on his father's farm. When he was almost nine years old, he accepted Jesus Christ as his Saviour at the family home. At fourteen years of age, and when just a freshman in high school, he announced his call to preach. He preached his first sermon the very next week on January 13, 1957.

Having grown up in a Southern Baptist church, he attended SBC schools and was pastor of SBC churches for the early years of his ministry. An anonymous gift subscription to the SWORD OF THE LORD came to his mailbox one day, and it changed his life and ministry forever. He set out on a course of bold preaching, strong leadership and personal soul winning which has resulted in thousands of souls saved.

In late 1978 he accepted the pastorate of a small church, the Church of the Open Door in Westminster, Maryland. For seventeen years he saw his vision fulfilled as "every dream I ever dreamed came true." From a small group of 200, the church grew to average between 1,500 and 1,600 under his ministry. The church became one of the great growing, thriving centers of fundamentalism and soul winning in the Northeast.

In April of 1995, Dr. Smith was elected to succeed Dr. Curtis Hutson as the editor of the SWORD OF THE LORD. Now in his role as editor, he travels as an evangelist to encourage pastors and Christian workers to win souls, and to assist fundamental churches in reaching their areas for Christ. In 1996 he preached in meetings in 81 cities in the U.S.A.

Dr. Smith preaches as an evangelist with the same candor, compassion, conviction and courage that he had as a pastor. He is a soul winner, a fundamentalist, a separatist and an independent Baptist.

XIV.

If the Church Catches Fire, Just Let It Burn!

SHELTON SMITH

"And when the day of Pentecost was fully come, they were all with one accord in one place.

"And suddenly there came a sound from heaven as of a rushing mighty wind, and it filled all the house where they were sitting.

"And there appeared unto them cloven tongues like as of fire, and it sat upon each of them.

"And they were all filled with the Holy Ghost, and began to speak with other tongues, as the Spirit gave them utterance.

"And there were dwelling at Jerusalem Jews, devout men, out of every nation under heaven.

"Now when this was noised abroad, the multitude came together, and were confounded, because that every man heard them speak in his own language.

"And they were all amazed and marvelled, saying one to another, Behold, are not all these which speak Galilaeans?

"And how hear we every man in our own tongue, wherein we were born?

"Parthians, and Medes, and Elamites, and the dwellers in Mesopotamia, and in Judaea, and Cappadocia, in Pontus, and Asia,

"Phrygia, and Pamphylia, in Egypt, and in the parts of Libya about Cyrene, and strangers of Rome, Jews and proselytes,

"Cretes and Arabians, we do hear them speak in our tongues the wonderful works of God.

"And they were all amazed, and were in doubt, saying one to another, What meaneth this?

"Others mocking said, These men are full of new wine.

"But Peter, standing up with the eleven, lifted up his voice, and said unto them, Ye men of Judaea, and all ye that dwell at Jerusalem, be this known unto you, and hearken to my words:

"For these are not drunken, as ye suppose, seeing it is but the third hour of the day.

"But this is that which was spoken by the prophet Joel;

"And it shall come to pass in the last days, saith God, I will pour out of my Spirit upon all flesh: and your sons and your daughters shall prophesy, and your young men shall see visions, and your old men shall dream dreams:

"And on my servants and on my handmaidens I will pour out in those days of my Spirit; and they shall prophesy:

"And I will shew wonders in heaven above, and signs in the earth beneath; blood, and fire, and vapour of smoke:

"The sun shall be turned into darkness, and the moon into blood, before that great and notable day of the Lord come:

"And it shall come to pass, that whosoever shall call on the name of the Lord shall be saved."—Acts 2:1-21.

Many average Americans will tell you the dullest hour of the week for them is 11:00 on Sunday morning. They go to church out of a sense of social obligation or religious duty. The organ plays a funeral dirge, and the people halfheartedly mouth the words of a hymn or two. They purr their approval to a clergyman who gives a light and less filling sermon. When the clock strikes high noon, they make a dive for the doors so as to beat the Catholics and the Presbyterians to the restaurant.

Boredom has replaced the blessing. Inertia is in; excitement is out. There are many empty seats. Rarely does anyone get saved. There are cobwebs in the baptistry. "Amens" are unacceptable. There's always somebody bent out of shape. The buses have been sold or carted off to the nearest junkyard. Visitation is a joke. The church has no vision, no goals, no burden, no direction.

In view of such a circumstance in literally thousands of places that call themselves churches across our nation, I ask myself, "What has gone wrong?"

When we jokingly refer to seminaries as "cemeteries," and everybody knows there is death in both places, something is amiss! When we expect people to struggle to stay awake on Sunday morning at preaching time, something is wrong! When the big to-do of the year is an uproar over the color of the paint in the choir loft, something is woefully lacking!

When I began preaching as a teenage boy in 1957, I knew nothing about soul winning, nothing about alive, aggressive churches.

By 1963, I still had not seen the "fire from heaven." I still had no idea what it would be like for the fires of God to burn within the church, within the preacher, within me.

Then something happened that literally changed my life and altered the direction of my ministry. Someone sent me a subscription to the SWORD OF THE LORD. I began to read in the pages of the SWORD what I had read in the pages of the New Testament. I discovered churches—red-hot, Bible-believing, Christ-honoring, soul-winning churches where the fire of God was burning. Some of those same pastors I read about then are still in the harness now.

My heart began to beat with excitement. What a thrill! I had never known a soul winner. I had never seen a soul-winning church. I had read about it in the book of Acts, but I was dubious it could be done in the twentieth century.

Thank God, I can stand here now and tell you that God revolutionized me, my life and my ministry. He lit a fire in my soul. I know today what I did not know then. The church in the book of Acts is the prototype, the model. It is nothing unusual for God. It is exactly what ought to be taking place at my place, at your place, and at every place that calls itself a church.

The church in your town in the twentieth century ought to be alive, afire, just like the church in Jerusalem was in the first century. Excitement should be the normal, usual agenda when Sunday comes. People ought to be getting saved routinely. People ought to be going through the waters of baptism.

It is obvious now that the lukewarm Laodicean church is not the New Testament norm. The lukewarm are tepid. The tepid are timid. The timid are not victorious, not happy, not fruitful. God expects my church and your church to be something altogether different.

Whoever says church is dull and uninteresting hasn't been in church at all or has been going to the wrong church. Whoever pronounced the death knell upon the pulpit and diagnosed rigor mortis within the church is mired in the dearth of a dry, dull and defeated ministry.

The full story of God's program for our time unfolds in the book of Acts to reveal local churches alive, local churches bold, local churches crusading, local churches dynamic, local churches excited! What's the difference? What are the dynamics that set it apart?

The passage I've read gives us the truly distinctive dynamic. It's the fire of Heaven, the fire of God. The church is set ablaze when the Spirit of God fills Christians with the person of Christ, the presence of the Holy Spirit and the power of God.

I. THE PERSON WHO MAKES THE FIRE

1. Fire is sometimes used in the Bible as a symbol to indicate the very presence of God. In Genesis 15, we see it expressed in terms of a smoking furnace and a burning lamp. In Exodus 3, God appeared through a burning bush—burning but not consumed. In Exodus 19, it seemed the whole of Mt. Sinai was on fire. "Mount Sinai was altogether on a smoke, because the Lord descended upon it in fire" (vs. 18). When fire burns, smoke will be rising from it. When the fire of God is burning in us, the presence of God will be evident. You'll see the smoke that signals His presence.

2. Fire is sometimes associated with God's working of miracles, as in I Kings 18. In I Chronicles, chapter 21, David prayed, and the Lord answered by fire. In II Chronicles, chapter 7, Solomon prayed, and the Lord answered by fire. In Exodus 9, in a contest with the Egyptian pharaoh, the Lord in support of His people sent a plague of hail mingled with fire.

When God sends fire and ice upon the enemy, it burns them out and cools them off. God was eager to display Himself in great power to a wicked king.

3. In Numbers 16:35, God answered Moses with a killing fire that took the lives of 250 of the enemy. Any man, either peasant or potentate, who seats himself in opposition to God or the people of God, puts himself in a grave circumstance.

In II Kings 1, Elijah, in confrontation with the enemy, said, "Send a captain and fifty of your people up." Upon a word from the prophet, a fire from Heaven fell and consumed them on the spot. Elijah was unhesitating with these confrontations. He called out again, "Send out another captain and another fifty of your men. Listen, you hit me once—shame on you! You hit me twice—shame on me!" Right?

But these fellows didn't learn easily. When Elijah issued the second challenge, like a bunch of dummies, they sent up another group of men. Tromping up the side of the mountain, oblivious to the perils awaiting, they drew closer and closer. Elijah called out, and the fire from Heaven came down. It scorched them and destroyed them. They, too, are all dead. Here are fifty dead; there are fifty dead.

Elijah stands up there and calls out again, "Send a captain, and send fifty of your men."

Way down below in the valley some little fellow calls out to Elijah, "Hold your fire!" He said, "We don't want to come up anymore. You come down and see us."

God answered by fire in full support of the man of God.

4. In the Bible, fire is also an instrument of eternal punishment. We read in Isaiah 33 of a devouring fire and an everlasting burning. Matthew 18:8 says, "It is better for thee to enter into life halt or maimed, rather than having two hands or two feet to be cast into everlasting fire." Jesus said, in Matthew 25:41, "Depart from me, ye cursed, into everlasting fire, prepared for the devil and his angels."

Someone asked me just a few weeks ago, "Preacher, do you believe there is real fire in Hell?"

I said, "Yes, I believe there is real fire in Hell. Hell is a real, burning inferno, a flaming furnace of fire, a place to be avoided at all costs."

Mark's Gospel says,

"If thy hand offend thee, cut it off: it is better for thee to enter into life maimed, than having two hands to go into hell, into the fire that never shall be quenched:

"Where their worm dieth not, and the fire is not quenched.

"And if thy foot offend thee, cut it off: it is better for thee to enter halt into life, than having two feet to be cast into hell, into the fire that never shall be quenched:

"Where their worm dieth not, and the fire is not quenched.

"And if thine eye offend thee, pluck it out: it is better for thee to enter into the kingdom of God with one eye, than having two eyes to be cast into hell fire:

"Where their worm dieth not, and the fire is not quenched."—Mark 9:43-48.

Jesus said the rich man in Hell cried out, "I am tormented in this flame" (Luke 16:24). The Bible says, "But the fearful, and unbelieving, and the abominable, and murderers, and whoremongers, and sorcerers, and idolaters, and all liars, shall have their part in the lake which burneth with fire and brimstone: which is the second death" (Rev. 21:8).

Now when the Bible talks about the literal fire of punishment in Hell for all eternity, I know what it is talking about. When I see lost men and women dying and going out of this world without Christ, and I know what they will be doing five minutes after death, it spurs me onward to do all that I can to draw men and women to the Saviour.

5. The Bible also says fire is a symbol of God's power. Many of us have never had the fire of God fall in power upon us. It is my prayer, my dream, my hope, my expectation that men and women and teenagers here will get a yearning for the burning. You can have the fire of God. You may be active in the church, faithful to attend; but if that thrill and excitement, that burning of heart, is not there, it is my prayer that you will get it today. You need a fire that will not be stopped by disappointment, that will not be stymied by defeat, that will not be squelched because of a few wet blankets.

The Person who makes the fire that can fill and empower your life is our great God, our Heavenly Father, the Almighty God. You'll not possess the fire until you by faith are possessed by Him who makes the fire.

II. THE PLACE FOR MAKING THE FIRE

Elijah called upon the prophets of Baal to call on their god and get him to put a fire on the altar. Well, they called and they called and they called. They cut themselves with lancets and knives until the blood gushed out, as was their practice to do; still there had been no answer from the gods of Baal; still there was no fire kindled on the altar.

Elijah responded in a mocking spirit, adding salt to the wound and insult to injury! 'Hey, fellows, cry a little louder. Maybe your god can't hear you. On the other hand, maybe he is talking to somebody and is not paying you any attention. Or maybe he is out chasing somebody and doesn't have on his earphones. Or maybe he is off on a trip and cannot hear you. Or maybe he is home but is asleep and didn't hear when you rang the bell' (I Kings 18).

Yes, Elijah made fun of them.

Then after he had them prepare the altar and put the water on it, Elijah said,

"Lord God of Abraham, Isaac, and of Israel, let it be known this day that thou art God in Israel, and that I am thy servant, and that I have done all these things at thy word. Hear me, O Lord, hear me, that this people may know that thou art the Lord God, and that thou hast turned their heart back again."—I Kings 18:36, 37.

The Bible says that, when Elijah called upon God, *"the fire of the Lord fell* and consumed the burnt-sacrifice, and the wood, and the stones, and the dust, and licked up the water that was in the trench." **The fire of God fell upon that place.**

In all probability I am talking to somebody tonight *who has never had the fire of God fall on his life*. It is likely somebody here has never seen a time when the great power of God was demonstrated in his life. We need that fire of God's power to fill us, to make us effective in what we do for Him.

We broke ground for a new building, but we cannot build without the fire of God's power to enthuse, fill, excite and generate the resources necessary to build. Tomorrow night our people will knock on doors to tell others about Jesus. Week after week, our people lead others to Christ.

The power of God, the fire of God's blessing, does not and cannot come until His people are willing to be filled and thrilled with the fire of God's blessing permeating them, filling them, penetrating them and empowering them. We cannot see people saved until the fire of God's power comes to bless, to fill, to thrill our souls.

I like Elijah's prayer to God: "Let it be known this day. . . that I am thy servant, and that I have done all these things at thy word." He prayed, 'If I be a man of God, then let the fire come down from Heaven.' And immediately "the fire of the Lord fell."

There are times when you and I must tell God, "God, if You don't do it, it can't be done." We can't orchestrate it. We can't engineer it. We can't make it happen. The programs fail. Every plan unravels. Everything falls flat unless there comes fire, the mighty fire of God.

O God, if I be a man of God and if this place be Your place and if there is going to be here what we need, then we must have a demonstration of the God of fire who unleashes power upon us.

III. THE FIRE GOD SENDS IS A PURIFYING FIRE

I know nothing to tell you tonight except what is here in this wonderful

Book, the Bible. I didn't come in here to review *Time* or *Newsweek*. It is not my intention to tell you thus saith the *Washington Post* or the Nashville *Tennessean*. I read their publications, but I can't know what I read is for sure. But what I do know, and know for sure, is what I find in my Bible.

The fire of God reflects His presence, His power, His punishment and also His purity.

"And the posts of the door moved at the voice of him that cried, and the house was filled with smoke.

"Then said I, Woe is me! for I am undone; because I am a man of unclean lips, and I dwell in the midst of a people of unclean lips: for mine eyes have seen the King, the Lord of hosts.

"Then flew one of the seraphims unto me, having a live coal in his hand, which he had taken with the tongs from off the altar:

"And he laid it upon my mouth, and said, Lo, this hath touched thy lips; and thine iniquity is taken away, and thy sin purged."—Isa. 6:4-7.

The whole house was filled with smoke (vs. 4) because the God of fire was there. Isaiah cried out (vs. 5), "Woe is me . . . I am undone . . . I am . . . unclean." God applied the red-hot purging from His own mighty hand (vs. 6) and declared him forgiven, cleansed and purified.

The ceremony of fire made the humbled Isaiah ready for his heaven-sent role as the servant of God—first, the purging, then the purity. Our desire for His power must always be preceded by our devotion to His purity.

Our God, the God of fire, is a consuming fire (Heb. 12:29). He burns up our pride. He burns up our sin. He burns up our worldliness, our carnality, our fleshly ways. The result is a purification that presents us clean and polished vessels suitable for use on the dining table of the King.

"But in a great house there are not only vessels of gold and of silver, but also of wood and of earth; and some to honour, and some to dishonour. If a man therefore purge himself from these, he shall be a vessel unto honour, sanctified, and meet for the master's use, and prepared unto every good work."—II Tim. 2:20, 21.

As Christians we still struggle with the flesh in that we await the redemption of the body (Rom. 8:23). In order to allow these frail and feeble bodies to be wonderfully employed and mightily used in divine service, the Lord:

—frees us (in redemption),
—feeds us (on His Word),
—fills us (with His Holy Spirit)
—and fires us (with His power).

John the Baptist declared with authority, "There cometh one mightier than I after me, the latchet of whose shoes I am not worthy to stoop down and unloose" (Mark 1:7).

IV. THE PURPOSE OF THE FIRE

The state of Maryland, where I live, is a very liberal state. The liberals are everywhere. People ask me questions all the time about Heaven and Hell and eternity. The liberals, the intellectual liberals, have done a thorough job of selling their philosophic garbage to our society.

There was a time, in the 1950s and into the 1960s, when, if a religious person didn't believe in Hell, everybody's antenna really went up.

But now, whenever you and I stand up to say we believe in a Hell where there is real, literal fire that burns and burns forever and ever and ever, they look at us askance and think we are oddballs and radicals. We have become the outcasts and the offscouring of society because it's not intellectually acceptable and politically correct to believe these things.

Hear me carefully: You can be very precise in your church (every *i* is dotted, every *t* is crossed) but have no power. You can sing and preach in a professional manner but have no life in it and no blessing from it.

Dear ones, it is my solemn conviction that, unless the God of fire breathes His fire, you and I are in for some serious and difficult days.

Look at my text, chapter 2 of Acts. What is the purpose of the fire? What is the profit of the fire?

(1) *The fire of God draws us together.* Verse 1 says, "When the day of Pentecost was fully come, they were all with one accord in one place."

Now today I'm hearing all kinds of voices sounding discouraged. We talk very defensively. We talk defeatedly as though there is no way out. I'm hearing disappointment. I'm hearing disillusionment. Brethren, this is the product of our behavior and our disunity.

I'm at the Southwide Baptist Fellowship tonight as I have been every year since I became a part of the independent, fundamental, Baptist movement. I want you to know: I'm independent, and I thank God for being independent. I learned the value of separating myself from some things from which I needed to be separated and paid a price to do it. Thank God I did! I'm an independent, fundamental Baptist and unashamed of the fact.

We have a great movement. God has been good to us.

Brother Bobby Roberson said he and his wife had a conversation on the way here. They were rejoicing together that they had the greatest church in all of America and all the world. But, Brother Bobby, Betty and I had a similar conversation on the way down here. She said to me, "You know, we have the greatest church in the whole wide world!"

I said, "I believe you're right."

I'm excited about it. I thank God for what He has done. Often I pinch myself, slap myself and say, "Is this really for real? Is it really true that all those folks came down the aisle last Sunday? Is it really true we're still baptizing folks week after week? Is it really true? With our parking problems, our space—all the problems—is it really true?"

It IS true. But it can stop if we start fighting, quarreling and kicking one another. You can't have a fight every Sunday and Wednesday and keep the fire burning. You can't have your hands around some deacon's throat and be reaching out to bring a lost sinner to salvation.

I have no talent for being a referee. I have no qualifications for sorting out people who are clashing like fighting roosters and stubborn bulldogs.

Listen! They were "with one accord in one place." This Jerusalem church had 120 members the day the fire fell. It's asking a lot of 120 independent-minded folk to be in one place and all of them to be of one accord; but, brethren, we have the New Testament model here, the prototype.

I'm not talking about being ecumenical. No sir! I'm not talking about ecumenicity. I'm not talking about your becoming a compromiser. No sir! I'm not talking about your selling your convictions down the drain. No sir!

I *am* talking about our standing together on the divine authority of biblical truth and letting harmony and unity prevail. The church needs to be sweetly together in one place, united in one accord. If the fire of God is to come on our ministry, then we have to do it. If our independent, fundamental churches are to get in gear and get things going, if things are to happen across the country like they ought to happen, we must be of one accord.

Our local churches must stop sowing discord, must stop spreading discouragement, must stop being satisfied with defeat. Sow such as that, and it comes back to haunt you.

Yes, the fire of God draws us together in one place.

(2) *The fire of God delivers us triumphantly.*

"And there appeared unto them cloven tongues like as of fire, and it sat upon each of them.

"And they were all filled with the Holy Ghost, and began to speak with other tongues, as the Spirit gave them utterance.

"And there were dwelling at Jerusalem Jews, devout men, out of every nation under heaven."—Acts 2:3-5.

There are three miracles here. Number one: the rushing mighty wind that filled all the house. Number two: the cloven, visible tongues of fire. Number three: After God had gotten their attention with the wind and the physical fire, He gives to them, supernaturally, the ability to speak real, known languages which they had never studied, so that these foreign visitors could hear the Gospel. Verse 11 says it was so that the wonderful works of God could be articulated.

That is what these tongues are all about here. God put the fire upon these people so that the Jews from at least seventeen different languages could hear the message of the Gospel and could take it back home after the holiday of Pentecost.

Now what happened here? The fire of God drew them together in one place; then God delivered supernaturally exactly what was needed so that His Word could go out quickly.

The fire did not create unintelligible utterances, no guttural gibberish here. There were no interpreters here, nor were they needed. The languages were perfectly spoken and perfectly understood.

This is real fire (real languages) in contrast to the charismatic wildfire (gibberish) in practice today.

The fire brought an enduement upon Simon Peter and the rest, and there was a great victory in that three thousand souls understood the message and were saved.

(3) *The fire of God distresses the onlookers.* Now what happens when the Word of God is given? As the excitement of the things of God begins to grow and mushroom, it distresses some folks.

"Now when this was noised abroad, the multitude came together, and were confounded, because that every man heard them speak in

his own language. And they were all amazed and marvelled, saying one to another, Behold, are not all these which speak Galilaeans? And how hear we every man in our own tongue, wherein we were born?"—Vss. 6-8.

The observers became distressed. The multitude was confounded.

They talk about us. They say things, sometimes true, sometimes false. Some become distressed when the work of God goes forward in a great way.

We have a ball team in Baltimore. The last two or three games, 52,000 people or 53,000 people showed up. All sorts of folks are there in all kinds of goofy weather. Sometimes it is so cold people come wrapped in blankets to watch those overpaid millionaires bat that little piece of horsehide around the field. Everybody thinks it's wonderful when the Orioles have a big crowd.

Then when we pull off a big day and have two thousand or more present—I mean, a *great* day, with people all over the place, with souls saved and baptized—some people say, "You know, that church is just too big."

Now what is happening? The Devil has sold a bill of goods to our people. He has lied to us, and we have believed him.

Everything in the whole world likes to grow, to make great strides, to reach new heights. How many in this building tonight do not like to draw big paychecks? Everybody in his right mind, and a lot of folks who are not, want big paychecks. If you went in to your boss tomorrow and said, "You know, I believe my paycheck has gotten too big. Will you cut it down some?" you would be hustled off to one of these places where your head is examined and all the rest of you, too.

But when it comes to the work of God, little offerings are just wonderful, little crowds are just beautiful.

Hey, think straight! Get right for God! The work of God is more important than your paycheck or any baseball team. Dream big, work hard and trust God for great things.

Not every place is drawing a big crowd. But you hang tough. Don't give in to the nay-sayers, and you'll get there.

"Well, I might be excited, too, if I had big crowds," you say. Listen! I was excited before I got big crowds, because the God of the fire gave me an excited spirit.

If you get stirred up by the God who answers by fire, it will not diminish you.

When we had thirty in Sunday school, I typed the bulletin. I blew the old, cheap ink dry. I folded it, stood at the door and handed it out myself because nobody else would do it. I used the typewriter that Noah had on the ark. I typed the bulletin on an open-air, back porch office because I didn't have a real office. That was just one item in a long list of other crazy, wild things I did.

When thirty-five people showed up for Sunday school, I got excited. I'm telling you, I was THRILLED! I was excited to be the pastor and to have a place to preach and to win souls.

Wherever God puts you, have that excitement. What I'm advocating is, let the God of the fire breathe His fire on you. Sure, it's going to create some difficulties. Sure, some folks aren't going to like what you do. They will even charge you falsely, as they did in verse 13 of Acts 2, "These men are full of new wine."

"In the last days, saith God, I will pour out of my Spirit." The resources of God are available and accessible so that you and I can do His work.

You may say, "I don't have everything I need." Keep on going. Use what God has given you today. I myself could spend ten million dollars if I had it, and it still wouldn't do everything we need to have done at our place. My prayer list is a lot bigger than ten million dollars. I believe God wants to do big things, and I'm praying He'll let me be one of His instruments to do it. I don't know His schedule, but I'm going to try to do everything He wants me to do today.

(4) *The fire of God demands a decision.*

"And it shall come to pass, that whosoever shall call on the name of the Lord shall be saved."—Vs. 21.

The God of fire breathes on us so we can get folks saved.

Recently a fellow preacher asked me, "Do you really give an invitation every Sunday morning?"

I said, "Yes sir. I give an invitation every Sunday morning, every Sunday night, every Wednesday night, the Labor Day picnic, the Sweetheart Banquet, anything and everything else we have."

Frankly, I have trouble understanding why any person, especially anyone called of God, would get up and preach the Word of God and not give some kind of an appeal. He makes "his ministers a flame of fire" (Heb. 1:7). The fire God gives is a hot fire. It will warm your heart. It will give you compassion. It is a holy fire. It will clean you and purify you and temper you. It is a heavenly fire. It will set your schedule with a divine agenda. You begin to be concerned for the things that concern the Lord.

Jeremiah said, "His word was in mine heart as a burning fire shut up in my bones" (Jer. 20:9).

On the Emmaus road, the disciples said, "Did not our heart burn within us, while he talked with us by the way" (Luke 24:32)?

The psalmist said, "My heart was hot within me, while I was musing the fire burned" (Ps. 39:3).

The preacher is not just the errand boy; he's the exciter, the one who will stir the work of God. He is the encourager. He is the coach, the counselor and the evangelist.

You say, "I want to teach the Bible to my folks." Well, teach it to them, then give an invitation and invite people to come to Christ. Give them the Gospel. Preach on creation or inspiration or tithing or whatever you please; but when you finish, tell them how to be saved, give an appeal. You might be surprised how God will breathe His fire upon what you have said.

The exciter, the encourager, the evangelist, the expositor—the preacher needs to preach the Word, teach the Word, explain to them what is in the Book.

One of the missing elements is exhortation. We are to exhort our people to flee from the world, to leave their sin and to cut out the nonsense. We are to exhort them to come to God, to live for God, to stand for God, and to do what they ought to do.

And the preacher is the enlister. I've never known a day when I've had all the workers I needed. I am constantly doing what I can to enlist folks to help me. The Almighty's fire in the pulpit will help to build fire in the troops so that we can keep on snatching brands from the awful burning.

V. THE PRIORITY OF THE FIRE

A few years ago I was in a meeting in a town not too far from here. The Sunday morning when I started the meeting, the church literally caught on fire when the furnace blew up. When I went in, the place smelled like smoke. Some of the walls were blackened with soot. They finally got the furnace back on, so we were able to have the service.

With a little crowd of about 150 people in the building, it was a very staid, sophisticated place. The pastor said they had not had a baptismal service in five years. I said, "Oh, my soul!" (I had agreed to preach for the next four days.) He said, "You'd better tell them what you want to tell them on Sunday morning, for most of them won't be back on Sunday night. We may have twenty or twenty-five Sunday night, Monday night, Tuesday night."

As I stood up on Sunday morning, I said, "Folks, I'm glad to be here. It's an amazing thing. The church house caught fire this morning, but the church meeting here also needs to catch fire."

What a mess it was! But God got hold of the thing. I preached to them like there was no tomorrow. I was surprised Sunday night when many came back—about the same crowd we had had Sunday morning.

I gave the invitation on Sunday morning, but nobody came forward. It was deader than last year's bird's nest.

I gave an invitation on Sunday night. Nobody moved. You couldn't get folks down the aisle. It was dead and waiting to be buried. Monday night—and to my great surprise, the same crowd was back.

What I didn't know was, two little ladies across the town square in a little apartment had been praying for three months that God would use the meeting to turn the church around.

Glory to God, on Monday night, we had some folks saved! Two men running for political office in the county, who had been fighting one another bitterly, got right with God and with each other. Those two men, one from the left side of the church and one from the right side of the church, left their seats and came to the altar and put their arms around each other.

In four days we had three sets of people cancel lawsuits against each other when they got right with God!

What took place at that church? For the next three months they did not miss a Sunday having people saved and baptized. What took place? An invasion by the God of fire ignited that old dead wood with His mighty power. Somebody just put a little gasoline on it, and it made an excellent fire.

That is what we are looking for. The God of fire is still alive and well. The fire of God is still powerful and necessary. For the work of God to be drooping and declining, dry and dull, defeated and dead is altogether unacceptable and inexcusable.

I'm appealing to you now, let's get back to having church with the fire burning. Let's have preaching with the fire burning. Let's go soul winning because we've got a fire burning.

When your heart burns with the fire of God, it will keep you driving nails to build the ark.

When the fire burns in your heart, it will keep you looking for a city whose Builder and Maker is God.

When the fire burns in your heart, it will keep you out of the shade of the juniper tree.

When the fire burns in your heart, it will keep you pressing on to Nineveh, no matter what your preference may be.

What I'm saying tonight is, let's fire the preacher with hot fire. Let's fire him with holy fire. Let's fire him with heavenly fire.

Let's fire the staff with hot fire, holy fire, heavenly fire. Let's fire the deacons with hot fire, holy fire, heavenly fire. Let's fire the choir with hot fire, holy fire, heavenly fire. Let's fire the ushers with hot fire, holy fire, heavenly fire. Let's fire the bus workers, the Sunday school workers and all the workers of the church. . . with hot fire, holy fire, heavenly fire.

O Lord, I want to do it, but first I want You to breathe Your fire on me. Lord, if You'll use me, fill me and anoint me, I want to keep on. I don't want my church to dry up, dwindle and die. I don't want the fire to be smothered out. I want folks saved every week. I want us to baptize every week.

Fundamental? Yes! Amen! Absolutely! But not without fire. Independent? Yes! Hallelujah! But not without fire. Baptist? Yes! Glory to God! But not without fire.

May the fire of God be upon you. Let it fill you full. Let it burn within you. Let it burn when you preach. Let it burn when the people come in. Oh, may the God of the fire anoint you and enable you with His fire power so you can do what He can do through you.

Let's bow together for a moment of prayer. Perhaps there are many, such as I, who need a fresh anointing of the power of God. Right where you sit, will you simply pray, "O God, fill me fresh tonight. Give me Your power tonight. Put the fire within me right now. Let the fire burn in my heart tonight"?

Preacher brother, dear deacon, dear Sunday school teacher, dear choir member, dear usher, will you ask God to fill you afresh? to fill you with His fire?

It may be that I'm talking to somebody now who is not saved. Listen to me. Jesus died upon Calvary's cross, was buried and arose from the grave so that you could be saved. He bought you with a price. He paid for your salvation. It is yours as a free gift if you will receive it. So right where you are, if you're not saved, I ask you to pray this simple prayer:

> Dear God, I'm a sinner. I need the Saviour. I need to be forgiven. I do believe You died on the cross and arose from the grave for me, and I'm trusting You as my Saviour right this very moment. Amen.

If you are now trusting Christ as your Saviour, please copy the decision form below in a letter, complete it, and mail it to me. I will rejoice with you in the salvation of your soul, and I will send you some free literature that will help you as you set out to live the Christian life.

Decision Form

Dr. Shelton Smith
Sword of the Lord Foundation
P. O. Box 1099
Murfreesboro, TN 37133

Dear Dr. Smith:

I have read your sermon, "If the Church Catches Fire, Just Let It Burn!"

Realizing I am a sinner and believing that Jesus Christ died for me, I here and now trust Him as my Saviour.

Please send me the free literature you promised that will help me as I set out to live the Christian life.

Date ______________________

Name ______________________

Address ______________________

____

For a complete list of books available from the Sword of the Lord, write to Sword of the Lord Publishers, P. O. Box 1099, Murfreesboro, Tennessee 37133, or call:

(800) 247–9673 • (615) 893–6700
FAX (615) 848–6943

E-mail:
102657.3622@compuserve.com